LLOYD PAUL STRYKER

THE ART OF ADVOCACY
A Plea for the Renaissance of the Trial Lawyer

EQUINOX
PUBLISHING
JAKARTA KUALA LUMPUR

EQUINOX PUBLISHING (ASIA) PTE LTD
No 3. Shenton Way
#10-05 Shenton House
Singapore 068805

www.EquinoxPublishing.com

The Art of Advocacy
A Plea for the Renaissance of the Trial Lawyer
by Lloyd Paul Stryker

ISBN 978-602-8397-31-5

First Equinox Edition 2010

Printed in the United States

1 3 5 7 9 10 8 6 4 2

TABLE OF CONTENTS

PART ONE

THE TRIAL

I

A New Case Arrives

THOSE OF YOU fortunate enough to have witnessed the fine acting of Paul Muni in *Counsellor-at-Law* will remember the last scene. One misfortune after another has befallen the lawyer—hero of the piece. His wife has left him, and he feels himself a hopeless man. Planning self-destruction, in his despair he climbs out onto the window ledge preparatory to a fatal leap. But as he is about to jump, the telephone bell begins to ring. The ringing interrupts his suicidal purpose. He decides to answer it. And as he answers it, he undergoes a sudden change; his back stiffens, his eyes flash, his voice loses its dull tone. The son of a great industrialist has just been arrested, charged with murder! Disconsolate and without hope a moment back, the lawyer suddenly has become like a spirited fire horse eager to throw his whole weight into the collar. His troubles are forgotten, a new case has arrived!

In the great law offices, with their innumerable partners, countless law clerks, and unfailing corporate retainers, a new case, I imagine, excites no such emotion. But for the lawyer who devotes himself to advocacy and nothing else, a new and interesting case is always an event. Perhaps it may arrive in the turmoil of other preparations or it may be during the trial of some other case or, as is sometimes the case with even the most successful advocates, it may punctuate a long drought. For while there is nothing comparable in interest, so there is nothing similar to the uncertainties of a trial counsel practice.

Webster once said that lawyers work hard, live well, and die poor. Martin Littleton fulfilled the first two parts of this apothegm; he worked hard, lived well, but he did not die poor. He had periods of feverish activity, and yet when he was at the very top of his career, there were days or even months when he was not busy. Lunching with him one day I said: "Martin, are you busy? I have not seen your name in the newspapers recently." "No," he said, "just now I am not busy at all; indeed it is so long since I have had an incoming call that yesterday I rang up the telephone company to inquire if there were any mechanical defect that prevented people reaching me. But they told me that my line was in perfect order." "Martin," I said, "in times like this do you ever worry?" "No," he answered, "I trust to the law of averages, and Old Man Average will soon come around."

But if Martin Littleton at the summit of his fame thus found himself, what of the young advocate just beginning? He will have long uninvited hours of idleness that undermine his hopes, yet these hours may be employed to cultivate the two most important essentials of success: courage and the constant improvement of the mind. By his desk Martin Littleton had built a small attractive bookcase, and it was always lined with good books. He turned to these when he was not engaged with legal work. Like John Marshall, he was convinced that "no lawyer is entitled to the honorable and conventional epithet of 'learned,' if his reading is confined to statutes and the law reports."

And this is especially true of the young lawyer in his early struggles. The legal neophyte has been a favorite of the novelists, and has not been forgotten even by the poets. Remember the Judge's song in Gilbert's *Trial by Jury*:

> *When I, good friends, was called to the bar,*
> *I'd an appetite fresh and hearty,*
> *But I was, as many young barristers are,*
> *An impecunious party.*
> *I'd a swallow-tailed coat of a beautiful blue—*
> *A brief that I bought from a booby—*
> *A couple of shirts and a collar or two,*
> *And a ring that looked like a ruby.*

But even this equipment seemed inadequate, as the Judge pointed out to the amusement of the crowded courtroom, crowded as all Gilbert and Sullivan's operas are with charming girls who sing well. Encouraged by their smiles he sang on:

> *In Westminster Hall I danced a dance,*
> *Like a semi-despondent fury;*
> *For I thought I should never hit on a chance*
> *Of addressing a British Jury—*
> *But I soon got tired of third class journeys,*
> *And dinners of bread and water;*
> *So I fell in love with a rich attorney's*
> *Elderly ugly daughter.*

The course followed by the Judge as an impecunious young barrister has respectable authority, and yet it is one that I would hesitate commending, for even though, as it seems from the remainder of this tuneful autobiography, it appeared to bring success, the engagement nonetheless lacked much attraction:

> *The rich attorney, he jumped for joy,*
> *And replied to my fond professions:*
> *"You shall reap the reward of your pluck, my boy,*
> *At the Bailey and Middlesex Sessions.*
> *You'll soon get used to her looks," said he,*
> *"And a very nice girl you'll find her!*
> *She may very well pass for forty-three*
> *In the dusk, with the light behind her!"*

With all its drawbacks the marriage undoubtedly possessed some advantages, for

> *The rich attorney was good as his word;*
> *The briefs came trooping gaily,*
> *And every day my voice was heard*
> *At the Sessions or Ancient Bailey.*
> *All thieves who could my fees afford*
> *Relied on my orations,*
> *And many a burglar I restored*
> *To his friends and his relations.*

For the young barrister not choosing this easiest way, there may be many third-class journeys and dinners of bread and water, but I think he will enjoy them better than a life with "a rich attorney's elderly ugly daughter." For those who choose the harder road, there lie many black hours ahead; if one quails at meeting these, he has made a cardinal mistake in choosing advocacy.

That important case is coming! On the most uncomfortable day of a long dry spell, Old Man Average will surely put in his appearance. Let us imagine the scene of his arrival, and let us suppose that you are a lawyer, at a stage in your career when your reputation and experience entitle you to expect important cases. The telephone rings, an attorney is calling you! It may be one whom you know well or one whom you hardly know, or it may be a stranger's voice. But in any event he is telling you that he is the attorney for Mr. Smith, and that he would like to discuss retaining you in this case in the United States District Court, now working its way upward on the calendar.

The "Smith case" may be one of which you have never heard, or it may be one that has already had wide attention in the press; let us suppose it is the latter. You tell the gentleman on the other end of the wire that you would be pleased to see him and his client.

Your interest is aroused, your faculties alerted, as you wait impatiently for the hour to come. Finally the appointed time arrives. You greet an old friend or perhaps a new acquaintance, and he introduces you to the man whose problem will engage your waking and your sleeping hours for many days, perhaps for many months to come. You look upon the face of the man whose liberty it will presently be your duty to defend. Yes, it is the face that you have often looked at in the press. And you are surprised how much more favorable is your impression as you see it now without the dark surroundings of hostile printer's ink.

A new case has arrived! A new planet has swum into your ken! There have been hundreds of others recorded in the books; they have some similarities but in greater or less degree they differ all from this one. Your new case stands on its own feet—alone!

After a few introductory remarks, you ask your potential client to state his case, to tell his story in his own way, and you settle back to listen. You will have in mind Quintilian's advice, as timely now as when it was given nearly two thousand years ago: "Let us allow plenty of time and a place of interview free from interruption to those who shall have occasion to consult us, and let us earnestly exhort them to state every particular off hand, however verbosely or however far he may wish to go back; for it is a less inconvenience to listen to what is superfluous than to be left ignorant of what is essential."

With the background of such knowledge as the radio, the television, and the newspapers have previously supplied you, you watch him as he talks. You let him talk without interruption. You encourage him to talk more. You make a note here and there as he goes along, but you do not interrupt him; you encourage him to open his whole heart to you, and still you listen. There is an art in listening. We all know that a good listener is the most sought after of all conversationalists. But it is not the accolade of a good conversationalist that you now seek; what you are looking for are the facts. And as the only way you can learn them is to listen, with every faculty alert you listen, and listening you still listen on.

What you want at this time above all else in the world are the facts. The facts, all the facts, and nothing but the facts. And the man seated now before you is the best person on earth to give them to you. The *facts!* Would that there were some way over and beyond italics with which I might stress, might shout aloud that word: *facts!*

After an hour or two you will have learned much. You will have learned much not only about the facts but about your prospective client. You may begin to see in all its stark significance not only the difficulties but the unpopularity of the cause that you are now being asked to undertake. But you will be a poltroon and not a man if you decline to represent him on the sole ground that he has been prejudged by the world. "In my practice at the English Bar," Lord Norman Birkett once said, "I have frequently had to undertake murder cases of the greatest complexity and difficulty, not because I wanted to, but because of the unwritten law that I would not refuse." The American advocate has more liberty of choice, but he is unworthy of the name if he declines a case on the sole ground that it is unpopular. For in the law unpopularity often is the post of Honor.

After listening to your prospective client for a long time, however, you may discern other grounds that adequately support your declination of the retainer. You may have heard enough to satisfy you that his position is totally dishonest, or you may decide that the case though honest is a hopeless one. In such a case, says Mr. John C. Reed, "I am clear that you should decline to make a fool of yourself." And I agree.

But assume that you have decided to espouse his cause. With unfailing patience you will have listened to his every word, and your natural tact has not permitted you to show weariness at his many repetitions. Tact, that sensitive perception and nice discernment of what is appropriate to do and say in dealing with others without giving offense, is a quality for which you will find much use. The absence of this gift has been the downfall of many otherwise predestined for success. You will be patient therefore, totally patient, and will never let the client think that you are bored or that your interest for one moment flags. Do not shut him off. "Do not," Bacon once said, "snub a client."

In what has passed in the case before it came to you, you may find that many things have been done that you wish had not been done, but you will never be so tactless as to say so. And above all, you will never criticize the lawyer who has brought his client to you. Nothing could be more ungracious or more useless, and, from the practical standpoint, such conduct on your part will certainly insure that no other case will ever come to you from that source.

As the client goes on with his narrative, you will bend every effort conscientiously to follow him, but you will do more than study what he says, you will study him. You will form opinions (tentative, let us hope) as to his veracity and the kind of witness he will make should you ultimately decide to call him. And the process will be mutual; he will be studying you as well. The impression that you begin to make upon him will tend to dictate your future relationship. For it is essential not only that the lawyer trust his client but that the client have abiding faith in the man who is to represent him on the battlefield of justice.

As he talks, you will make many notes, dates, names of potential witnesses, addresses, and telephone numbers, and you will dictate to your secretary after each interview a full memorandum of all you have learned. Before he leaves, however, you will ask him to bring next time all the letters, diaries, or other papers he has mentioned and, as he is taking his departure, you will exude such honest hope as you can muster.

On his return the next day you will ask him to repeat again all that he has already told you and you will listen with renewed interest and attention, noting whether he now contradicts himself, and how and in what respect the repeated narrative may differ from the first, or whether the two are so mechanically identical as to suggest that all his story has been learned by rote. And then you will invite him once more to tell his whole story over again.

You have become familiar with it now, and as you begin to question him more closely, new facts will emerge. You repeat this process day after day until you know his narrative as well as he does. Long before this, however, your associates, especially the younger ones who served upon the law reviews, have begun plying you with "the law." Some, indeed, start telling you about it long before you have attained anything like a mastery of the facts, ignoring the simple truth that there is no law in your case in the abstract. What statutes and decisions are in point depend upon the peculiar facts and circumstances of your case and nothing else.

The really difficult problem in the preparation of the case is to learn what the facts are, and no matter how long or conscientiously you work, you will never know them all. The law seldom decides the issue, the facts do; and as contrasted with the ascertainment of the facts, the law is relatively easy to discover. There are a hundred good researchers of the law to one who has a genius, I may say a nose, for the discovery of the true facts.

Some young lawyers have a tendency not only to minimize the study of the facts but to treat them as of inferior importance to what they are pleased to call the "law." Such young gentlemen I think regard the facts as a field beneath them, a department belonging to the lesser brains of a detective bureau, or the untutored labors of a private operative. But the experienced advocate has learned that facts are the foundation, the only sure foundation, of his case and he has found out, too, how complicated and how difficult it is to dig them out.

"More and more," Judge Cardozo once observed, "we lawyers are awaking to a perception of the truth that what divides and distracts us in the solution of a legal problem is not so much uncertainty about the law as uncertainty about the facts—the facts which generate the law. Let the facts be known as they are, and the law will sprout from the seed and turn its branches toward the light."

Voicing an understandable impatience with the enormous collection of court decisions, containing as they do innumerable contradictions, an able and charming professor, Fred Rodell, of Yale, a few years ago wrote an interesting book which he called *Woe unto you, Lawyers!*

He there defined the law as "a big balloon of inflated nonsense"—a "mass of hokum"—and referred to it as a "mighty fraud" and an "impressive abracadabra devoted to the solemn manipulation of a lot of silly abstractions." Of course I do not agree with these strictures, and I don't believe that Fred Rodell himself does. He wrote them, I am sure, with his tongue in his cheek as a kind of antidote to smug complacency with our so-called legal science. His observations are a kind of twentieth-century echo of the eighteenth-century aphorism attributed to Alexander Hamilton that the law is "that which has been confidently asserted and boldly maintained."

We have a Government of laws; without law there can be no ordered freedom. To those who go into court without knowing the decisions applicable to their case, I would say with Fred Rodell, "Woe unto you, lawyers."

You must acquire a feeling for the law as much as for the facts. It must become a part of you and you must translate it into common parlance for instantaneous and ready use.

One of the most interesting things that you will find is the vast difference between the law of the library and the law in the forum. "The law," Mr. John C. Reed well said, "as written in the textbooks and as revealed in the adjudged cases is not the same as that assumed by its administrators. The reports over which we pore day and night have no presentation of the faces, characters, voices, dress, deportment, and evident bias one way or the other of the parties and witnesses. The glance of intelligence of a juror unconscious that he is watched, the frown of another, and the smile of still another—all these are missed. But they are the signs by which the lawyer was guided almost unconsciously . . . and thus there is a different law from that which is found in Blackstone and Story and this law is to be learned by him who would be a successful practitioner."

The law is not an exact science. At the most it is a kind of guiding star whose light suggests rather than defines the way. But for those industrious enough to track the principles of jurisprudence to their sources, and with imagination enough to discover not only the governing rules but their true application to each case, it will become a beacon and a guide. It will be not only a guide to the ascertainment of the rule but a chart and compass for marshaling the facts from which the law must spring. While then you will push your study of the decisions, the statutes, and their legislative history to the limit of your strength, as well as that of your associates, you will give your first, your last, and at all times your unflagging efforts to finding out what the facts are.

For these reasons I cannot too strongly stress unlimited and never-ending talks with the client himself. Sometimes after long weeks of preparation, perhaps on the very eve of trial, he will drop a comment that throws a new light on the whole case, or he may mention a name heretofore not given, which may perhaps make a difference between victory and defeat. I shall never forget a circumstance of this kind when, as a young man under thirty, I was preparing to defend Rocco Carnavalle on a charge of murder in the first degree.

Contrary to the practice of English barristers who leave these difficult and unpleasant tasks to the solicitors, I spent many hours with this defendant in the counsel room of the Tombs, trying to learn and understand his case. The theory of the prosecution was that Rofrano, a member of Mayor Mitchel's cabinet, had employed Carnavalle as a kind of murder broker to procure a gunman by the name of Tony Montimagno to shoot a henchman of an important Democratic leader.

The District Attorney contended that my client had had a conference in a Brooklyn flat at which Montimagno was present and in which he agreed to do the killing. In one of my last talks with the defendant, he repeated what he had told me before, namely, that he had had a conference in this flat but that it did not relate in any way to a plan to murder, and that Montimagno was not present, indeed that he had never met him, and I asked him then to name again all those who had been there. He cudgeled his mind, evidently having heretofore considered it unimportant, and then rather casually remarked that in that conference there was present a man named Tony *Mongano*. The similarity between the names *Montimagno* and *Mongano* struck me and I remembered it; it was well that I did so, for, as I shall presently explain, it saved my client's life.

At the trial I called the defendant as a witness in his own behalf. He was not a very literate Italian and he had some difficulty with the English language, in addition to which—as what man on trial for his life would not be—he was extremely nervous. I asked him the usual introductory questions and he, of course, denied that he had participated in the remotest way in the homicide. I then asked him if he had attended a conference in a Brooklyn flat; he admitted this but said it was in no way related to any murder. I then asked him to enumerate the persons present at that conference, feeling that a stronger impression would be made upon the jury by having him tell those who were there rather than asking him first if Tony Montimagno (the acknowledged killer) had been present.

To my dying day I shall never forget the scene that followed. Quite confidently he reeled off half a dozen Italian names. He paused for a moment and then said there was "also present Tony Mon—" and stopped, turned red, and snapped his fingers, giving everyone the impression that he was about to say Tony *Montimagno.* The District Attorney looked up and smiled broadly and knowingly at the jury. His eyes (if not his voice) were saying, "You see, gentlemen, the truth will out."

It was the dramatic highpoint of the trial. The situation called for instant action. Something had to be done—at once. To have ignored the incident, hoping that it would be forgotten, would have meant the electric chair. To have passed it by for the present, and having later learned his explanation, then to have re-called him would have been just as fatal. Something had to be done then—then or never!

The situation called for instantaneous action, but it called even more for a weapon with which to destroy the bad impression the defendant had just made. I had that weapon, one supplied by what my client previously had told me, and my recollection of it. And so while the District Attorney was still smiling at the jury and the twelve pairs of eyes were focused on the witness, without letting another instant pass, I asked, "Rocco, in telling us who was present at that conference, you just said 'there was Tony Mon—' and then you stopped. Were you about to say Tony *Mongano?*" The sun seemed to break through his dark clouds and he became a relaxed and different person when he answered "Yes." Then in order to emphasize the similarity between the two names and thus the occasion for his confusion, I went on: "You said Tony *Mongano* was there; was Tony *Montimagno* also there?" To which with clear and steady voice he answered "No."

His life was saved and although he was convicted of murder in the second degree, I obtained a reversal by the Appellate Division which the Court of Appeals affirmed. A man in whose innocence I believed went free.

I could enumerate many other incidents in my own practice as well as in that of abler lawyers, all of which in one way or another illustrate the incalculable importance of personal preparation, not by proxy, but by the advocate himself, who is to present the case. One such instance came in my defense of the District Attorney of one of the great counties of New York City against whom charges had been preferred, looking to his removal by the Governor.

I had never met my client until he asked me to defend him. I therefore began at the beginning, searching out his background, his education, his family life, and his career. I spent two whole uninterrupted days and parts of two nights on this before even considering the facts in the case. I wanted to know what manner of man he was, whether I trusted him, and whether others, particularly the Governor before whom his case would come, would be justified in believing in him. Were there any dark corners in his life? Was he an honest man?

As a result of a prolonged and detailed inquiry I was able to answer these questions to my complete satisfaction and I came to the conclusion that he had never been guilty of any wrongful act, let alone one that was criminal. My trust in him became absolute. And now let me tell you in what stead this supreme confidence was to stand him.

The trial came on in the large executive chamber in Albany before Governor Lehman. The room was crowded with spectators and representatives of the press. Before the trial wide publicity had been given to the charges, and as the trial progressed, it filled the front pages of all the leading newspapers of the state. Some of them had shown marked partisanship and were loud in excoriating this unjustly accused official.

In this atmosphere my client took the stand, preserving, as he had every reason to do, his composure. He was and looked an honest man. If grave doubt could be cast upon his character, my opponent not only felt that this would furnish fuel to the flames but hoped that public opinion, thus aroused, might not go unnoticed by the Governor. With this hope evidently in mind, he began his cross-examination:

"Mr. District Attorney, I understand that you went to Ireland last summer?" "Yes, sir." "What line did you travel on?" The witness told him. "Who paid for your passage?" "I did." "Did you pay for it by check?" "No, I paid cash." "Oh, cash!" the prosecutor exclaimed with glee. "Where did you get the cash?" "I obtained it from a box in my house." "Oh, you had several thousand dollars in cash in your house?" The purpose was evident and I waited until it became plainer still. It was clear that the prosecutor was now seeking to convey that there was something wrong in this. It was the era when we had been hearing so much about tin boxes.

And so at this point I stood up and objected. "What is the ground of your objection?" the Governor asked me. "Your Excellency," I said, "the first ground is that the question is irrelevant. There is nothing in the specifications alleging any financial wrongdoing of any kind on my client's part and the question in its plain implication suggests that there was some wrongdoing in this transaction, that perhaps this cash had been obtained by some illicit means, possibly as a result of being bribed."

And then in a room now dead silent, I went on. "But before

I finish with my objection, I wish to couple it with this further statement. Although we have now been engaged for more than three weeks in this trial, and although there is no charge before us justifying this question, if my opponent, even at this late day, wishes to amend his charges so as to allege bribery or corruption, I will consent to the amendment and I will withdraw my objection."

Governor Lehman looked at my opponent and said: "Do you wish to amend your charges?" "Let me first confer with my associates," he answered. He then sat down to engage in a long whispered consultation with his assistants. As they conferred, the clock ticked loudly, and we all waited. During this interlude I happened to glance at some of my client's Assistant District Attorneys and the look I read in their eyes was not encouraging. I could almost hear them saying, as they stared at me: "This idiot! Haven't we enough trouble already without inviting a charge of bribery?" But I was not worried because I had no doubt that if such a charge were made, I could destroy it utterly, and if on the other hand the prosecutor now declined to allege that which he was implying, it might destroy the whole prosecution.

Finally, after what seemed to me a half hour's conference with his associates (although in fact it was not more than four or five minutes), the prosecutor got to his feet and the Governor again asked him if he desired to amend the charges. "We do not wish to amend," he answered, and the chief executive brought down his heavy gavel on the desk with a resounding bang. "Very well," he said, "the objection is sustained."

The case dragged on for many days and resulted finally in a complete vindication and exoneration of my client, but I am sure that the case was really decided when that objection was sustained. This little story illustrates, I think, several things. First, that it is of the highest importance to have studied the client so as to reach a definite conclusion as to his fundamental integrity, and second, the willingness at a crucial time in the trial to stake your whole case on the correctness of your estimate.

An English barrister, removed as he is from personal contact with his client, would be deprived, it seems to me, of so sound a basis for making such a decision. I'm sure you remember how poor Mr. Pickwick worried about the breach of promise case Mrs. Bardell had brought against him. His solicitor, Mr. Perker, had engaged the great barrister Serjeant Snubbin to try the case, and Mr. Pickwick asked for the privilege of a personal interview with his famous counsel.

Aghast at so radical a proposal, Perker finally stammered in amazement, "See! Serjeant Snubbin, my dear sir! Pooh, pooh, my dear sir, impossible! See Serjeant Snubbin! Bless you, my dear sir, such a thing was never heard of, without a consultation fee being previously paid and a consultation fixed. It couldn't be done, my dear sir. It couldn't be done!"

But Pickwick was adamant and a few minutes later Dickens ushers him into the chambers of the great Serjeant Snubbin himself. On being invited into the inner sanctum, now on the eve of trial he met his counsel for the first time and told the surprised barrister: ". . . I have come here because I wish you distinctly to understand, as my friend Mr. Perker has said, that I am innocent of the falsehood laid to my charge, and although I am very well aware of the inestimable value of your assistance, sir, I must beg to add, that unless you sincerely believe this, I would rather be deprived of the aid of your talents than have the advantage of them!"

I am sure that in like circumstances any of us would have felt as Mr. Pickwick did; and you will remember that Serjeant Snubbin lost the case. Perhaps he might have won it had he taken more time with his client.

But let's get back to the new and important case that has reached your office and in which you have now been engaged in preparation for many weeks. You have worked every waking moment, and even while you slept, your subconscious mind has been wrestling with its many problems. You have literally absorbed the facts.

Asked why he read the Greek authorities, Antonius replied, "Well, . . . just as when walking in the sunshine, . . . the natural result is that I get sunburned, even so, after perusing these books rather closely, . . . I find that under their influence my discourse takes on what I may call a new complexion." So you will have become literally sunburned from your exposure to the facts.

Meanwhile you will have been obsessed by a thousand details in your collection of the proofs. You will have tried to assemble every paper, every letter, every affidavit, every particle of previously given testimony, and you will be annoyed and harassed at the difficulties and delays in bringing them together. And as your records grow toward a completion, you will see to it that your plan of arranging, filing, and cross-indexing your material for ready, instant use has been carried out. For what good can all your researches do if you are unable to lay your hands on the desired document. You will not adopt, I hope, Lincoln's filing system. He kept one envelope labeled: "If you can't find it anywhere else, look in here."

Do not rely upon your acquired skill in advocacy to surmount the embarrassment and delay at some hour of the trial when you cannot find a needed paper. "Orderliness in the arrangement of the documents in a case," says Lord MacMillan, "has far more importance than is generally realized. Which of us has not seen the confusion produced by a paper going missing just at the moment when it is wanted, or the irritation of the judge when he finds his copy of the document differently arranged and paged from counsel's copy? The thread of the argument is interrupted, tempers are upset, and half of the effect of a good speech may be irreparably lost. All this can be avoided by a little forethought and system. . . . But . . . when what I may call the mechanical apparatus of a case works easily and well, the mind of the judge is inevitably favorably impressed. He follows easily what is presented to him and he is predisposed to accept what is so well-ordered."

But you will have many other difficulties confronting you. Among which not the least is the problem of public relations. The newspapers will be constantly calling you for information; reporters will be dropping in seeking to entrap you into an interview. Magazine and fiction writers will beg you for material with which to ply their trade. And no matter how annoying all these interruptions are, you will somehow hold a strong rein on your temper, you will treat all with courtesy.

Meanwhile you will press quietly on in mastering the facts, all the facts of your case; for do what you will, you may never learn them all. You will keep on learning them up to the eve of trial, you will learn many in the trial itself, and indeed you will be the exception if you do not learn still more after the verdict is recorded. And so, amid your hopes and fears, your moments of elation and despair, like a good infantry soldier, you will slog along hour by hour, never wearying and never giving up your dogged resolution to find what the facts are.

Why should this be so difficult? One reason is that every

accused person seeks to put his best foot forward with you. He has rationalized many things, he has colored others in his own mind, and he has forgotten still more.

From long experience you will have learned that one of the most difficult tasks confronting the good lawyer is the handling of the client. You must possess a shrewd and thoroughly penetrating discernment in dealing with him. You can be firm and still not be offensive. You must deserve and win his confidence and, more than all else, his respect. You will study his real character, the good parts and the bad, even as he will be studying yours. A great doctor, I have heard it said, is one who inspires hope and confidence in his sick patient. This is equally true of a good lawyer.

But there is this vast difference between law and medicine; the patient is necessarily more tractable than the client because the patient is in a realm in which he knows that he is ignorant. What does he know about the progress of a brain tumor, the inroads of cancer, or the true significance of a blood clot? The client, however, is apt to feel quite capable of forming judgments, since he is fully cognizant of the facts; he is quite certain that he can appreciate their true significance as well as you, and often considers himself as good a judge, sometimes a better one, of what should be done as you are.

Right here lies one of the great problems confronting every conscientious lawyer. He must receive and honestly consider every suggestion that his client makes to him, and sometimes the suggestion is a good one, one perhaps that had not previously occurred to him. But more often he knows from his experience that it would be unwise, perhaps even folly; and not infrequently the client will seek to press his views, often abetted by the lawyer who has brought the case or by some nameless counselor whom he knew at college or whom he has met recently at a cocktail party. Again you will be patient, but firm.

And right here your powers of persuasion, your ability as an advocate, may undergo more ruthless testing than that experienced within a crowded courtroom. It is right here that you will display your power of advocacy or your lack of it. You will summon up your lessons of experience, you will argue with the best logic you possess, you will cite illustrations from your previous practice, you will endeavor to explain the vagaries and the prejudices of the average juror, and the probable reception of the course of conduct now so sedulously pressed upon you, with the full realization that if you do not do what is wanted and the case is lost, you will be forever blamed, if not damned, for your refusal. You will nonetheless continue in your opposition to what you know is a poor plan.

Whether you prevail or not in the conferences will depend upon your strength of character and your client's estimate of it; this may cause you to persuade him where no art of advocacy would suffice. For did not Aristotle tell us twenty-two hundred years ago that character is the best means of persuasion an advocate possesses?

You will probably convince your client that he is wrong, but if you fail in this, you will then once more review your own position and it may be that you will conclude that the point is sufficiently in doubt to enable you to say to him: "It is your liberty and not mine that is at stake. You are an intelligent man and I respect your reasoning although I do not agree with it. I will then, if you wish, follow what you propose and I shall do so with the same zest as though the idea had my approval, which it does not. But you must remember that the course suggested is yours and not mine, and you must be prepared to take the consequences, my predictions of which I hope and trust will prove wrong." It is likely that he will then acquiesce in your advice, but if not, you go ahead as promised. What your client wants done, however, may be so fantastic and so futile that you are unwilling to stake your reputation on a course so hopeless. In such a case you will say to him: "I will return your retainer to you. The thing for you to do is to engage a lawyer who agrees with you."

But if you surmount this difficulty, you will not permit the argument to dull your zeal and you will go ahead. By this time you may conclude that you are sufficiently acquainted with the case to put your client through a dress rehearsal cross-examination. You will then proceed to cross-examine as you imagine the United States Attorney will ultimately do. You will ask your questions in the most barbed form you can contrive and listen to his answers without comment until the ordeal is over.

When you are through, you point out where you have tripped him, and by going back over the records show him how he can truthfully answer without being tripped. At this point I often simulate the witness and ask one of my associates to cross-examine me and to unhorse me if he can. It is a great exercise, in the performance of which I have often found that I did not do so well as I had hoped. My failures and the reasons for them are then discussed, and I now ask my associate to change places with me and I then cross-examine him. From this, new ideas are developed while all the time the client is looking on and listening. He probably is saying, "Let me try again." And you will then go through the whole process once more. This time he does far better.

It is a method indispensable to giving the defendant confidence. If finally he can come off with colors flying, he stands in less dread of anything the prosecutor ultimately may ask him at the trial. His hope and courage are built up. His morale is strengthened, and the morale of your case is of all things the most important, even as it is in war.

And now finally the time comes when you go through a dress rehearsal of the defendant's direct examination, and you go through it step by step, even as you will presently be doing at the trial. You see how he gets over the hard spots (I have never seen a case without hard spots in it) and how generally he conducts himself. When he is through, you go back, perhaps for the fiftieth time, over the awkward places, re-examining his previous testimony and showing him how he can surmount his difficulties though still staying well within the truth, the whole truth, and nothing but the truth.

Then you will seat him opposite you and go through the whole narrative once more. This time he will do better, but his manner and deportment could be much improved, so you pretend again to be the client and ask one of your associates to put you through the direct examination, and as you tell the story, you pretend that the jury sits before you and you will not look at them as a whole but select individual members, making an impression first on one and then upon another.

Throughout all these days and weeks of preparation you will be thinking, thinking about your case.

One of my associates on the District Attorney's staff, when I was twenty-four, was a young man named George Medalie. He became a great trial lawyer and finally a judge of the New York Court of Appeals. Before he left the bar to assume the less onerous and less difficult judicial life, he said to me: "You know, Lloyd, there is no substitute in the handling of a case for good hard thinking, and I have long made it a practice after I have probed every corner of the problem, of lying on my office couch with the door closed and just thinking, thinking about my case."

I have always followed the same practice. By thinking, imagination will be whetted, and from thinking and imagination ideas will spring, and those ideas may become the keys to a successful verdict. By thinking, you will evolve the strategy and tactics of your case, and a campaign in the courtroom is as dependent upon strategy and tactics as on the field of battle.

Strategy has been defined as a science of combining and analyzing the means which the different branches of the art of war afford, for the purpose of forming projects in directing great military movements. Strategy is generalship. Tactics, we are told, is the science or art of disposing military or naval forces in order of battle and of performing military or naval maneuvers with them. Other writers have defined the term as the art of inventing and making machines for throwing missile weapons. These are military definitions but they are as applicable to the art of advocacy as to the art of war.

The conduct of a trial has been likened to a game of chess and the two have many similarities. But there is this great difference: chess is pure mathematics, pure skill without any element of chance. But in war and litigation, chance plays an enormous if incalculable part. "If we contemplate a litigation closely," says John C. Reed, "we see that it is more like warfare than a game." Advocacy without the most minute study and patient preparation is nothing. Without these it is a snare and a delusion. No eloquence, no quickness of wit, no knowledge of the law can be a substitute for a mastery of the facts. For important as words are, advocacy rests not on words but on the facts which words describe. A skillful handling of the facts is advocacy.

And now I see you in your office, carefully tying up your papers (well indexed and well arranged, let us hope) and waiting for your day in court—your client's day. You are now prepared for this, as well prepared as you will ever be. Tired from your long labors, there may come upon you in your weaker moments misgivings, and a depression that breeds fear. But you have assumed the task; you have put your hand to the plow and you intend to follow the long furrow to the end. Only stupid unimaginative men have not experienced fear, but as a great voice once told us on the radio, "There is nothing to fear but fear itself." In those dark hours I suggest that you reread one of the most dramatic stories in the Old Testament.

You will remember that one day when Moses was tending the flock of Jethro, his father-in-law, he drew near to the Mountain of Horeb and there saw a burning bush. The fire blazed but the bush was not consumed, and as he moved toward it, the Lord spoke to him from the bush and said: "Draw not nigh hither: put off thy shoes from off thy feet, for the place whereon thou standest is holy ground."

You have enlisted for the duration; there is no turning back. Maintain with all your strength the courses that you have charted. Fight it out on the lines you have prepared. Do all within your power to defend the position you have taken. "The place whereon thou standest is holy ground."

CHAPTER

II

─────────

In Court at Last

W HEN BROADWAY puts on a play depicting a great trial
scene, the box office is usually in for a long harvest. The
customers flock to see a good actor cast in the role of the defendant's counsel or the prosecuting attorney. There is something
about a scene of this kind that kindles the imagination of all
playgoers; there are many in my recollection that still live. *The
Winslow Boy*, a dramatization of Carson's famous defense of
young Archer Shee, delighted us a season or two ago. But the one
that I remember best was *Libel*, a colorful and skillfully produced case of mistaken identity.

Alexander Woollcott invited me to attend this play with him
and, between the acts, took me backstage to meet Mr. Edward
Lawton, who played with rare ability the defendant's counsel.
Himself the son of a distinguished English barrister, he was a

very talented and brilliant man. I told him how much I was enjoying the fine play and his admirable acting, and he asked me
if I had noticed anything wrong. I told him that I had attended
many trials in the Old Bailey and that I could see no flaw. "Ah,"
he said, "but did you notice where my junior sat?" "Right beside you," I answered. "Yes, yes," he said, "but you know the
junior never sits beside his senior—he always sits behind him."
He then went on to discuss the many changes that had befallen
England in late years, and added, "But there is one thing that
has not changed—the English Bar. The old Bar of England will
remain unchanged, unshaken, come what may."

So strong is the average American's addiction to trial scenes
that he will even attend the dreadful Hollywood concoctions that
so monstrously distort and parody proceedings in a court—those
dreadful films in which the part of trial counsel is played by
some girl whose sex is not unstressed, with good-looking legs and
wearing very high-heeled patent leather pumps. I have seen
sickening performances of this kind and so have you. They are
enough to cast ridicule on the administration of justice.

But if the public finds drama in these imitations of the stage,
how much more dramatic are real trials of real cases in real
courts. There was once a time, before the advent of the movies
and the radio, when in the small communities at least the courthouse offered better entertainment than the theater.

Yet the average citizen, despite his avid interest in imaginary
trials produced upon the stage, takes little interest in the law;
the subject bores him. He might listen politely while you are
pointing out that there could be no liberty without law, and that
it is the law that through the centuries has given us such civilization as we have. Should you continue on a little further and
try to tell him that in greater or less degree, in all countries

and at all times, the law has been a governing force, he would begin to yawn, and were you to persist enough to inform him that this was true under the Code of Hammurabi, the earliest national code in the world, that it was true of the Decalogue brought down by Moses from Mount Sinai, that it was equally so with the Chinese under the Regulations of Chow Li, with the Hindus under the Laws of Manu, with the Romans under the Twelve Tables, and that the seventeen Maxims of Shotoku performed a similar office for the Japanese, as did the Sayings of Mohammed for the Arabians, the Judgments of Caratnia for the Celts, the Code of Justinian for the Roman Empire, and the Year Books for the early English—were you to tell the average man these things, he would be fast asleep before you were half done.

But though the average citizen takes little interest in the law and even less in the history and philosophy of jurisprudence, his fascination in seeing and hearing what actually goes on in a courtroom before a judge, or preferably before a judge and jury, never ceases. And he will read the great trials of history with equal interest.

Who has not thrilled to Plato's great account of the trial of Socrates or wept at the ordeal of Jesus before Pontius Pilate or shuddered at the infamous injustice visited upon Catherine of Aragon by Henry VIII and Cardinal Wolsey, who served his king far better than his God? Who has not sympathized with Mary, Queen of Scots, when she was persecuted by Elizabeth? And what man who has ever read a page of history has not been stirred by Macaulay's great portrayal of the trial of the Seven Bishops and his even more colorful account of the seven-year ordeal of Warren Hastings? Since juries are made up of average citizens, many of the twelve listeners are as alertly interested in the real drama as they have been by those presented in the theater, and as intelligently critical.

But your trial—the one I have imagined you preparing—will not have footlights to illuminate it. Your D Day has come, and it is the real thing. Your client's case, his good name, his liberty are now finally in your hands, and it is not only your client and his case that are about to go on trial—but you. All your character and courage, all your skill, all past experience, all that you know and are, all that you have been, will be on trial.

You leave your associates to see to it that your papers are in court and decide to walk by yourself to the place that now awaits you. You move on to Nassau Street and each step brings you one yard nearer to the courthouse. What thoughts cross your mind as you press forward! Are you ready for trial? Are *you* ready? Have you done all within your power to make ready? Is your trial brief as good as you could make it? Do your memoranda of the law contain every statute and decision that could help you? Has every last corner of the law been scientifically explored? Have your researches probed to the utmost the legislative history of the statutes that confront you? Have all the law reviews of all the schools been studied and digested? Do you know your facts? Have you tested out your plan of action and are you satisfied with it? Are you ready for trial?

And as every step draws you nearer to your destination, you think again for the hundredth time of the judge who will preside. Have you been before him on some previous occasion and thus learned of his peculiarities, his prejudices, his whims? And if you have not learned to know him in this way, have you sat patiently in court in other cases to make note of the manner of man this judge of yours really is?

At this stage in your career, you have long since learned that trial by jury is a trial by a judge *and* jury and that the judge is just as important to you as the twelve men who will decide your case. Although he does not accompany the triers of the fact into the jury room to deliberate upon the verdict with them, his every word and look and intonation will, in the course of the trial, weigh with the twelve men as much as, if not more than, his final charge. He has often been described as a thirteenth juror and he is indeed that, especially in the Federal court, where great latitude is given him in commenting on the evidence. But since he is a man, he is human too—just as human as the laymen whose names the wheel has brought finally into the box.

Judges, like other men, are products of their environment, their education, and inherited predilections; they have their hopes and fears, aspirations and ambitions, and their weaknesses and strengths, their susceptibility (however they resist it), to the impact of public opinion. Mr. Dooley once quipped that even the Supreme Court follows the election returns. In short, no matter how intellectually honest a judge may be, he is still not an abstraction but a thing of flesh and blood—in short, a man. Laws are made by man and those who administer them are only men. For it is human and not divine justice that in your case will be done—and there is quite a difference between the two. How important then is it that you should have learned all you can of human nature, for on its strange vagaries your client's liberty will presently depend.

Perhaps you may be thinking of that shambles of injustice which was the first trial of Police Lieutenant Charles Becker, under the aegis of Mr. Justice John Goff. I have often thought of him as I walked to court. I shall later tell you something more about him.

But although some of our modern judges have less humanity

than others, the days of bloody Jeffreys are no more. I know of no John Goff now sitting on the bench. Yet the problems of psychology are still with us. A trial still presents the struggle of one mind working on another, and the laws of psychology govern the judicial mind like those of lesser men. He has been sworn to do justice but in so doing he has not, because he cannot, divested himself of the usual attributes of human nature. His mind has not become a machine. For the advocate, therefore, of equal importance with knowing his case well is knowing all he can about the judge who will preside.

Nearly two thousand years ago, Quintilian wrote: "I should also wish if possible to be acquainted with the character of the judges. For it will be desirable to enlist their temperaments, in the service of our cause where they are likely to be useful, or to mollify them if they are likely to prove adverse, just as accordingly they are harsh, gentle, cheerful, grave, stern, or easy going."

Lord MacMillan, recognizing this truth, once wrote: "I used to find *Who's Who* quite a useful volume to consult before addressing a Parliamentary Committee with whose members I was unacquainted. It is unwise to attack too violently the practices of landowners when that invaluable manual has informed you that a member of the committee owns three thousand acres or to assail the methods of a trade in which it tells you that another member is engaged, or even to deride a recreation in which another member has actually confided to the public that he indulges."

And as you walk on toward the courthouse, you will be thinking too of the prosecutor who will oppose you, the man who will seek to bring you to your knees, and strike down and destroy your client. What manner of man is this lawyer for the Government? Perhaps you know him well, and it may be that you have felt his blade in other contests. If not, you will from other sources have learned all you could about him, and will no doubt have attended in the courtroom some of his other cases to watch his methods and to learn all that it was possible to learn about his skill, his weaknesses, and his strength, even as Napoleon and Robert Lee were wont to study and thereby to discern the true nature of an opposing general. This stood them in good stead, and whatever you may have learned of your adversary will be of vast moment to you when at some crucial hour of the trial you may be called upon to make an instantaneous decision that wrongly made will spell disaster for your client, or if rightly made may mean his vindication and his triumph.

And as you dodge traffic and try not to knock down the swirling passers-by, and you approach your ordeal ever nearer, you will no doubt be pondering that inarticulate major premise of public opinion. For public opinion will permeate the courtroom and subconsciously your jurors' minds. We have a constitutionally guaranteed free press and it is well that it is so, yet I believe that it is anything but well that we have discarded the restraints under which the British courts hold English newspapers. Jury tampering is a crime, yet palpable attempts through the press to persuade jurors in advance of a trial as to what verdict they should render is one of the great and thus far unchecked evils of our day.

We have now with us the half sister of lynch law: the trial by newspaper. It is an outrage and a blot upon our civilization, and it is one with which no advocate can contend on equal terms. He finds himself simultaneously engaged in two trials, not one. One is taking place before the judge and jury, where witnesses may be cross-examined and documents and other evidence that are irrelevant, excluded. But in that other trial, the trial by newspaper that runs concurrently, there are no restraints of legal evidence nor the administration of its rules by a fair judge. In this newspaper trial, abetted now by the radio and soon (if the sponsors have their way) by television, no holds are barred. From the morning papers the jury may read the full documents excluded the day before, or follow in detail what a witness, not allowed to testify, would have sworn to if he had been permitted.

Thus are the rules of evidence both thwarted and surmounted, and if there is any part of our jurisprudence more indispensable than another to the administration of justice, it is the law of evidence. Through the centuries there has been put together, bit by bit, by Anglo-American judges, the rules that govern what may and may not be put before the jury in the courtroom. Based as they are upon the principles of inductive logic, the philosophy behind them is that laymen are not logicians and therefore should be prevented from hearing facts from which illogical conclusions are irresistible.

These rules of evidence are not the mere technical inventions of judges and lawyers, they are the instruments with which the jury system is made to work and without which a jury trial would be a shambles not unakin to mob rule.

On your walk to court you have been thinking of many things. Your mind so long occupied with your case seeks a moment's relaxation. Pictures of your whole past life come trooping in a flash before you, bringing back the bright untrammeled hours of childhood when books seemed more real to you than life itself. Perhaps you may be recalling something of the delight derived from your first encounter with Bunyan's *Pilgrim's Progress*, the only allegory ever written that possesses strong human interest, so strong that when you read it as a child, the allegory was completely missed and the narrative seemed only the story of a brave adventure.

For by this time on your walk up Nassau Street, you have reached the cheap and gaudy stores from which blare the radios and the loud raucous singing from innumerable victrolas, and by the din you are reminded of Vanity Fair, that picture of this world which Bunyan has so finely drawn. And you may be thinking of the trial of Faithful before Lord Hategood and a jury composed of personified vices of which Mr. Blindman was the foreman, and Mr. Highmind, Mr. Liar, Mr. Enmity, and Mr. Malice were among the other jurors. You will be recalling how the people of the town of Vanity were the subjects of Beelzebub and how from their midst this jury had been drawn. And you may be thinking of how Bunyan led you by the hand behind the scenes to listen in on the deliberations of the jury and to hear from its various members such exclamations as "Hang him! Hang him! He is a rogue." "Hanging is too good for him!" "Let us forthwith bring him in guilty of death."

You will hark back to the horror awakened in your young mind when you read how the mob took this prisoner from his cage, fastened him to a stake and burned him alive, and you will remember all your youthful consternation in learning that such things happen on this earth. And as you walk along you may be reflecting that this trial of Faithful at Vanity Fair was all but merciful compared with that of Alice Lisle and with innumerable other horrible miscarriages of justice with which later you became familiar. You will be recalling too how when you grew older you rejoiced to find Macaulay expressing for you your own opinion of *Pilgrim's Progress* when he wrote that it is "invaluable as a study to every person who wishes to obtain a wide command over the English language. The vocabulary is the vocabulary of the common people, yet no writer has said more exactly what he would like to say."

Reflecting upon man's cruelty and inhumanity to man, your mind may turn back to the most celebrated trial in history when Pontius Pilate, a weak judge, chose to yield to public clamor. Looking back to that far distant scene, you may be wondering what a great advocate might have done had there been one to defend the prisoner. Could Erskine, perhaps, or Daniel Webster, or Lincoln or Rufus Choate, or Edward Carson have beaten down the clamor of the mob, stiffened the weak spine of Pontius Pilate, and have shamed him into doing right? Weak judges and weak juries both before and since have been led to follow a brave advocate. What might have been the result in the trial of Socrates had he had such an advocate? Or in that of Joan of Arc or Mary, Queen of Scots, or Marie Antoinette?

In your progress toward the courthouse, you have now passed City Hall Park and are approaching Foley Square at last, and it is high time that you lay aside all these reflections and think not of other cases but of your own. Your case, your client, these and nothing else must now absorb you and possess you to the exclusion of all else. You will long since have marked out your strategy; the hour for tactics is at hand.

Other lawyers are now rushing along to court; they greet you and wish you well. Clerks of the court are hurrying to perform their several duties. Some of these may stop and speak to you, and perhaps a passing judge or two greet you. And as you approach the Federal Courthouse, you notice that the mounted police are out this day in force. Some of them may know and hail you. On the sidewalk, directly in front of the long granite steps, you see the newspaper photographers scurrying about. You run the gamut of their flashing bulbs.

There is a long queue of would-be spectators hoping somehow to crowd their way into a courtroom that will not hold a hundredth of their number. There will be law students who step out of line to beseech your aid in getting them into the trial. Others there may pretend to know you, and you are importuned by them in turn. You do your best to help them all.

Good will is infectious; you can neither have nor display too much of it. It carries with it a special atmosphere of its own—an atmosphere that may somehow temper the climate of opinion in the very courtroom itself. If you are in truth a friendly, kindly man, the fact that you are will somehow become well known. In every honest, decent way, do all you can to create this atmosphere, for in addition to your other tasks, you must be a kind of public relations expert for your client. I have often said that you should begin trying your case by the time you have come within a thousand yards of the courthouse. If by your very conduct and deportment as you approach the great task confronting you you have somehow attained good will and won friends from the very bystanders, this will help you and sustain you and may give you countenance before the twelve pairs of eyes that presently will search you through and through.

You will finally have gotten through the crowds into the courthouse itself and will have worked your way into the crowded elevator. It stops at the appointed floor; you are about to enter court at last.

There are innumerable stories of the way in which great lawyers have made their dramatic entry. Marshall Hall was a tall and singularly handsome man, a noticeable figure in any gathering. He was popular with the crowds. They watched him as he entered court, and whispered and made way or sometimes roared with vehement applause as he hurried into the Old Bailey.

But long before his arrival, a clerk had brought in his air cushion and had carefully arranged it for him. A row of bottles containing smelling salts and other medicines was then set upon his desk, while beside these would be placed an exquisite eighteenth-century box containing some invaluable pill. A nose spray occupied a prominent place, while beside it several blue, green, and red pencils were laid out in a neat row ready for the great man's use. When all of these stage properties were in order, and while the judge waited, the famed barrister made his dramatic entry.

As an attempted justification of all this, Edward Marjoribanks has said that an advocate "must be something of an actor, not indeed playing a well-learned part before painted scenery, but fighting real battles on other men's behalf. . . ." Marshall Hall himself once declared: "My profession and that of an actor are somewhat akin, except that I have no scenes to help me, and no words are written for me to say. There is no backcloth to increase the illusion. There is no curtain. But out of the vivid living drama of somebody else's life, I have to create an atmosphere—for that is advocacy."

Atmosphere, that nothing, that vague and intangible something, that everything, is a vital element in the trial, and within limits the advocate may stimulate it, for whether he would or no, there is a general feeling that permeates the courtroom, the judge, and above all the jury—a kind of indoor climate of opinion. If favorable, it can help, sometimes more than any evidence. But if it turns hostile, the strongest proofs may not prevail.

A trained advocate knows this well and a large part of his effort will be directed, through every legitimate means within his power, to help make that atmosphere a favorable one. One way of doing this is through one's obvious feeling of good will. Your friendly attitude is displayed toward all who see you, and yet underneath your smile there must appear a real and un-shakable courage and the evident conviction that you are in earnest—that you intend, come what may, to fight your client's cause with manly intrepidity and unyielding resolution.

Different men convey this in different ways even as they enter court. But in every great advocate, in one way or another, a strong determination is apparent, so apparent that all who see him feel it. Thus it was when Bourke Cockran stepped out upon the field of battle and thus it was with John B. Stanchfield, Jim Osborne, William Travers Jerome, Max Steuer, Martin Little-ton, and so many others.

Of all these the least dramatic was Mr. Steuer. He seemed desirous of not courting notice. Everything he did was quiet. He came with no fanfare, no equipment of expensive brief-cases; he carried an old brown envelope in his hand. There was about him an innate modesty, bordering on humility. He was dressed modestly; he was modest. He seemed to be saying, "Pay no attention to me. I am not important; my case is, but I am not." Thus he afforded a sharp contrast to the opposing army. He brought few assistants with him, more often none, and if any did accompany him, they never by any chance were permitted to interrupt or prompt him. He resented interruptions, he never needed prompting.

It was as though he said, "See, I am here alone against a multitude. I do not know how I can worst this Goliath who now laughs and sneers at me, but insofar as lies within my power, I will play the part of David, even with my little sling." And when finally he spoke, it was with a voice so low that few within the courtroom heard him and the jurors had to strain to catch his words. Yet he created an atmosphere that few men at the bar have succeeded in achieving.

And now as you are entering the court, you will have your part to play. You will be dressed neither like a race track tout nor an undertaker's assistant. You will have on a dark suit and an inconspicuous tie. You will not be thinking how the great advocates of the past conducted themselves; you will not be imitating Erskine or Webster or Littleton or Steuer. You will be imitating no one; you will be yourself. Whatever that may be, you will prefer the genuine article to an imitation.

Your years in the court will have taught you your short-comings, and you will have found the things you can do well. You will long since have put aside the disappointment that you do not look like Daniel Webster, or Rufus Choate or Abraham Lincoln; you will have learned to endure the face God gave you with philosophy and resignation. And you may be helped in this by the recollection that some men at the bar who looked like titans, when the crisis came, proved dwarfs.

Your strength will come from the knowledge that you know your case, all of it, inside and out, and that your lines of strategy have been thoroughly developed and that from long previous experience you feel yourself equipped to meet the exigencies of tactics. Your client enters and you step forward to greet him. You engage in none of the formalities of encouragement; rather by the way you grip his hand and look him smilingly in the eye do you transmit to him your own quiet confidence.

You know that in this struggle now impending morale outweighs all else. Your client must have it; you must convey it in every word and action, for all are looking at you now, especially the gentlemen of the press, who sit with pencils poised to record all they see and hear—and sometimes much else. They will be watching you to determine whether your confidence is real or feigned, even as the jury presently will do. And as you sit now waiting for the court to open, you will try to remember one thing only: be yourself, be simple, avoid pretension.

The door behind the bench swings back. The marshal raps for order, directing everyone to rise. The judge is coming in! He comes at last, he is here—a man of dignity and sober mien, clad in his black judicial robe. He bows to counsel and quietly now takes his seat. The trial has begun. The jury wheel is turning, and as the clerk draws out the names, the talesmen answering to them move swiftly to the box. Twelve are soon seated and then two alternates. You watch them, studying their faces, trying to discern those to whom you would entrust your client's fate as well as those whom you most certainly will challenge—for cause if you can find it, peremptorily if you must—and you will be remembering that you have ten peremptory challenges and no more.

Who are these men, any one of whom may be your nemesis, or perhaps your staunch ally and defender? You will find, by glancing at the list just handed you, that they are all very respectable citizens—very! There will be assistant tellers from the great Wall Street banks, trusted executives from the utility companies, railroad men, and some not too friendly housewives, all well fed and with good coats on their backs. Their looks suggest that they consider themselves the spokesmen of society, the vindicators of law and order.

As you look at them, you long for the old days when you were permitted to examine every talesman separately and under oath, and were thus afforded opportunities of watching his reactions and noticing his expression as he answered you. In this way, in the State courts, and formerly in the Federal courts, you could, if you had had enough experience, sometimes make shrewd estimates of the man and often form an accurate opinion as to whether he was one to whom you would be willing to entrust the liberty of a fellow citizen.

The old system, I think, worked well, but there were abuses; some lawyers needlessly prolonged their examinations and so delayed the trial. When, therefore, the new Federal Rules of Criminal Procedure were adopted, Section 24A was written into them. It provides, among other things, that:

> The court may permit the defendant or his attorney and the attorney for the Government to conduct the examination of prospective jurors or may itself conduct the examination.

In the Southern District, at least, the judges seldom permit counsel to conduct the examination, allowing the lawyers merely to hand up questions which the judge may ask or may not ask as he sees fit. Nowhere in this questioning do you have the old opportunity of watching how a talesman may respond to the questions which you put to him, or of determining how he reacts to you. You sit there like the lawyers in the Continental courts, who must permit the judge to cross-examine for them. For the time being, you are one of the least important persons in the courtroom; the talesmen ignore you; you are little better than a spectator.

The twelve are now sworn and then the two alternates. Sworn before Almighty God to render a true verdict according to the evidence, and you look even more intently at what is now a jury —twelve judges of the facts. Twelve men among whom you hope no Mr. Blindman, as in Faithful's case, will be the foreman, and that among them will be found no Mr. Enmity nor Mr. Malice, and no Mr. Cruelty. Your next feverish weeks will be spent before them and you hope and pray that somewhere in their hearts there may be a sense of justice and humanity, and possibly some feeling of compassion. But whatever they may be, they are the jurors whom by every legitimate means within your power you will try somehow to persuade. That is why you are there.

Now the judge is bowing to the United States Attorney and asking him to proceed with the Government's opening. You settle back to listen. You settle back because there is nothing else you can do, for up to this time in the trial, you have been little better than a bystander. "Mr. Foreman and gentlemen of the jury," your adversary is saying, and the twelve look up at him with eager expectation, wondering how all that they have already heard on the radio or read during long weeks in the press will now be presented by the lawyer for the Government. You feel singularly isolated and alone; you realize perhaps as never before what a lonely role the defendant's counsel plays.

You stand between the citizen on trial and the massed power of society. The very title of the action dramatizes this: "The United States of America against John Smith." A hundred and sixty million people against one man. The odds are heavy, the contestants seem ill-matched. Thus far a hundred and sixty million—and the twelve members of that enormous mass who now sit before you and who feel themselves their representatives —have for months listened to one side, the side of the prosecution. Now the prosecutor is stating it again, more pointedly, more distinctly than it has yet been stated.

In a tense and crowded courtroom you listen as he marshals

every fact he is promising to prove. Everything that could be held adverse is paraded with consummate skill and care. The story bit by bit is put together until finally the canvas on which the character is being drawn stands forth in the darkest colors. Every favorable circumstance is glided over; every adverse fact is dwelt upon with loving care. The main witness for the Government may be a scoundrel and a villain, yet as the prosecutor gives his preview of his testimony, the narrative stands forth stripped of the low character of him who presently will unfold it on the witness stand.

And there is nothing you can do about all this but listen and suffer and hope that by the time your turn finally comes the jury will not have been so poisoned as to refuse to listen. Each of them is looking at you now with curiosity to watch how you take it. Few of their looks are friendly ones, many not far removed from downright hatred. They appear to say what many of the spectators in the courtroom seem with their eyes to be saying: "How dare you sit there and defend so terrible a man?"

And so, trying not to lose your composure and trying even harder not to look as though you had, you suffer through an hour or two or perhaps three of the one-sided story with which the courtroom rings. All your senses are alert, your eyes, your ears, and, as you think of the perjury that may be used as evidence against your client, your nose. With every faculty you have, you listen and watch the effect the prosecution's opening is having on the jury, and as an experienced trial counsel, you will not spend much time in taking notes; a date, a fact, a name, a phrase perhaps, but little more.

Sir Charles Russell, one of England's greatest advocates, one day glanced around at his junior and said, "What are you doing?" "Taking a note," was the answer. Russell looked at him and said: "What the devil do you mean by saying you are taking a note? Why don't you watch the case?" Watch the case! I agree with Judge Parry who, in recounting Russell's observation, declared it to be "the golden rule."

The United States Attorney is now working himself up to a climax and the walls reverberate with his denunciation. It soon will be over now. Your turn is coming. And so he finishes at last, and he has timed his closing peroration so that by no chance will it fall at the end of a session and especially not at the end of the day. To do so would give you a chance to rest and to collect yourself, but no such opportunity will be given you. He will close at eleven thirty in the morning or a little after three in the afternoon so that your request for an adjournment will fall upon deaf ears. The judge will direct you to proceed.

And so, as you pull yourself to your feet and look directly at the jury, you realize that you are as yet a stranger to them, and that they had almost forgotten that with all the United States of America against your client, there was anyone to speak for him. What can you do to lift the heavy gloom that hangs about you? What will you say to dispel the poisonous atmosphere? With what sentence can you startle your twelve listeners or shock them into the realization that there are two sides to this case and that your side has not yet been heard? As you glance about the jury, you feel as though a cold blast from the north had chilled you. Twelve pairs of hostile eyes now stare, and as you look into their pupils, they seem to shine and glint like the bright points of twenty-four sharp bayonets. What will you say? How will you say it? The answer to these questions will reveal your knowledge of the true nature of advocacy.

CHAPTER

III

The Opening Address

Too LITTLE has been said or written on the importance of the opening address. It presents many dangers and, at times, rare opportunities. It is a prelude, an introduction, and a preface, or as they say in movie parlance, a preview of the case about to be presented. It is a distinct and special art, differing in many essentials from the closing speech or any other task incumbent on the advocate to perform. And especially is this true of the opening for the defense in a criminal trial.

When a prosecutor has concluded, he has left (if his task was well performed) a picture in the jury's mind that, if allowed to linger there unaltered, can only spell disaster for your client. He will have told the jury every fact and circumstance that spell out guilt. He will have painted in the darkest colors the portrait of a villain and a rogue—a man so deaf to the dictates of decency and honor that to look at him is to recoil from an archenemy of mankind. And he will, if he is skillful, have done this so quietly and with such restraint as to persuade the jury of his fairness, indeed, of his sad regret to have been called on to perform so necessary yet so unpleasant a duty. The jury will have been made to feel that it was with pain and sorrow that the prosecutor has spoken. But you, as you listen, may be thinking of the Walrus and the Carpenter who, having invited the Oysters for a stroll, sat down to eat them, sorting out with sobs and tears those of the largest size.

The prosecutor has no ax to grind, his apparently dispassionate manner seems to indicate. He is the mere servant (sometimes, he will suggest, the ill-paid servant) of the Government, sworn to see that those who break the laws are brought to justice, and that to bring this particular person to justice is not only his duty but that of every juror in the box. His narrative of the facts will have been long but clear; every essential piece of evidence which he says that he can prove will have been dilated on with consummate thoroughness and almost loving care, and each act of the defendant will have been presented in the blackest form.

And the jury will have strained forward to listen, already prejudging your client's case before a single word of testimony has been uttered. In this forbidding and most hostile atmosphere, which you must somehow dispel before it irretrievably disposes them to convict, you rise to make the opening address for the defense.

You sat through the long ordeal of your opponent's opening speech with such composure as you could command. You suffered under the pointed arrows from the prosecutor's quiver, and winced inwardly as his sharp barbs sank home. But you

have steeled yourself to cover what you feel by the appearance
at least of imperturbability. You have been hurt but you do not
look hurt. And now, whatever you have felt is quite forgotten in
the opportunity awaiting you to fight back.

This is the first chance you have had to be heard. Your participation in the drawing of the jury has been negligible. The jury
has hardly heard your voice. You are just one of the anonymous
people at the counsel table, and if the jury have thus far noticed
you at all, it was to let you share in the cold, furtive looks of
disapproval they have been casting on your client.

You must do something now, at once, to dispel the poisonous
aroma of your adversary's speech. Now is your chance, now!
You are all too well aware of the surcharged atmosphere of the
courtroom. As though furnished with antennae, you sense all the
overtones of the case, the hatred of the crime and the consequent
hatred of your client, although he stands as yet merely charged
with its commission. All this and much else has intensified the
contagion of prejudice. You must dispel it and you must do it
now.

By the look in your eye, your firm but not aggressive posture,
and by your first simple and well-chosen words, you must somehow create and disseminate a new and different atmosphere.
You must be strong and bold and yet withal conciliatory; somehow you must begin to change the thinking of the twelve who sit
before you. This is your task. This is your excuse for being
there.

Your first words must arrest attention and arouse interest. I
remember one case in which I opened somewhat in this manner:
"Mr. Foreman and gentlemen of the jury, I am sure that we
have all been fascinated with the extraordinarily able speech
just now concluded. You and I—all thirteen of us—have

watched with interest a very able prosecutor and have been carried along by his most excellent command of English."

And I went on: "Every word he uttered, I am sure, he thinks is true, but none of us, as we have been swept along by his eloquence, has, I hope, forgotten that he is not a witness and is telling us nothing that he knows himself. He was not there; he has no firsthand knowledge. All he knows is what his witnesses have told him, but whether what they have told him is the truth, he knows no more than you. Indeed, he knows far less than you will know when you have heard *all* the evidence, instead of that small part of it on which he asks you to convict. The man who sits before you, my client, the defendant, your fellow citizen, a citizen of the United States, carries with him and around him that cloak of priceless value, more glorious than the robe of any king: the presumption of innocence. By his plea of not guilty he has denied the charges against him and has asserted before God and man that he is innocent.

"Not only has he said that he is innocent, but he has said it with a voice far more entitled to be believed than that of the rascals (for I shall prove them to be such) who will here testify against him. He is at least as creditable as they are, and I will satisfy you by evidence that you cannot doubt that he is ten times more so.

"As you are all, of course, aware, neither my opponent nor I nor you may decide what the law is; that is the function of the judge. But I am sure he will not object to my assertion that the defendant is presumed to be innocent of all charges against him, and that that presumption is not a mere legal phrase, a word without real meaning, an idle expression to be uttered and forgotten, but a clear command of the law of the United States, mandatory upon all of us—upon you.

"As His Honor on the bench is untrammeled in judging what the law is, you are equally as free in your determination of the facts, for you are the sole and exclusive judges of the facts. And as you place those facts in the scale of justice, you will never forget that with them on the defendant's side is the added weight of the presumption of his innocence.

"My purpose here this morning is to tell you what our evidence will show the facts to be. But before I begin with this, I ask you to rejoice with me that we are living in a land where men's lives and liberties cannot be taken from them by a prosecutor's speech. And so I beg you here at the beginning to have and to maintain an open mind, and to remember as you listen to the evidence that you can strike down and destroy this man only if with all your consciences, with God to judge you, you can say that you have no reasonable doubt as to his guilt—that you are so sure that your minds no longer entertain a doubt which any honest man would call reasonable."

This part of the speech is what rhetoricians call the exordium. It is that part of your opening intended to make your listeners heed you and to prepare them for that which is to follow.

The foregoing paraphrase of the first part of an opening address I once made is not laid before you as a model. It is only an example (and perhaps not a very good one) of how one lawyer in one case tried to catch the initial attention of his jury. I can think of many just criticisms that could be leveled against it, not the least of which is that it is not short enough, although as a great writer on rhetoric once said: "It is impossible to reach the desired result without making the process of persuasion somewhat long."

But what is too long or too short? You remember that when Lincoln was asked how long a man's legs should be, he replied:

"Just about long enough to reach the ground." If your opening really reaches Mother Earth, if it walks upon the ground with a firm tread, it will not be too long.

An effective advocate takes care not to begin by striking too high a key. Monotony at all costs must be avoided. If at the beginning too high a note is struck and the pitch is sustained to the end, monotony will be the sure result. But if, on the other hand, that pitch is not sustained, the result is anticlimax, and in persuasion the principle of climax should never be forgotten.

And now, having finished your exordium (and let us here take leave of that most stilted word), you are ready to plunge into the main body of your address. There are, of course, technical limitations that curtail you, for the function of an opening address is to inform the jury what you intend to prove. The opportunity that it presents is, therefore, a far more limited one than that which will be afforded by your summation. In the latter case, any legitimate argument that may be drawn from the facts is permissible. But the opening address is not supposed to be an argument at all. It must remain within the framework of an outline of your promised evidence. And many judges will hold you very rigorously to that.

I shall never forget what happened to me in the Gene Tunney case—the case of Mara against Tunney. Martin Littleton appeared as counsel for the plaintiff, Emory Buckner for Mr. Tunney, and I represented his codefendant and former manager, Billy Gibson. Mr. Littleton had opened for the plaintiff, Mr. Buckner for Gene Tunney, and then it came my turn. It was a good many years ago, and I was less experienced then. I started off in the conventional manner, but as I went on, I became more and more aroused by the merits of my case, until soon, I fear, my opening resembled more a summing up. Suddenly I felt an arm around my shoulder. Mr. Littleton, my friend (and this time my opponent), had placed it there, and he was saying to the court: "Much as I love this man, I cannot permit him to go on with this summation which he is making in the form of an opening address." He was right and, of course, the judge sustained him. I had learned a lesson—one that has stood me in good stead ever since.

As I reflected on this incident, it came to me one day that the result which I had failed to achieve could still be accomplished in a different way: by making a plain narrative of the facts argue for me. For evidence itself is eloquence, and the facts, if properly arranged, will make the argument which you are not allowed to make as such. The facts, if put together right, will shout louder than you could; they may be made more eloquent than you possibly could be. "Short explanations," says Professor Hill, "vivid descriptions, happy illustrations, indirect suggestions, all may be instruments of persuasion, if they are so used as to advance the main purpose."

Suppose you were defending Jean Valjean. If you could tell his story as Victor Hugo told it in *Les Misérables,* your opening address would live forever as a classic, and what is more important, could not fail to reach the reason and the hearts of all your jury.

Suppose that you had represented Dred Scott or some other slave a hundred years ago. A dry treatise on slavery might have left your listeners cold. But if you could have set your subject all alight, had you portrayed the facts as Harriet Beecher Stowe portrayed them in *Uncle Tom's Cabin,* you could not have failed to take your jury with you, even as she persuaded the great jury of the North. Lincoln understood this when one day she called upon him at the White House and he said, "So you are the little woman who started this great big war."

In your opening you are engaged in one of the most important parts of advocacy. And despite the limitations surrounding it, you may find here an opportunity greatly to advance your cause. Whether you do or not will depend not only on your knowledge of the facts but on your ability so to arrange and marshal them as to make them argue for you.

Your task is not unlike that of a writer who sends an outline of his book to the publisher, hoping that it will be accepted. The book is what he wants to sell, but his selling it may depend on whether the outline he has written interests the publisher; and whether it does or not may be determined in large measure by the way in which the outline is composed and phrased. It must be so done as to make the publisher believe that the author really knows how to write and that in his promised book he has something to say worth saying. So your opening speech must arouse in every juror's mind the belief that you are not only telling the truth but that you can really prove what you are promising to establish.

One of your greatest problems will be a shrewd appraisal of the manner of men who sit within the jury box. Your study of them will help you to determine their particular susceptibilities and to select the pitch and key of what you say. The true advocate is sensitive not only to the character and quality of the jury he is addressing but to the changes and passing moods of the twelve men who hold his client's fate.

There are many things that juries generally approve. They like good sportsmanship and good humor. They warm to a man who can laugh at his own mistakes; they applaud the good manners of a gentleman in his courteous and tactful conduct not only toward the judge but toward the opposing counsel.

All this you will not forget as you make your opening speech —or at any time in the trial. But now that you are moving into the main body of your address, you will be thinking how you can make the facts so tell your story as to enlist not only interest and attention but sympathy. And yet how subtly and shrewdly this must be done!

How should you present your facts? There are a thousand ways, and yet for each case there is undoubtedly one best way —the only way, if it can be found. The great forensic speeches of the past demonstrate how great advocates met such problems. The great playwrights and novelists succeed in describing similar situations. They are inimitable and, therefore, quite literally, cannot be imitated.

Remember that it is not just a speech that you are making; what you are trying to do is to persuade a jury, and this is your first opportunity in the trial to begin winning, if you can, twelve men to your side. For the accomplishment of this you have two weapons: your character and your words. Of these the first is by far the more important. For what the jury think of you will sometimes be the controlling factor in their verdict. Make no mistake that you yourself are not as much on trial as your client and his case. If you can make your judges of the facts believe in you, you probably will not fail in making them believe in your defense as well.

In the course of many days, perhaps even weeks or months in court, a jury listens to many words, sometimes to scores of thousands. And the human mind, particularly the very human minds of jurors, cannot always recall with clarity from whose mouth words that struck them came. Thus, although you are not a witness, what you say may be recalled as though it came from the witness stand instead of from the bar.

Perhaps the most useful lessons ever offered me have come from jurors after the case was over. From them I have learned what they thought about the witnesses and how they appraised the facts. I have learned what they thought of the judge and my opponent, and often what they thought of me. Legion are the stories concerning the reactions of jurors.

An English juryman was once asked about Scarlett and he answered, "He is a lucky one because he is always on the right side." A Yankee juryman said of Rufus Choate: "I did not think much of his flights of fancy; but I considered him a very lucky lawyer, for there was not one of those five cases that came before us where he was not on the right side." Be on the right side, if you can, and be sure that the jury thinks so.

An advocate's most potent weapons are his character and his words, the kind of words he uses and the way he uses them. They are the keys to the magic portals of the jury's verdict. If you have a fine sense of English, use it; yet never let the jury think that words are your first concern, for if they see that you are thinking of your style alone, they may follow you with interest but you will never move them. And if you do not try to move them, why come to court at all?

As you open to your jury, you will have in mind, as Justice Vanderbilt has well said, "the intellectual environment" of your case; and you will not be deaf to the "assumptions of the age" in which you live and speak. For you are not talking in a vacuum to men without previously formed views. You cannot flout or ignore public opinion—an opinion that is made up of accepted principles, even though you know that many so-called convictions are no more than the rationalized prejudices of the times.

I have followed the expression of this idea with fascinated interest in Albert V. Dicey's *The Relation between Law and Public Opinion in England during the Nineteenth Century.* "The whole body of beliefs," he writes, "may generally be traced to certain fundamental assumptions which at the time, whether they be actually true or false, are believed by the mass of the world to be true with such good confidence that they hardly appear to bear the character of assumptions."

In Salem, Massachusetts, three hundred years ago, it would have been idle to argue to a jury that witchcraft was a myth and a delusion, though some progress might have been made in an endeavor to persuade them that the elderly lady at the bar, all things considered, was not a witch.

In certain Southern states today, if you were defending a Negro before a white jury, you would not try to persuade them that black men are the social or intellectual equals of the whites. The fundamental assumptions, inherent since the days of slavery, would be idle to combat. The firmly rooted prejudices of your jurors and their inherent convictions would not yield to persuasion. Yet you might find a ready and generous attention to the plea that the man on trial had not done what was charged against him.

I can give you something of an illustration of this, not from South Carolina or Mississippi but from the city of New York. Bourke Cockran, a celebrated orator of his day, had been assigned to defend a Negro for murder committed in the course of a rape on a white woman. He made no pretense of ignoring the fact that his client was a Negro. He knew the jury would not ignore it. I can still remember the impact of his extraordinarily moving final plea. He was tall and strong and handsome; he had a leonine head crowned by a great shock of white hair. He had a piercing eye, a flashing wit, and he talked with a slight Irish accent. His final words were: "Do justice to this boy. I do not ask you to treat him as though he were a white man; give him the shrift that you would give to a dog, give him only that much and you must acquit him." The verdict was not guilty!

So you, in your opening speech, in addition to all else, must have a clear perception of the convictions, the sentiments and firmly rooted prejudices of the twelve men in the box. You will fail in this at your peril.

There is a chemistry of communication, there are things which a jury will somehow divine though unspoken. Never imagine that advocacy is a bag of tricks. The only trick—and it is not a trick—is to give the jury the result of long and patient study and a lifetime of educating and building and developing your mental processes, your character, and your courage.

What you say in your opening address will give the jury its first awakening to the fact that there are two sides to this controversy. You must be a kind of great chorus explaining to the audience what the play is about—the play they have not yet seen but presently will witness. Your feel for the facts is not skin-deep; it must become obvious that it is not skin-deep, but that it permeates the inner recesses of your very being. You know the facts now better than anyone in the world. They are a part of you. What has happened is so vivid in your imagination that you all but believe you personally had been a witness to the events.

Tell your story as though it were a narrative of occurrences which you had actually seen and of which you yourself had been a part. Your sympathy for your client must be such that you step into his shoes, you become him. You are the man on trial! Let the jury feel that you are not just a paid spokesman brought on to say a piece. You embody the defendant, you are the defendant. Let them see your courage in standing up against so mighty an antagonist as the plaintiff in this litigation—the United States of America. Let them know that though the whole one hundred sixty million people are against you, you are not afraid, that you have the valor of righteousness and the sober faith that justice will prevail, the conviction that right makes might. To do all this you must possess an indefinable something that will make what you say seem credible just because you say it. Draw the robes of your own character about the shaking shoulders of your client. Let the defendant become merged in you.

Great advocates of the past have set a high value on the opportunities an opening address affords; they have also recognized its dangers. There are dangers, not the least of which is striking a sour note here at the very beginning of your trial. If here at the start you do or say anything that may alienate your jury or even some member of it, mountains of evidence and weeks of testimony may not undo it.

There is also the danger of misstating a fact (however honestly), a misstatement that will never be forgotten by your adversary and which he will never permit the jury to forget when, in summing up, he compares the proved fact with what your opening statement of the fact was. Then there is the danger of making an unnecessary admission. Twice in my life, in trials far removed in years, a District Attorney, in opening his case, after lauding his main witness, added: "Of course, if you do not believe him, that is the end of the case."

On each of these occasions, I never let the jury forget the admission and concentrated all my efforts by cross-examination in an endeavor to prevent the jury from believing him.

What is a good opening depends on an incalculable number of factors: What facts, what kind of facts, are you going to prove? What kind of jury have you? Are they college graduates or day laborers? How does your case fit into the current climate of opinion? Have you a popular or an unpopular cause or client? What is the feeling in the courtroom—that very local climate of opinion? How receptive do the jurors seem to you? These and innumerable other factors will determine the nature of your opening speech and whether or not you embrace the opportunity it affords.

There is, of course, always the danger that you may give away your case too early, thereby enabling unscrupulous witnesses to mold their testimony accordingly. In criminal cases the Government perforce must often rely on the testimony of abandoned rogues, the kind of men who have had long experience in lying and have acquired a marked proficiency in perjury. Such men, if they read your opening in the newspapers, will study it with care and contrive a cunning story to refute your narrative. Too much detail, therefore, in an opening may be dangerous; too little may destroy its force.

At the trial of Bardell against Pickwick, Dickens has given us a good example of overstating a case. To create sympathy for his widowed client, Serjeant Buzfuz spoke feelingly of her late husband who had been a minor employee at the custom house. "The plaintiff, gentlemen," he said, in soft and melancholy voice, "the plaintiff is a widow. . . . The late Mr. Bardell, after enjoying for many years the esteem and confidence of his sovereign as one of the guardians of his royal revenues, glided almost imperceptibly from this world, to seek elsewhere for that repose and peace which a custom house can never afford."

He "glided imperceptibly from this world"—it was a telling

phrase. But it became less telling when it was proved that this had scarcely been the manner of Bardell's departure, for he had been killed in a barroom brawl.

There is never a case in which there is not some unanswerable fact or circumstance that is strong against you. Face it boldly, bravely, at the start. It will sound far less damaging for you to tell it. "Why, this can't be so bad," the jury is saying to itself, "or why should the man's own lawyer be telling us about it?" So tell it, tell it all, even as you would pluck out a splinter from an infected finger. It is over and done with then and it will become a stale and twice-told story when your adversary mentions it.

Perhaps I have already said enough to cause you to agree with John C. Reed when he wrote: "Strange as it may appear, there is nothing more difficult in the art of advocacy than to effectively open a case to a jury. The proof of this is the rarity of the exhibition. How few of our advocates accomplish it to the entire satisfaction of a critical listener! How few possess the faculty of marshaling facts in their natural order, and taking up and so interweaving distinct threads of a story as to form a clear, intelligent narrative."

The high estimate Erskine placed upon the efficacy of an opening address is revealed by the fact that in both the Hardy and the Horne Tooke cases he left the summation to his juniors and chose instead to make the opening address.

But the best example of an opening I have ever read was made by Brougham in the defense of Queen Caroline, perhaps the most celebrated case in English annals.

The marriage of George IV to his German princess had not been a love match. He accepted her reluctantly and only as a means of getting his debts paid. He soon came to hate her, and so at last resorted to the House of Lords where Lord Liverpool had introduced a bill of divorcement. Its preamble recited that the Queen, during an Italian tour, had carried on "an adulterous intercourse" with one Bergami, her courier. Thus, the Queen's trial was in reality a form of examination wherein witnesses were brought forward to establish the recitals of the bill.

Now Brougham knew that the King, while still the Prince of Wales, had secretly been married to Mrs. FitzHerbert—a fact which explains Caroline's remark when she first heard of the bill's recital: "I am not altogether blameless, for I have committed adultery with Mrs. FitzHerbert's husband."

Days of the trial were consumed by the Crown's lawyers in examining Italian witnesses, but finally the Crown's case was closed and Brougham stood up before the House of Lords to open for the Queen. He knew of the FitzHerbert marriage and he knew that if it should become known, the Act of Settlement would forfeit the King's throne.

The fascinated gaze of the entire House was focused upon him when he exclaimed: "I call upon you to pause. You stand on the brink of a precipice. If your judgment shall go out against your Queen, it will be the only act that ever went out without effecting its purpose. It will return to you upon your own heads. Save the country. Save yourselves. Rescue the country; save the people, of whom you are the ornaments, but severed from whom you can no more live than the blossom that is severed from the root and tree on which it grows."

And as the Lords strained forward, Brougham launched into this final exhortation: "Save the country, therefore, that you may continue to adorn it. Save the Crown which is threatened with irreparable injury. Save the aristocracy which is surrounded with danger. Save the altar which is no longer safe when its kindred throne is shaken. You see that when the church and the throne would allow of no church solemnity in behalf of the Queen, the heartfelt prayers of the people rose to Heaven for her protection. I pray Heaven for her, and I pour forth my fervent supplications at the throne of mercy, that mercies may descend on the people of this country, richer than their rulers have deserved, and that your hearts may be turned to justice."

Brougham's handling of the Queen's case displayed an advocacy unparalleled in English annals. The witnesses produced by the Crown in support of the bill were for the most part Italian servants who did not speak English and were forced, therefore, to testify through an interpreter. One Majocchi was not only the first but the most important witness for the prosecution. He testified as to the sleeping arrangements in one of the palaces they visited and gave considerable description of the rooms occupied by Bergami and the Queen, and how in the nighttime he had seen the Princess enter the bedroom occupied by her courier.

For his cross-examination Brougham did not have much to go on, but he adopted the obvious line of asking the witness to describe the sleeping arrangements in other palaces. Among his first questions Brougham asked the witness whether he remembered another English servant who, as well as Bergami, had dined at the Queen's table, and the witness answered, "I do not remember." His actual words were in Italian: *"Non mi ricordo."*

Brougham now plied Majocchi as to his memory of the names of other servants, and then asked: "In the Princess's house at Naples, where did William Austin sleep?" And the answer came: *"Non mi ricordo."* Asking for names, dates, and places which the witness would have known had he told the truth on his direct examination, again and again Brougham elicited the response, *"Non mi ricordo,"* until the very galleries rang with this Italian answer. The phrase became a byword in the streets. "Everyone," wrote the Princess Lieven a day or two later, "is using the catchword *'Non mi ricordo.'* " In England it is still remembered.

Mistaking another room for his consultation chamber, Brougham entered it one day to find the Duke of Clarence and Sir Walter Scott in conference. He started to withdraw, but the Duke good-humoredly invited him to come in. The conversation drifted to the *Waverley Novels,* the authorship of which was then unknown, and the Duke began plying Scott with questions on this subject. "Sir," replied Sir Walter, "I must give Your Royal Highness the favorite answer of the day, *'Non mi ricordo.'* "

In my life of Erskine I have endeavored to describe the Queen's trial. There is not room for more of it here. The vote on the third reading showed one hundred and eight votes for the bill and ninety-nine against. It had been carried by the small margin of nine votes, and Lord Liverpool, because of this small margin, moved to proceed no further with it. "I move," he said, "that the further consideration of the bill be adjourned to this day six months." From that day to this it was never taken up. The Queen was acquitted.

IV

Cross-Examination — A Bulwark of Liberty

NEW YORK CITY had been sweltering through a torrid Indian summer. The very elements had conspired to render the ordeal of Police Lieutenant Charles Becker more intolerable. To be on trial for his life would have seemed agony enough without the added torture of a suffocating day. But torture more intolerable still awaited him.

It was September of the year 1912, an epoch that in retrospect seems almost Elysian. No wars were raging, nor were there any threats of war. The Kaiser was a faintly amusing figure, and the Czar of all the Russias seemed permanently entrenched. It seemed an era of perpetual peace. Woodrow Wilson was running for President for the first time, and talked of how he would improve and brighten the domestic scene. Americans heard little of our foreign policies and cared less. It was a pleasant world for most of us, but it was not a pleasant world for the defendant Becker.

We sat in the criminal branch of the old courthouse, now happily demolished. Upon the wall behind the judge's chair there was a fairly creditable painting depicting Justice with her usual accouterments. But this figure of Justice proved a mockery of what was taking place before her.

Upon the bench sat an old man with long white hair and piercing, cold, blue eyes. A superficial glance might have given the impression of quiet kindliness and serene benignity. Some said that he resembled a figure in a stained-glass window, yet how mistaken and how tragic an allusion this was appeared on the very first day of the trial. He had a cold heart and a sadistic joy in suffering. During the impaneling of the jury (as I learned years later), he beckoned a young Assistant District Attorney to the bench and spoke to him in a low whisper: "Have the shades drawn low. There is not enough gloom in the courtroom."

All that he did throughout the trial now stands recorded in the two hundred and tenth volume of the New York *Reports*. The opinions of the Court of Appeals constitute a veritable Magna Charta of fair trials. With fierce indignation, our highest court excoriated and denounced this judge as one who had so conducted the trial of a man accused of murder "as to insure a verdict of guilty regardless of the evidence." Because of his rulings, the high court said, the defendant "never had a fair chance to defend his life, and it would be a lasting reproach to the state if under those circumstances it should exact its forfeiture."

But the Court of Appeals would have searched in vain for expletives of denunciation had they seen this old man in action as I saw him. For, as one of Becker's junior counsel, I sat at the defendant's side throughout the trial. The judge who at first had seemed a saint was now revealed as one intent on striking down a fellow citizen, no matter how. From his face the mask of benignity was soon laid aside, and as I gazed up at the bench, I felt like some four-footed denizen of the jungle that suddenly stares into the cold visage of a python. His countenance revealed a coldly calculated purpose to strike down a fellow human being no matter by what foul means—or, to use the more temperate but equally clear language of the Court of Appeals, he conducted this trial "so as to insure a verdict of guilty regardless of the evidence."

He shared with Jeffreys what Macaulay called "the most odious vice which is incident to human nature, a delight in misery merely as misery." And as the trial moved on, like the great historian's portrayal of Alice Lisle's tormentor, "ferocity sat upon his brow. The glare of his eyes had a fascination for the unhappy victim on whom they were fixed." No one could have seen him as I did without thinking of Lord Jeffreys. But his real character and purpose did not fully reveal themselves until the cross-examination of the people's witnesses. "Dangerous and degenerate," the Court of Appeals later called them.

The leader and the worst of these was Jack Rose. Called by the District Attorney, he was fawned upon by the court. By every look and intonation, the judge revealed how much he wanted to obscure the fact that this man was not only a cunning, shrewd, calculating, dangerous criminal, but a self-confessed murderer who, in return for his testimony, had secured from the District Attorney, with the sanction and approval of the court, an agreement whereby he would go scot-free for the murder that he acknowledged he had helped to bring about.

I sat enthralled as John McIntyre, our chief counsel, began

the cross-examination. Upon the witness stand before us there sat a rogue who needed cross-examining if any scoundrel ever did. I had heard many cross-examinations but never one so deft and sure and brilliant as that which our chief counsel now began. But he was blocked, interrupted, and at every moment interfered with by a judge who resented every thrust at this self-confessed murderer on whose word a human life depended.

Unawed by the cold frown of a hanging judge, unabashed by his sarcastic interruptions, undaunted by the continuous admonitions to "go along," to "get along," and "time is too precious," Mr. McIntyre, like the brave and skillful advocate that he was, pushed forward undeterred.

He was a master of every field of cross-examination, but he excelled perhaps in that in which he now engaged: the discrediting of a witness by showing from his own mouth that he is unworthy of belief. Every question searched some dark chamber of this rascal's life, reached into the putrid cesspool of his past, turned the light upon his meanness, his depravity, and his crimes. Every question sought to reveal this creature of the underworld for what he was. It was a slashing and a brilliant effort. It was fast, staccato, and never for one moment lagging. He laid his questions on as with a lash. They were as sharp and pointed as a dart, as ensnaring as a harpoon, as lethal as a rifle, and as businesslike as a machine gun.

Never for one moment pausing, he hurled question after question, and every time the witness cowered under the assault or was upon the point of breaking, Judge Goff came to his rescue. The defendant's counsel was making too much headway, he was breaking down, he was destroying the foundation of the prosecution. And so a judge intent on obtaining a conviction, "regardless of the evidence," decided upon still harsher and more lawless methods.

During the cross-examination, it developed that Rose, before the trial, had prepared and given to the District Attorney a confession showing his participation in the murder and that this confession had been published in the New York *World*. Counsel now asked the District Attorney to produce the original statement for the purpose of cross-examination. Judge Goff sharply refused to allow it to be produced. An effort, then, to use this confession, as published in the *World*, for the same purpose was similarly prevented by the judge.

But even this judge finally came to the realization that what he had done was so flagrantly opposed to the most elementary requisites of the law as to insure a reversal of a much desired conviction; he, therefore, reversed himself and allowed the District Attorney to give us the confession after forcing us, however, to agree that it be placed in evidence in its entirety. Judge Goff further commanded that we should not refer to it as a confession but only as "a paper."

Rose had begun his direct examination at ten o'clock in the morning under the friendly nods and encouraging smiles of the prosecutor's judge. He told of the so-called Harlem conference held in a vacant lot where he asserted Becker had conferred with Rose and the other assassins. The picture drawn was like that in which Macbeth had plotted with his hired murderers.

At half-past two, Mr. McIntyre had begun his cross-examination. He continued without a break or a request for an indulgence until six in the evening. I shall never forget that afternoon. It was a steaming day and in a stifling courtroom, hour after hour, our chief counsel relentlessly pressed on. His collar wilted and sweat streamed down his face as he confronted one of the worst men who ever lived. At six o'clock, counsel asked for an adjournment. "Mr. McIntyre," Judge Goff thundered, "we shall have no further discussion about the matter," and forced him to go on.

He was exhausted in his long effort, but he went on; he was defending a man's life. No time was accorded for refreshment or even the ordinary demands of nature. It was cold, calculated, deliberate oppression. Two and one-half hours passed, and Mr. McIntyre, glancing at the courtroom clock, noticed that it was now half-past eight. He had not yet even touched the Harlem conference.

It was now ten minutes before nine. Turning from the clock to the equally impassive judge, he once more asked for an adjournment and said that his exhaustion was now such that he was unable to proceed. In sharp, clipped words, Judge Goff replied: "No good reason whatever appears for adjournment. There yet remain three hours. Counsel may have them." And on counsel's stating that he was too spent to continue, the judge declared the cross-examination closed and dismissed the witnesses.

I shall never forget that trial. Its incidents were impressed on me forever. I had witnessed a great advocate in a very great performance. I saw what part courage played in advocacy. I watched and listened to a great cross-examiner.

When, a few months later, the Court of Appeals reversed the conviction, I understood what they wrote about cross-examination as no book and no law course could have made me understand. Quoting from Wigmore, Judge Hiscock said: "For two centuries past, the policy of the Anglo-American system of evidence has been to regard the necessity of testing by cross-examination as a vital feature of the law. The belief that no safeguard for testing the value of human statements is comparable to that furnished by cross-examination, and the conviction that no statement (unless by special exception) should be used as testimony until it has been probed and sublimated by that test, has found increasing strength in lengthening experience."

I had seen a monstrous curtailment of that right. I had witnessed a repudiation of a vital feature of our law—by the destruction of the right of cross-examination, its value to the cause of liberty became doubly manifest.

I had sat through an unfair trial, and that phrase has been to me ever since no mere form of words. Having seen it, I responded with every fiber of my being to the denunciation by the Court of Appeals of the means employed to bring about a verdict. I understood, as no law school could have made me do, what Judge Hiscock meant when he wrote: "In the presence of such dangerous and degenerate witnesses as have been described and under all the conditions attending and surrounding his case, the defendant certainly was entitled to a scrupulously fair and impartial trial where nothing should be done to prejudice his case or to obscure in the minds of the jurors the elemental question whether the evidence justified them in reaching the conclusion that he was guilty of the grave crime with which he was charged. . . . We do not think that the defendant had such a trial."

I understood, as I never could have had I not witnessed the conduct of a hanging judge, why the Court of Appeals granted a new trial because, as Judge Miller said, the verdict was "shockingly against the weight of evidence . . . because the trial was so conducted as to insure a verdict of guilty regardless of the evidence."

What a rare education this trial afforded me and how I wish

that I had profited by it better! No case book on the law of evidence, nor even the most brilliant teacher of the subject, could have given me so much; for when you read the cases or follow the great learning of Professor Wigmore, the subject taught is still abstract. You do not see the witnesses nor watch them; you have not before you all the problems of the case or the reasons underlying the decisions which the lawyers made in dealing with them.

No book can teach why a question is well put, and no book can ever explain just how the question should be asked or exactly at what time it should be put. No book can teach you until you see and hear how advocacy and cross-examination are related and how it is that the great cross-examiner makes his questions ofttimes far more eloquent than his final speech.

Until the "Glorious Revolution" of 1688, prisoners in treason and felony cases had no counsel. But even when counsel finally were allowed, they were not permitted to address the jury, although they were allowed to cross-examine. And so, debarred of one means of advocacy, they sought another, and, said Sir James Stephen, ". . . their cross-examination therefore tended to become a speech in the form of questions, and it has ever since retained this character to a greater or lesser extent."

Such was the cross-examination of Mr. McIntyre in the Becker case. Realizing that the questioning of an adverse witness, particularly one so debased as Rose, is the most important part of advocacy, that the way the questions are composed, their timing, the demeanor of the questioner work as a kind of foil to the man questioned, that the questions must be so short and clear as to make it impossible for the witness to misunderstand them, Becker's chief counsel gave a supreme exhibition of the art. He knew that he must make his points as he went so that the jury could not miss them. He knew how much more persuasive was this method than to await for weeks the opportunity to make them in his closing speech. By his posture, his voice, the look in his eye, the cross-examiner who is a true advocate must not only be but must appear to be a brave and fearless man. Such was the man who defended Becker. To stand resolute and unafraid before so despotic a tyrant as Mr. Justice John Goff required character and courage to a high order. Mr. McIntyre had them both.

He had had his early training as an Assistant District Attorney under the celebrated Delancey Nicoll. There were titans in those days and many of his assistants later achieved national celebrity at the bar. Among these was Francis Wellman. Fifty years ago he published his first edition of *The Art of Cross-Examination.* There have been many editions since and the book has now become a classic. It is an invaluable book not only to the student but to the veteran lawyer as well, and its clarity, simplicity, and appealing style have caused it to be read by laymen with almost the same appreciation as that accorded it by students of the law.

With Professor Wigmore he knew that cross-examination is "beyond any doubt the greatest legal engine ever invented for the discovery of truth." But since he recognized it as an art, he knew how difficult is the acquisition of proficiency in this, the most exacting duty of the advocate. The art of cross-examination, he wrote, "requires the greatest ingenuity, a habit of logical thought, clearness of perception, in general; an infinite patience and self-control; power to read men's minds instantly, to judge of their character by their faces, to appreciate their motives; ability to act with force and precision; a masterful knowledge of the subject matter itself; an extreme caution; and above all the instinct to discover the weak point in the witness under examination."

This paragraph is so complete and so profoundly true that a would-be cross-examiner might well commit all of its wise maxims to memory. If you count them, you will see that he has listed twelve requirements, each essential to the mastery of the art. The absence of any one of these could well prove fatal to the examiner. Of what use would he be if he were incapable of logical thought? For it is often by sheer logic that the fallacy or falsehood of an answer is exposed. If he had no ingenuity, he would be lost, for often, in default of all other weapons, he must, by sheer intuition, divine the true field for the attack. If he lacks patience, he will not last out the ordeal. A lack of self-control can be as fatal in the courtroom as in the prize ring. If the cross-examiner cannot read men's character by their faces, he may not understand what manner of man he has to deal with—whether he is honestly trying to tell the truth, is honestly mistaken, has honestly forgotten or whether he is concocting a deliberate lie. A mistake as to which it is may be a fatal one.

If the cross-examiner is not cautious, he may, by one false move, destroy his client's case. If he lacks courage to act at any given moment with force and precision, he may be overcome by a tyrannical judge or a determined witness. And last of all, if he does not possess the instinct to discover the weak point in the witness or his testimony, he would be like an artist who had mastered color and design but lacked the innate skill and in-tuitive ability that somehow enable him to transmit to the canvas that special blend of colors that the true portrayal of countenance or scene demands.

And this is true, because, as Mr. Wellman well explains, "One has to deal with a prodigious variety of witnesses under an infinite number of differing circumstances. It involves all shades and complexions of human morals, human passions, and human intelligence. It is a mental duel between counsel and witness." Every lawyer of experience knows this well, and none but the inexperienced would ever doubt the truth of Professor Wigmore's dictum that cross-examination "is beyond any doubt the greatest legal engine for the discovery of truth."

If there be any still in doubt as to the efficiency of this vital weapon in skilled hands, let him attend a trial in a French court. There the judge and not the advocate is the cross-examiner, and there, amidst the general turmoil, he is permitted to engage in relentless sarcasms and exhortations that would sicken an American or English lawyer. The French judge is a frank partisan, though not so frank as he might be, and so, having taken a leading part in the conflict, debars himself from ordering an impartial trial.

The absence of a sense of sportsmanship, more noticeable in a French court than elsewhere, perhaps accounts for the conviction of an innocent Dreyfus and his incarceration for long years on Devil's Island. Whereas the whole policy of Anglo-American law (so our oft-quoted master of evidence informs us) "is more or less due to the inborn sporting instinct of giving the game fair play even at the expense of efficiency of procedure." For, he continues, ". . . the common law originated in the community of sports and games and permeated essentially by the instincts of sportsmanship . . . it has contributed a sense of fairness, of chivalrous behavior. . . ." The feature of all games and sports, he says, "has influenced profoundly the policy of the common law."

In Professor Wigmore's praise of cross-examination he also spoke of its abuses. Among these are bad manners, harsh conduct, and an insulting behavior toward the opposing witness or his counsel. These abuses usually carry their own punishment with them in the shape of an adverse verdict; for the lawyers who adopt methods of this kind forget that as between the witness and the examiner the sympathy of the jury is often with the witness. They feel that he is at a disadvantage with the lawyer because he cannot talk back but must confine himself solely to the answering of questions. Nothing could be worse or more unjustified than the abuse of a witness.

This is not to decry an attack, when justified, upon the credit of a witness. It is, however, an attack that never should be entered on without justification. The old maxim "Do not strike a king unless you can kill him" applies. If, however, you really have a true and honest basis for this assault (however infrequently this may happen), do not be afraid to make it. In such a case, advance boldly to the affray. Attack with no holds barred. If you know, for instance, that the witness whom you must cross-examine is a deliberate perjurer or a thief or a murderer or a traitor, treat him as you would a snarling beast. But if you embark upon this course, you must succeed; failure here will discredit you forever with your jury.

Although it won him a short-lived verdict—a verdict that was reversed by the Court of Appeals—Joseph Choate's famous cross-examination of Russell Sage is a notable, a classical, illustration of this method. *Laidlaw* v. *Sage*, before even I can remember, was once the talk of the town, and reading the cold opinion of the court without the living context of all the facts and all the current opinions of the hour illustrates anew how difficult it is to understand a case—really to understand it unless you were there in court and heard it or at least had the opportunity to read every word of the testimony, the exhibits, and the briefs as well as all of the contemporary newspapers. Few of us have had the time, the industry, or the inclination to do this in many cases other than our own.

Choate's cross-examination of Russell Sage, however, somehow succeeds in conveying to us that great lawyer's contempt and scorn for one whom he considered a mean and grasping miser. If you are sufficiently sadistic to enjoy torture and to watch with interest the methods of the torturer, you cannot fail to find enjoyment in this cross-examination. Yet who is there so heartless as not to feel some sympathy for this much-badgered witness?

Let us turn back, then, to the fourth of December, 1891. It was three weeks before Christmas and a little early for the appearance of Marley's ghost, although there were not wanting those who felt that Russell Sage could adequately fill the role of Scrooge. He was seventy-four years old and after his fashion had prospered mightily. He had amassed millions of dollars, and if the way in which he did it made him a success, then success in this world was indeed his. He had started as a grocer up in Troy, and from this had graduated into banking and finally into operating, if not manipulating, railroads. It was the age of Hetty Green and John D. Rockefeller, Sr., and his Standard Oil Company which Ida Tarbell has so brilliantly described. It was a pleasant era for those who knew their way around, and Russell Sage was one of these.

He was no spendthrift; indeed, those who knew him and were well versed in the art of understatement described him as a frugal man. Such facts as have come down to us seem to make this statement no exaggeration. When I was very young, I heard a minister describe a social evening at his home. After a few hours of arid conversation, Mr. Sage asked his guest if he would not like some refreshment. On his assent, the host moved into the pantry. The tap was heard to run and presently he returned, bringing one glass of tepid water and a rather moist saltine.

December 9, 1891—no, it was not quite Christmas Eve, but if Marley's ghost had as yet put in no appearance, there was another caller. He walked into an office with its roll-top desk and its old-fashioned letter press and filing cabinet, such as no self-respecting junkman of our times would dare display. But it was an office that commanded more ready cash than could be counted in many sumptuous business establishments of today.

The caller's name was Norcross and he gained admittance by sending in word that he bore with him a letter of introduction from Mr. John D. Rockefeller and that he desired to see Mr. Sage about an important business matter. I hasten to add that he, of course, bore no such letter with him. In his hand instead was a note of quite a different tenor, as Mr. Sage was presently to learn. He learned this when he left his private office and went out into the outer reception room where his caller stood awaiting him.

William R. Laidlaw, an office clerk, at this moment came into the room where Sage and Norcross stood and waited for an opportunity to speak to his employer. He had not heard the conversation which had just previously ensued between the two, and he most assuredly had not read the letter Norcross had presented. It was an amazingly frank and forthright communication, reading: "The bag I hold in my hand contains ten pounds of dynamite. If I drop this bag on the floor, the dynamite will explode and destroy this building, and kill every human being in the building. I demand $1,200,000, or I will drop the bag. Will you give it? Yes or no?"

Mr. Sage had quietly read this letter and had handed it back to Norcross, saying that he had a gentleman in his private office and would be through his business with him shortly, and would then give the matter his attention. To this Norcross had replied, "I rather infer from your answers that you refuse my offer," and it was just at this point that Laidlaw entered. It was a cardinal mistake and, as it proved, a nearly fatal one. What happened then was later many times recounted by Laidlaw on the witness stand. Upon his entry, Sage, who had seen him come, walked over and pressed his hand on Laidlaw's shoulder, then dropped his left hand and took Laidlaw's right hand in his and gently moved him in such a way as to interpose his body between that of Sage and Norcross, thereby making him a kind of human shield.

There was then a sudden flash and a sound like thunder; the room was blown to bits and the building itself trembled. When the explosion ceased to echo, it was found that Norcross had been completely torn asunder. Sage was on the floor unhurt and Laidlaw, seriously injured, found himself sprawled on top of the millionaire.

As soon as he could reach a lawyer, he brought suit against his erstwhile employer. The celebrated case of *Laidlaw* v. *Sage* had begun. It was tried four times. After a verdict for $25,000 and a reversal, the case came on for the fourth time. On this occasion, Joseph Choate was counsel for the plaintiff.

It was a case to delight the nephew of the great Rufus. The conduct of Russell Sage seemed a shade less than an example of the most perfect sportsmanship. The financier had used poor Laidlaw (at least so Laidlaw claimed) as a shield to defend his own body. It was something far removed from cricket, and Choate recoiled from this base example of unequaled meanness. He did not like Russell Sage. There were many others who did not, among whom, I suppose, Mr. Laidlaw should be prominently mentioned.

A graduate of Harvard and the scion of a distinguished family, Joseph Choate—a typical school-tie product—with an aversion for mere trade and an antipathy to those who through menial pursuits had risen high in the financial world, took up this case with zest and relish. To him the former upstate grocer was a representative of everything that seemed mean and low, a particularly offensive representative.

It was, then, with distinct pleasure that on a March day of the year 1894 he stood up before Mr. Justice Patterson and a New York jury to cross-examine Russell Sage. He probably enjoyed himself in this undertaking more than in any other of his long and highly successful career at the bar, more than his dramatic fight against the Tweed Ring, more even than his later experiences as Ambassador to the Court of St. James's where, until years later when John W. Davis captured London, his ambassadorial career shone in isolated splendor.

But he was in no diplomatic mood when he stood up to face Laidlaw's erstwhile employer. One of the greatest attributes an advocate can have is charm. Choate had this to a marked degree. His personality was a winning one and his distinguished career and long experience as a lawyer seemed to accord him many privileges that certainly would have been denied a young and unknown advocate. And so, for example, instead of remaining standing as he cross-examined, he sat on a table immediately behind his chair, idly swinging his legs and smiling at the witness. It was no smile of friendship.

He asked the witness where he lived; it was on Fifth Avenue. He asked the old man his age; he had passed the first flush of youth, having just turned seventy-seven. The first questions were asked in a low tone of voice, but Sage found no difficulty in hearing them. Mr. Choate then raised his voice and asked: "Do you ordinarily hear as well as you have heard the two questions you have answered me?" "Why, yes," the witness answered, almost inaudibly. And then, like a pistol shot, came the next question: "Did you lose your voice by the explosion?" And the answer, "No," and then these:

Q. Do you wear a watch?

A. Yes.

Q. And are you ordinarily carrying it as you carry this one you have at present in your left vest pocket?

A. Yes, I suppose so.

Q. Was your watch hurt by the explosion?

A. I believe not.

At the outset, Mr. Choate had established that Sage had come through his ordeal relatively unscratched, thereby drawing a strong contrast with the fate of Laidlaw. He now pressed forward with this line, gradually broadening it to an attack on the miserliness of his victim. Sage now swung his glasses in his hand and the alert advocate saw another opening. "I see you wear glasses," he said, but Sage merely closed them and replaced them in his pocket, arousing this comment from the cross-examiner: "And when you do not wear them, you carry them, I see, in your vest pocket." And then:

Q. Were your glasses hurt by the explosion which inflicted forty-seven wounds on your clerk?

A. I don't remember.

Q. You certainly would remember if you had to buy a new pair.

The crowd in the courtroom more than caught the point and roared with laughter and the answer from the witness went unheard. Delighted with this sally, Mr. Choate went on:

Q. These clothes you brought here to show—they are the same you wore that day?

A. Yes.

Q. How do you know?

A. The same as you would know in a matter of that kind.

Q. Were you familiar with those clothes?

A. Yes, sir.

Note the infinite art in the use of the word "familiar." It was a perfect word to convey the cross-examiner's thought and innuendo. It stressed the idea of miserliness. By one flash of connotation, it brought to the jury's mind the rather sordid, if not disgusting, thought of old clothes and their attendant odor and the distaste which one naturally would have for the penuriousness of a miser who by preference walked about in garments that should long since have been discarded. And the word could not fail to remind the jury of the shopworn saw: "Familiarity breeds contempt." It was contempt for Russell Sage that Choate now sought to breed. In addition to all this, there was a suggestion that if the witness was not "familiar" with these clothes, he was lying when he said he was.

After gaining the rich man's admission that he was "familiar" with these old clothes, the questioning proceeded:

Q. Have you had them three or four years?

A. No.

Q. How long have you had them?

A. Oh, some months.

Q. And wear them daily except on Sunday?

A. I think not; they were too heavy for summer wear.

And the idea was left to the jury that if his much worn clothing were given a respite in summer, they had done yeoman's service on all weekdays through the cold months.

From this Mr. Choate now pushed on to inquire about "puts" and "calls" and "straddles." "Oh, you are a moneylender? You buy puts and calls and straddles?" he asked, and Sage answered, "They are a means to assist men of moderate capital to operate." And his tormentor then inquired, "A sort of benevolent institution, eh?"

He then read from a newspaper that "Mr. Sage looked hale and hearty for an old man—good for many years of life yet." "Is that true?" Mr. Choate asked, and Sage answered: "We all hope to hold on for as long as we can." And the cross-examiner shouted out: "You speak for yourself when you say we all try to hold on for all we could get." It was hardly a fair comment or one justified by the answer.

The cross-examination was a long one in which every effort was made to ridicule and belittle an old man and hold him up to the contempt of the jury. Mr. Choate no doubt believed that Russell Sage sought to save his life at the expense of Laidlaw's and, believing this, was trying to establish that the defendant's denial of this despicable act was not true. As we read the long interrogation, however, we cannot fail to feel a certain sympathy for Russell Sage in the ordeal to which he was subjected.

Invoking in every way within his power the public sentiment against the aged millionaire, Choate carried his jury with him. They were fascinated by his winning personality and delighted by his wit, and so they brought in a verdict of $40,000 for the plaintiff.

In the Court of Appeals, however, the defendant's lawyer argued broadly for a reversal on the ground that the cross-examination had exceeded all fair bounds and was a gross abuse of the privilege, and the high court agreed with him and reversed the jury's finding largely for that reason. In its opinion, written by Judge Martin, the court said: "We think the plaintiff's counsel was permitted to go beyond the legitimate bounds of a proper cross-examination. . . . It has ever been the theory of our Government and a cardinal principle of our jurisprudence that the rich and poor stand alike in courts of justice, and that neither the wealth of the one nor the poverty of the other shall be permitted to affect the administration of the law."

This famous cross-examination was directed to the credit of the witness and consisted of a vitriolic attack upon him. Sage was not a rogue or a murderer or a traitor. He was just an old man who had grown rich by legitimate, though much disfavored, means. To attack him on purely personal grounds, to lampoon him for his miserliness or for his wearing of old clothes was hardly a fair assault upon his character or credibility. It was a brilliant example of cross-examination but as it turned out in the end, not a successful one. It exemplified what Professor Wigmore meant when he spoke of the "abuses and mishandling" of the art.

Yet in spite of this and similar abuses, no better means have ever been invented for the discovery of truth than that of cross-examination. No more efficacious test of credibility has ever been devised. It is a typically Anglo-Saxon weapon.

It is a sword for cutting through and destroying perjury. It is a bulwark of liberty. Let us find the men to man this rampart and hold it at all costs.

CHAPTER

V

Cross-Examination — An Incomparable Art

EXCEPT PERHAPS for the confessional of a priest, there is no better vantage ground for the study of mankind than a court of justice. There is no seat where humanity reveals itself more clearly than in the witness chair. There is no better laboratory for the dissection of human character and motives than the crowded scene that daily is unfolded before some judge and jury. To the lawyer is accorded the supreme opportunity for this study of men and women. Here, day after day, he looks at human nature in the raw, and it is here that he may learn to distinguish between sincerity and sham, the genuine and the spurious, truth and falsity, half-truths and those undiluted.

How well, then, has it been said that a good cross-examiner is the product of a generation of witnesses. His education never ends and each witness called affords him a new study. Each one presents the problem: Has he told the whole truth or only part of it? Has he tried to give his honest recollection and is it only the fallibility of memory that has interfered? Is he testifying from some bias that even he does not appreciate? Is there something he has omitted that would be helpful to your client? And finally, is he an out-and-out perjurer, a bold and intentional liar under oath? On the advocate's answers to these questions will depend the nature of his cross-examination. On the correctness of his answers hangs the client's fate.

And what are the materials afforded you for answering these questions? They are the facts that you have learned about your case before you came to court and all that you have previously found out about the character, the life, and the activities of the witness, but the most essential material is his testimony upon direct examination. What he has said and the way in which he has said it—this will be the primary basis of your questioning because here the jury has been afforded the same opportunities for studying him as you. Yet it may be that you will largely ignore his direct testimony and make your attack upon him a collateral one.

A thousand imponderables go to make up a jury's verdict, not the least of which is their observation and impression of the advocate. If they see him flustered and unnerved, they attach weight and importance to an incident, which they would not otherwise have done. It may be, then, that an opponent's unskillful examination in chief and his reaction to an unexpected answer will be of great assistance in your determination of the kind of cross-examination you will conduct. But there are many other keys to the solution of the problem, among the most important of which is your observation of the manner in which the witness gave his evidence.

The general deportment of the witness, not only what he says but the way he says it—this, if carefully observed, will give you many clues. Did he hesitate? Did he look off into space? Did he moisten his lips and seem perturbed? Did he stammer and needlessly repeat himself? Was there an honest or a shifty expression on his face as he answered? And above all, what is your impression as to how the jury reacted to him? Did they seem to believe him or were there some jurors, at least, whose expressions spelled incredulity?

What answers has your observation given you? None, unless you have watched with every faculty alert. None, if you have not similarly watched the jurors ranged before you—yes, and the judge too. None, if you have been so busy taking notes that all of these things have passed you by. Still another key to the kind of cross-examination you should conduct is your estimate of what the jury thinks of you; for remember that in a popularity contest between the witness and the advocate, the jury's sympathies are almost always with the witness.

Sometimes you will have nothing to go upon except the direct examination and your estimate of the witness whom you must cross-examine. I had such a case not long ago in which I represented the husband against a guilty wife in a divorce case. The evidence of adultery was so conclusive that finally it was not contested, but the real problem came over the question of the custody of two young daughters, the children of this unhappy pair. The lady was quite attractive, and I could see that the judge, a very fatherly old man, felt sympathy for her. She had admitted on her direct examination that she had had intercourse many times with a gentleman who was a visitor in this country. The question was whether she was a fit custodian for her daughters. From the way she looked and acted, I thought that she would brazen out her conduct with the corespondent, and so I asked her:

Q. In other words, you a married woman, supported by your husband, and with growing daughters, thought that you would see how you liked living with this Frenchman who himself had a wife in France and children?

A. Well, that is one way of putting it.

Q. You think what you have done here was perfectly moral and fine?

A. I think it was moral under the circumstances, yes.

The cross-examination then proceeded:

Q. Do you feel at all that the inculcation of decent moral principles is important in the raising of a girl?

A. I certainly do.

Q. Is it one of your principles that the only way to know a man is to live with him?

A. For me, yes.

Q. And that is in your opinion a moral and ethical principle, is it; yes or no?

A. For me, yes.

Q. That, however, would not be a good principle for anyone else in the world but you?

A. I didn't say that.

Q. I am trying to get your standard, as the person who wants to have the custody of children. Is that principle that you expressed a principle applicable, not only to yourself, but to other women as well; yes or no?

Seeing the dilemma in which she was thus placed and that she could not claim a principle applicable to her alone, she answered:

To full-grown adults, yes, but not when they are young—to full-grown adults who are mature and who know something about life and who understand people. Then I think they are free; otherwise they have no right.

Q. What is your definition of a full-grown adult?

A. I feel a full-grown adult—

She hesitated, having now to improvise. Her answer then proceeded:

I don't think any woman is a full-grown adult until she reaches the age of over twenty-eight.

Q. Then it is your standard and moral principle that a woman over the age of twenty-eight is following proper ethical standards who chooses to sleep and have intercourse with a man other than her husband; is that right?

A. If she wishes it, it is right.

A little later she stated:

A. I think it is wrong for young girls to go out and have intercourse with men. I do.

The cross-examination then proceeded:

Q. But not after twenty-eight?

A. You know, people vary. There are some people of twenty-eight who never grow up and there are some people who are younger that are matured.

Q. Then for some persons it would be all right to go out and do what you did at an age considerably younger than twenty-eight?

A. I wouldn't want my children to do it, no.

Q. At any age?

A. I wouldn't want them to do that *until they were absolutely fully grown.* As a matter of fact, I wouldn't want my daughters to do that *until they reached the age that I gave you, or over.*

To my surprise the trial justice nevertheless awarded custody of the children to this woman, and what surprised me even more was that his decision was affirmed by the Appellate Division with but one dissent. However, I am able to report that by the judgment of the Court of Appeals, the guilty wife was finally deprived of custody.

During the direct examination of a witness, you will never be guilty of that very common fault of inexperienced counsel, namely, that of making ill-timed and useless objections. Rarely, for example, object to a question merely because it is leading. Let trivial and unimportant breaches of the rules of evidence pass unnoticed and never, never make an objection without good grounds for believing that it will be sustained unless it relates, of course, to some fundamental legal proposition in your case in which you must have a ruling to preserve some basic right upon appeal. For every time you are overruled, the jury thinks that you do not know your business or that you are merely there to obstruct, and every answer given after an unsuccessful objection is doubly emphasized. No knowledge of the rules of evidence is too much; you must know and feel the rules, feel them in your very knee joints. But you are not there to display that knowledge. Never for an instant forget your jury and remember that they do not like objections to the evidence, believing in their lay fashion that these are mere excuses for attempting to conceal truth.

I am imagining you in court as the direct examination is coming to an end and where presently it will be your turn to take over. Before you rise, you will have finally made your estimate of the witness and the most important decision you arrive at will be the fundamental one: Should I cross-examine him at all? The decision to cross-examine or not to cross-examine (excepting possibly, the determination to call or not to call your client to the stand) is the most difficult and important one you will make. Taking it for all and all, has the witness really hurt you? Has he told the truth which you are unwilling or unable to refute? Has his version of the facts paralleled your own understanding of them? Has he perhaps inadvertently put a better aspect on the case than your own witnesses could do? If so, why cross-examine him at all?

To decide this question rightly, a broad understanding of the law and the clearest grasp of the facts are indispensable. You must *know* that the witness has not hurt you, not merely *believe* that this is so. Uncertain of themselves and of their mastery of the whole case, many lawyers fear to waive a cross-examination. Feeling that their client will not understand, or will later criticize what seems to them inaction, they plunge into a long and unnecessary questioning. I have heard some start aimlessly at the beginning of the story just unfolded and ponderously plod through to the end, strengthening at each step the testimony previously given, with every question enabling the man upon the witness stand to embellish, enlarge, and expound what he has said before. Such lawyers learn thus the hard way how delicate and how dangerous a weapon cross-examination is. It is only the truly skilled who dare decide not to cross-examine.

Let us suppose that you are one of the skilled; you will rise and say something like this: "Is that all? Nothing! No questions. Step down!" I have heard this done with great effect. There is little that you can do that will more impress your jury who will be saying to themselves, "There couldn't be much in that testimony if the opposing lawyer does not even wish to question it."

Once, a few days before Christmas, I was presenting a criminal case for the prosecution in which the late Abe Levy was the defendant's counsel. I had called an important businessman to the stand and thought his testimony most impressive, but Mr. Levy evidently did not think so. And so, rising with a winning smile and the charming manner for which he was so justly famed, he bowed to the witness and said: "Thank you for coming here. Other than to wish you a very Merry Christmas and to express my hopes that you may have a prosperous New Year, I have no questions," and sat down. My witness did not weigh much with the jury after that.

From this and many other lessons which he gave me, I began to see that the manner of the cross-examiner is sometimes more important even than the matter of his questioning. A friendly smile, a look of good nature, quiet courtesy are all assets of inestimable value in this field. However categorical and short your questions are, they still can be put in such a way as to avoid all needless offense. You will win friends with the jury by this method.

But I am anticipating your decision that you must cross-examine. As you rise to do it, you will have previously thought out your first question, for the first question may be the most important one. And this especially is true in an attack upon the character and credit of the witness—an isolated field to which I shall shortly come. It is a field which you will traverse rarely and then only of necessity. Let us assume for the moment that this is not what you intend to do. Perhaps your purpose is to assail the memory of the witness, or his bias or his accuracy, or it may be that a quiet deflation is in order. Cockiness and arrogance do not endear themselves to any jury, and this witness perhaps in testifying has managed to display an aloof or patronizing disdain of you. If you can take him down a peg or two, the jury will enjoy it, and they will give less heed to all that he has said if you can make them laugh at him.

Carson once cross-examined such a witness in this wise. With his thick and charming Irish brogue, he asked, "Are you a drinking man?" "That's my business," the witness haughtily replied. "And have you any other?" Carson shouted. The jury roared. The witness was demolished.

Mr. Wellman tells a good story of this kind about a doctor in Chicago who had given damaging testimony. The opposing lawyer did not attack his testimony or him, but instead questioned him as follows:

Q. Doctor, you say you are a practicing physician. Have you practiced your profession in the city of Chicago for any length of time?

A. Yes. I have been in practice here in Chicago for about forty years.

Q. Well, doctor, during that time I presume you have had occasion to treat some of our most prominent citizens, have you not?

A. Yes. I think I have.

Q. By any chance were you ever called as a family physician to prescribe for the elder Marshall Field?

A. Yes. I was his family physician for a number of years.

Q. By the way, I haven't heard of him lately. Where is he now?

A. He is dead.

Q. Oh, I'm sorry. Were you the family physician of the elder Mr. McCormick?

A. Yes, also for many years.

Q. Would you mind my asking where he is now?

A. He is dead.

He then asked about eight or ten others whom the doctor once had treated, all of whom were dead. As the jury smiled, he looked politely at the doctor and said, "I don't think it is necessary to ask you any more questions. Please step down."

It is in the field of memory that perhaps the best fruits may be garnered, for of all the functions of the human mind, the most fallible is memory. Witnesses are historians and autobiographers; on the witness stand they are reconstructing past events. Many of them to the best of their ability attempt to do it honestly, but it is not strange to find the grossest imperfection even in the memory of an honest man. Not only may his hearing and his eyesight be defective, but all his recollections ofttimes are the product of an association of ideas, commingled and confused with rationalization, and all his memory may be tinctured by a bias, sometimes subconscious, or colored by suggestion.

Professor Münsterberg of Harvard, in a book which he called *On the Witness Stand,* explains all this by scientific tests and fascinating illustrations. That the memory of the ordinary man is imperfect, and his ability to describe in words the incidents occurring two or three years before he testifies even more so, becomes less astonishing as we review the works of great historians. They sometimes make mistakes in dates and facts and ofttimes provide faulty and distorted pictures. Macaulay's great essay on history describes all this. If possible, to set straight the memory of a witness is, then, one of the great tasks of the cross-examiner.

There are innumerable other fields equally dissociated with an attack upon the character and veracity of the witness. Among the most important of these is bias. If you can show that the testimony on direct cross-examination has been colored, however unintentionally, by a leaning toward one side, you will go far toward destroying all the force of that to which the witness testified.

Cross-examination is not a thing that can be learned by rote. Each cross-examination differs from all others because the facts are different, the witnesses are different, the jury is different, the judge is different, everything is different. Each cross-examination is a new adventure, a foray on an uncharted ocean.

Learn when to stop. When you have really scored a direct hit, forget your other points and sit down. Do not try to gild the lily. Don't spoil all that you have done by asking that one last fatal question. A rather pompous lawyer was once cross-examining a witness in an assault case. The charge was that the defendant had bitten off the complainant's ear. A stupid and reluctant witness had testified that he had seen the affray but that he did not see the incident in question. With unction, the defendant's counsel rose to cross-examine. "Well, my good man," he said, "you have told us that you did not see my client bite off the complainant's ear; now, just what did you see?" "Well," the witness drawled, "as I was coming along the road I just happened to see him spitting the complainant's ear out of his mouth."

Dickens was not only a novelist but one of the ablest of our legal historians. As a newspaper reporter, he had haunted the courts in his youth. The unfortunate cross-examination which he describes in *Bardell* v. *Pickwick* was no doubt founded upon some actual observation in the Old Bailey. Mr. Phunky was a young barrister who had been briefed as an understudy to the great Serjeant Snubbin and had been assigned the task of cross-examining Mr. Winkle.

"Did you," he complacently asked, "ever see anything in Mr. Pickwick's manner and conduct toward the opposite sex to induce you to believe that he ever contemplated matrimony of late years, in any case?" "Oh, no, certainly not," replied the frightened Mr. Winkle.

It would have been a good place to stop, but Mr. Phunky, in his inexperience, desiring to improve the point, already sufficiently well made, pressed on to inquire whether the witness had ever seen Mr. Pickwick behave toward women other than as a father to his daughter. And here the witness hesitated as he answered, "Not the least doubt of it. That is—yes—oh, yes—certainly."

But the young barrister continued to inquire: "You have never known anything in his behavior towards Mrs. Bardell, or any other female, in the least degree suspicious?" By this time the junior had intercepted Serjeant Snubbin's wink and was about to take his seat, but he did not regain it before Mr. Winkle answered, "N—n—no, except on one trifling occasion which, I have no doubt, might be easily explained."

The young lawyer here sat down. What followed would not have taken place had he stopped earlier. In vain did Serjeant Snubbin hastily inform the witness that he might leave the box, but it was too late, for Mrs. Bardell's counsel, Serjeant Buzfuz, was on his feet to stop him. "Stay, Mr. Winkle, stay!" he said, and turning to the judge: "Will your lordship have the goodness to ask him what this one instance of suspicious behavior towards females . . . was?"

Poor Winkle tried to remain silent, but the judge forced him to speak, and thus he faltered out: "The trifling circumstance of suspicion was Mr. Pickwick being found in a lady's sleeping apartment at midnight; which terminated," he believed, "in the breaking off of the projected marriage of the lady in question, and had led," he said he knew, "to the whole party being forcibly carried before George Nupkins, Esq., magistrate and justice of the peace for the borough of Ipswich." Small wonder that poor Pickwick lost his case.

The *Pickwick Papers* lay many decades in the future when, on an autumn day in the year 1770, John Adams sat preparing for the defense of the British soldiers whom all Boston thought guilty of a massacre. But how well he understood the principle illustrated in the Bardell trial (as all good lawyers from time immemorial have understood it), appeared in his admonition to his junior, young Josiah Quincy, Jr. "You, Josiah," he said, "are a man of zeal. In the heat and inspiration of your cross-examination, do not, my young friend, press your examination beyond the necessity of the case," and when Quincy demurred, John Adams cut him short. "Cases at law," he said, "are often won by what is left unsaid."

Echoing the wisdom of the ages, Sir Norman Birkett once admonished, "Above all do not ask that one question too many."

A word, a phrase, sometimes captures the imagination and may become more eloquent than all the testimony. With ingenuity you will be listening for the important word. Marshall Hall brilliantly illustrated this in his defense of Annie Dyer. The girl had been seduced by a married man and when her unwanted child arrived, she asked the visiting nurse: "How can anyone get rid of a baby like this?" A little later she took the child to bed with her and it was never seen alive again.

Marshall Hall defended her in her subsequent trial for murder. With a stroke akin to genius, he concluded that emphasis on one word might transform a seeming confession into a defense, and so when he asked the nurse on cross-examination, embodying the phrase used by the prisoner, Hall put his question thus: "Did she say how *can* anyone get rid of a baby like this!" The witness acknowledged that that was not only what the mother said but that she had said it with the same emphasis on "can" that he had used. His client was acquitted.

Cross-examination is like firing a Roman candle. First you light it and, holding it in one hand, you make sure that the sparks do not get into your eyes. As you rotate it very gently, in a flood of fire a ball emerges with a loud report. Thoroughly alight, the sparks now burst out in a flood and every now and then there is a ball. But if you hold the candle inexpertly, or if it is itself defective, the ball, instead of gracefully describing a parabola in the sky, may fire backward up your sleeve and burn you badly.

Sometimes the most impressive cross-examination is that wherein the witness pauses for a long time to answer. Let him pause, tell him to take his time—take plenty of time. Sit down and wait, and as the seconds tick, every instant brings him lower with the jury.

The most hazardous undertaking in cross-examination is the direct attack on character and credibility. No lawyer can ever be excused for making this assault upon an honest witness who he believes has told the truth. No lawyer will long survive in the courtroom who does that.

Let us suppose that the witness who now sits before you is a rascal who, by his deliberate perjury, has been trying to destroy your client. With such a one, you have but one duty: advance upon him as you would (if you were brave enough) upon a rattlesnake. Taking courage in both hands, determine that you will destroy him once and for all—destroy him where all men can see and hear. Destroy him so that no juror, however hostile heretofore, would dare to rest a verdict on his word.

Cross-examination, Sir Norman Birkett once well said, "to a very large extent must depend upon the kind of man you are." It will depend, too, very largely on the kind of man the witness thinks you are, for it is in every real sense a duel between counsel and the witness. You must dominate him, overcome him, conquer him, if you hope to save your client. Throughout his direct examination, rivet him with your eyes—rivet him and make him look away.

A lying witness finds difficulty in looking you full in the face; he shifts and changes his position and stares out into space. Judah Benjamin, it is said, cross-examined with his eyes. "No witness," an observer tells us, "could look into Benjamin's black, piercing eyes and maintain a lie." The eye is not only the window of the soul, it is the revelation of man's character, and your character is now pitted against that of the lying witness. With it you must conquer him, for you are engaged now in mortal combat. Either you or he must prevail. All that your client has is staked upon this duel.

To vary the simile but a little, you are in the prize ring, and while you are sparring for the opportunity of a knockout blow, you must keep your guard up. I have seen knockouts both in the prize ring and in the courts of justice; I have seen them at the very start of the encounter. If you can do it, it is of vital importance that you knock the witness down in the first round.

Of all the cross-examinations I have ever read, Carson's destruction of Oscar Wilde is the most perfect and complete.

In the year 1895, Oscar Wilde, the prototype of Gilbert's "Bunthorne," was at the top of his literary fame in London. Success and depravity had hardened him. His features had become gross and coarse, even as the portrait did in *Dorian Gray*. He was large and fat, and heavy sensual lines marked his debauched face. For four years, young Lord Alfred Douglas, the third son of the Marquis of Queensberry, had been on terms of close intimacy with Wilde, much to Queensberry's disgust. Twenty-four-year-old Alfred Douglas was as beautiful as a woman, although he did not show effeminacy.

When ugly rumors flew connecting his son's name with that of Wilde, the old Marquis determined that the time had come to act, and thus it was that on the last day of February, 1895, he appeared at the Albermarle, one of Wilde's many clubs, and handed the porter a card on which in a large scrawl he had written, "Oscar Wilde, posing as a Sodomite." With a white flower in his buttonhole, Wilde lost no time in walking into a police court to prefer a charge of criminal libel. A little later, the grand jury indicted Queensberry and on April third the trial began.

Carson had known Wilde slightly at Trinity College, Dublin, and when he was offered the brief in defense of Queensberry, he was in doubt whether he should take it. He sought out Lord Halsbury's advice. "The great thing," the old Lord ex-Chancellor told him, "is to arrive at justice, and it is you, I believe, who can best do it." And so Carson accepted.

In the interval between the police court hearing and the trial, Queensberry's detectives had been making many inquiries, and one day, almost by accident, they encountered a prostitute and asked her if she was prosperous. Replying in the negative, she said that both she and her friends were in sore straits owing to the competition which she attributed to Oscar Wilde. And before she left them, there was a hint that they break into a certain flat, the location of which she gave them.

Promptly following this advice, Queensberry's men broke in and there found names and addresses of many young men of low origin, and documents connecting them with Wilde. Though Bernard Shaw attempted to persuade the popular writer to abandon the prosecution, Wilde refused, looking forward as he did with keen anticipation to the court encounter. The trial would enhance his reputation, he thought; victory would be easy. As for poor old Ned Carson, what did he know of literature—or of life for that matter?

And so, on an April morning of the year 1895, a courtroom of the Old Bailey was crowded to suffocation as Mr. Justice Collins, in his robes of scarlet and ermine, took his seat upon the bench. Young Lord Alfred Douglas was there, and Oscar Wilde, accompanied by many friends who waited for the triumph of a great literary figure, soon appeared.

Sir Edward Clarke, whose fame then far outshone that of Carson (a comparative newcomer to the English bar) was counsel for the prosecution. Opening to the jury, he said that the indictment had been brought against the Marquis because Wilde could not let Queensberry's expression, "posing as a Sodomite," pass unnoticed even though the words had not directly charged a criminal offense. Wilde had had trouble of this kind before, it seemed. He had often been blackmailed. Men by the names of Allen and Clayborn had sought money from him for the surrender of a letter he had written to young Douglas.

Referring to this letter, Sir Edward Clarke now said that its words "may seem extravagant to those who are in the habit of writing commercial correspondence." The jury laughed and Sir Edward then assured them that they need "place no hateful construction on it." Sir Edward, knowing well how much the defense would seek to make of it, adopted the wise strategy of reading the letter himself, hoping in this way to remove the sting.

This was the letter addressed by Wilde to the twenty-four-year-old Alfred Douglas, which Sir Edward now read to the jury:

> My own Boy,—your sonnet is quite lovely, and it is a marvel that those red rose-leaf lips of yours should have been made no less for the music of song than for the madness of kisses. Your slim gilt soul walks between passion and poetry. I know Hyacinthus, whom Apollo loved so madly, was you in Greek days. Why are you alone and when do you go to Salisbury? Do go there to cool your hands in the grey twilight of Gothic things, and come here whenever you like. It is a lovely place—it only lacks you; but go to Salisbury first—
> Always with undying love,
Oscar Wilde

Smiling, and with great assurance, Oscar Wilde now stepped into the witness box to give his evidence for the Crown. His age, he said, was thirty-nine, and no one took special notice of this answer,—no one but Edward Carson who looked straight into the witness's eyes as he made a careful note. Sir Edward then asked Wilde about his interview with the blackmailer. The man had said to him that "a very curious construction could be put on the letter," and Wilde now told how he had replied: "Art is rarely intelligible to the criminal classes."

He was then asked if there were any truth in the charges (set forth in the specifications that had been served on him) of immoral conduct with young men, and it was a very confident and assured Oscar Wilde who answered: "There is no truth in any of them." He turned a patronizing smile on Edward Carson as he rose to cross-examine. For a long time this advocate had been puzzling to select an effective question as his first.

The note that Queensberry had written charged Wilde with *"posing* as a Sodomite." In the age he gave, was Wilde making still another *pose?* Carson had Wilde's birth certificate with him and so his first question was, "You stated that your age was thirty-nine. I think you are over forty. You were born on the sixteenth of October, 1854. Did you wish to *pose* as being young?"

A. No.

Then Carson shot:

Q. That makes you more than forty.

But Wilde was not to be taken aback so easily. "Ah," he drawled, as if congratulating Carson on his mathematics. "How old was Alfred Douglas?" Carson asked, and the witness admitted that he was just twenty-four, and that he and Douglas had been seen together at many times and places throughout the past three years.

Carson now began to ply the witness about the corrupting influence of his writings. Approaching the large theme of moral purpose in literature, Carson asked him: "You are of an opinion there is no such thing as an immoral book?" The witness replied in the affirmative. "May I take it that you think *The Priest and the Acolyte* was not immoral?" Wilde answered, amid the loud laughter of the entire court, "It was worse—it was badly written."

Carson was getting much the worst of it; the clever Oscar Wilde seemed more than a match for him, but he pressed on, asking the writer about his *Importance of Being Earnest*. He put the salacious details of the story before the witness, but Wilde merely shrugged his shoulders and said that he could hardly remember it, adding, "I have only read it once, in last November, and nothing will induce me to read it again." Carson then asked him if the story was not blasphemous, and Wilde replied that it was "disgusting," "horrible," but not "blasphemous." With every answer Wilde was making headway and Carson was losing ground.

In his questions he now used the word "pose," more than once asking him: "So far as your work is concerned, you pose as not being concerned with morality or immorality?" And Wilde answered: "I do not know whether you use the word in any particular sense."

Carson then asked:

Q. It is a favorite word of your own?
A. Is it? I have no pose in this matter.

Carson noticed that Wilde's answer was a little less self-assured and so he began questioning him about his *Phrases and Philosophies for the Use of the Young*. Carson inserted some of these phrases in his questions: " 'Wickedness is a myth invented by good people to account for the curious attractiveness of others,' you think that is true?" he asked, and once more, amid laughter, the witness answered, "I rarely think anything I write is true."

Many had now begun feeling sorry for Edward Carson as Wilde scored point after point at his expense. The atmosphere in the court was becoming surcharged with pleasure in the brilliant witness, but Carson gave no evidence of his discomfiture, no sign that he was being worsted.

He now questioned Wilde about *Dorian Gray* and referring to one of its characters who had adored another man madly, asked the witness whether he had ever entertained such an adoration. Amid even louder laughter, at Carson's expense, Wilde answered, "I have never given adoration to anybody except myself."

Once more the courtroom shook with laughter. But Carson treated the witness with cold scorn. He was angry now but he did not allow his anger to unsettle his determined purpose to bring this charlatan to his knees. Another sentence of this book was, "I have admired you passionately," and when Carson asked the witness about this, Wilde answered with another question intended to be funny: "Do you mean financially?" Thoroughly aroused at last, Carson answered, "Oh, yes, financially, do you think we are talking about finance?" With even greater gusto, Wilde replied: "I don't know what you are talking about." "Don't you?" said Carson. "Well, I hope I shall make myself very plain before I am done."

Advancing with cold fury upon the corrupter of young men, Carson now directed his attention to the letter Wilde had written Douglas. "I think," said Wilde, "it is a very beautiful letter. It is a poem. You might as well cross-examine me as to whether a sonnet of Shakespeare was proper." "Apart from art?" pressed Carson. "I cannot answer apart from art," the self-confident witness answered. "Suppose a man who is not an artist had written this letter, would you say it was a proper letter?" "A man that was not an artist could not have written that letter," Wilde answered.

Roars of laughter greeted this sally. The crowd was fascinated with Oscar Wilde and was delighted by his wit and was increasingly scornful of the man whom Wilde was worsting. Carson by now was surging with cold fury, but never for one moment let it get the best of him. "Can I suggest, for the sake of your reputation, that there is nothing very wonderful in this 'red rose lips' of yours?" Carson's Irish accent, perhaps because of his anger, seemed now more noticeable, and Wilde, taking advantage of this, answered, "A great deal depends upon the way you read it." Ignoring this most pointed jibe, Carson continued, " 'Your slim gilt soul walks between passion and poetry.' Is that a beautiful phrase?" "Not as you read it," Wilde answered, and this time Carson shot back, "I don't profess to be an artist and when I hear you give evidence I am glad I'm not."

He then immediately picked up another letter Wilde had written Douglas, asking, "Is that an ordinary letter?" Wilde answered with a condescending smile, "Everything I write is extraordinary. I do not *pose* as being ordinary."

Not the packed courtroom only but all London was watching now. Unless Carson could somehow floor this literary trickster, Wilde's triumph would be complete and Carson's defeat would probably destroy him as an advocate. What was he to do now? He had the evidence that this great slobbering Bunthorne had consorted with valets and grooms and bootblacks in curtained perfumed rooms. Should he save all this for his own case or should he use it now?

Carson decided to use it then and there, and he began plying Wilde with questions as to his extraordinary companions and asked him about the ten shillings he had paid a blackmailer. Wilde said that he had given it out of contempt. "Then your way to show contempt is by paying ten shillings?" And Wilde gained still further adherents from the court by answering, "Yes, very often." There was another young man employed in a publishing house whom the author had taken to a hotel and given an expensive dinner. Referring to this, Carson asked, "Was that for the purpose of having an intellectual treat?" "Well, for him, yes," Wilde answered, and Carson was now almost laughed out of court; yet he stood his ground, undismayed and undiscouraged.

He had facts, names, circumstances, and specific dates, and Wilde now appeared less confident as Carson began to use them. Wilde had made gifts of jewelry to some of the young men whom he had corrupted. "Did you know that one was a gentleman's valet and the other a gentleman's groom?" Carson asked. Wilde answered in the affirmative. The questioning continued: "What enjoyment was it to you to be entertaining grooms and coachmen?"

A. The pleasure of being with those who are young, bright, happy, careless, and original.

Q. Had they plenty of champagne?

A. What gentleman would stint his guests?

Once more the courtroom laughed, but it was for the last time. The audience grew sober as Carson exclaimed, "What gentleman would stint the valet and the groom!" And now the tense atmosphere took on a positively somber hue as Sir Edward Clarke interrupted to offer a "very ordinary respectful letter" from a young man named Packer. "Never mind that," Carson growled. "Packer himself will be in the box and the jury will see what he is like."

One of the greatest arts in cross-examination is the timing and the use of a document or a circumstance. It may be done with no effect, or in the hands of a master of the art it may become the lethal blow. Some lawyers prefer to use a letter or a fact by offering it as a part of their own case, but those who really understand their business will use it in their cross-examination. Professor Wigmore never said a wiser thing than when he wrote: "The difference between getting the same facts from other witnesses and from cross-examination is the difference between slow-burning gunpowder and quick-flashing dynamite; each does its appointed work, but the one bursts along its marked line only, the other rends in all directions."

But Carson did not need Wigmore to teach him this. His long experience had taught him. And he has left for us a perfect example of this truth. He had asked Wilde often about his base associates and the witness had never faltered. And now, as if with a swift saber thrust, Carson, after mentioning by name a young serving boy at Oxford, asked, "Did you ever kiss him?" It was here that Wilde made his fatal answer: "He was a particularly plain boy. He was unfortunately very ugly. I pitied him for it." By this single answer he had exposed himself. Had he now stood naked before the jury, he could not have revealed his filthy character more clearly. Carson's question was a stroke of genius.

Like a great fighter in the ring who has just delivered a shattering blow, Carson followed his advantage with many others of the same kind. Ignoring all the teaching about not asking "Why?" Carson closed in on the witness and asked him question after question as to why he had mentioned the boy's ugliness. Why had he said the boy was plain? Like the cur he was, Wilde now literally turned tail and ran. He was not only a cad, he was a coward. Carson had mastered him totally, completely, and forever.

So total was the rout that the next day Sir Edward Clarke withdrew the prosecution against Queensberry and the defendant was discharged. And it was not long before Wilde himself was indicted and convicted and sentenced to two years at hard labor in Reading Gaol.

Cross-examination in the hands of a great master had once again been proved the strongest of all weapons in the arsenal of justice.

CHAPTER

VI

The Closing Speech

THE LAST DOCUMENT has been marked in evidence; the final witness has been cross-examined. Both sides have rested. The time for the summation has arrived. Your last opportunity to address the jury is now at hand. Your final effort at persuasion, it will be yours now to make. What you say or do not say, and how you say it, may bring liberty to a fellow citizen or fail to prevent his ruin. It is your last chance—and his! And since in the case I am imagining you are conducting, you are appearing for the defendant, it will be your duty to speak first.

Every night throughout the trial you have dictated notes of those things which may be useful for your summing up so that by this time you have a skeleton covering the main points on which you expect to dwell. Your associates will somehow have found the time to digest the testimony day by day and will have cross-indexed it for ready reference. If your memory has been well trained, you will remember the main parts of the evidence and many expressions of the witnesses will stick there in verbatim form. You are ready to embark upon this final effort to acquit your client.

The summation is the high point in the art of advocacy; it is the combination and the culmination of all of its many elements. It is the climax of the case. It is the opportunity to rescue a cause until that time perhaps seemingly lost. It calls for every skill the advocate possesses. It calls for more than skill—it is a summons to his courage, a testing ground of his character, a trial of his logic and reasoning powers, his memory, his patience and his tact, his ability to express himself in convincing words; in short, it is an assay of every power of persuasion he possesses. Small wonder, then, that there have been few great summations.

And so, as you stand up for this final foray, you realize the staggering weight of your responsibility, and your heart beats fast with the fear that you may not measure up to it. Why are you there at all? Dr. Johnson once answered that question in these words: "As it rarely happens that a man is fit to plead his own cause, lawyers are a class of the community, who by study and experience, have acquired the art and power of arranging evidence, and of applying to the points at issue what the law has settled. A lawyer is to do for his client all that he might fairly do for himself if he could."

An advocate is one who has been called to the aid of a fellow citizen in deep trouble. You are that advocate, and your one, sole, and single aim is to aid that fellow citizen with all your heart and soul and mind.

The jury is watching you with an even greater scrutiny than that with which they looked at you while you were making, now so long ago, your opening address. They remember what you promised them; they have a good recollection of the evidence that followed and they are challenging you to persuade them that you have proved all that you promised them you would prove.

But if they have been studying you, your scrutiny of them has been no less intense. You will remember how they looked when certain evidence was introduced, how they reacted to your cross-examinations. Some one or more of them may have asked questions of a witness on the stand, and you will be thinking now, as you thought then, of the significance of those questions and the way in which the questioner received the answers. If you have succeeded thus far in the trial in establishing some credit with the jury, if your firmness, your good manners, and your complete integrity have won you some measure of approval in the jury box, you will strain now to avoid everything that may forfeit that good will and you will do all within your power to strengthen it.

If you have decided to sound your keynote at once and to make it as telling and provocative as you are able, you will be fortified in this decision by Scarlett, one of England's greatest advocates, whose habit always was, he said, "to state in the simplest form that the truth and the case would admit, the proposition of which I maintain the affirmative and the defendant's counsel the negative." Suppose that your client has been charged with perjury and that the main witness against him has admitted many false swearings under oath. The clear and simple issue, then, is: Has your client lied or is it his accuser who has committed perjury?

In such a case, your first words might well be: "Gentlemen of the jury, this is the first time so far as I know when an American citizen has been charged with perjury on the uncorroborated testimony of a perjurer. This is the first time when an American jury has been asked to strike down and destroy a fellow citizen on the word of a professional liar, a man who has trained himself in false swearing for the better part of his disreputable life, and has become in this particular field of crime an accomplished adept from long experience and from habit—a man whose predilection for perjury has made him an outstanding criminal in this field. It is on his word, gentlemen, that the prosecution will seek your verdict of conviction."

By some such opening as this, you have come to the very heart of your case, you have defined the issue, sharpened the point to be decided, and in the same breath have recalled to all the jurors' minds your cross-examination of the Government's main witness. You have thereby stressed and underlined your main contention: that no fair mind could fail to have a reasonable doubt as to whether the accuser had told the truth. You have paved the way for convincing them that they must have a reasonable doubt as to whether, on this isolated occasion, the Government's main witness has departed from his protracted career of perjury long enough this once to have told the truth.

A summing up may be likened to the writing of a book. Before an author dares commit his thoughts to paper, he has first gone through long, painful months or perhaps years of hard, laborious research. He has culled his facts from every source available. He has corrected every date, verified every reference, weighed and considered every proof, and resolved all questions of conflicting evidence.

The trial, for the lawyer, is what research is for the author. Histories and biographies, letters, memoirs, diaries, and the archives of great libraries are the material from which a book is made. The evidence, documents, and the demeanor of the witnesses are the stuff from which the advocate's summation must be constructed.

But the author works leisurely and alone, with time for reflection and for reconsideration. The advocate is denied this luxury; he must, as it were, write his book in the floodlight of the public gaze and send it forth to the public—his jury—forthwith, without correction or amendment, and yet, withal, he must be as accurate, as clear, as logical, and as interesting as the author, and his book must be so written as to withstand the hostile reviewer in the person of opposing counsel.

In one respect, however, the lawyer's task in summation closely resembles that of the author. He has the same problem of selection. A great writer, after he has canvassed his whole subject, chooses from his material those facts and incidents that illuminate and explain his central point. His researches have covered a wide and varied field and he usually is embarrassed by a wealth of facts. Some are totally immaterial, others important, and still others of less consequence.

As he is writing a book and not an encyclopedia, the limitations of a single volume dictate and prescribe his choice. How well he chooses and describes will determine whether or not the public reads him. His arrangement of his facts and the language in which he presents them make the difference between a great writer and a lesser one. So, too, the lawyer, from perhaps six or maybe thirty weeks of testimony, must be able to discern which are the points worth dwelling on when he sums up, and just how those facts should be marshaled.

But there is one respect in which the advocate has an advantage over the author: he has seen and watched the jury—his reading public. The author casts his book adrift and, except through it, never meets his readers. He cannot watch them as they read, and change his text to suit their moods.

The advocate, on the other hand, observes from second to second those who listen to him and knows from their expression and a kind of thought transference whether what he is saying is having its effect or is creating the desired impression. The advocate has direct contact with those whom he is seeking to convince and for whom he molds and shades his words and sentences as he proceeds. In this way, if he has the talent, he will find the keys that will unlock their feelings and the road that leads unerringly into their hearts.

Facts, unlike the men whom Jefferson envisioned, are not all equal. There is no democracy in this field. Some facts obviously are of more importance than others. Some are aristocrats; some are members of the middle class; some are nothing more than serfs. Some are obvious leaders; others mere followers in the ranks. By instinct and by intuition, the advocate must discern their proper rank and treat them accordingly. "You will find," John Quincy Adams once said, "hundreds of persons able to produce a crowd of good ideas upon any subject for one who can marshal them to the best advantage."

A piano has its octaves, its white keys and its black, its sharps and its flats. An advocate is a pianist whose white and black keys are the facts. His task is to play them. Set up a grand concert piano on the stage of an auditorium and a little child may step forward and with one finger haltingly pick out a tune, and the vast caverns of resounding melody within the instrument remain unexplored. But let a Paderewski sit down before this instrument and what has seemed a thing of wood and ivory and metal strings springs suddenly to life and finds its voice. On an instant the great instrument's whole soul is set awake. It responds to the true artist as Adam answered to the voice of God. The great musician causes it to sob and shout, to sing and to cry out, until all who listen are subdued like ghosts from an enchanter fleeing.

Such is the opportunity of a great advocate; such is his power if he embraces it.

You stand there speaking for your client because you can say for him better than he can say for himself all that can and should be said in his behalf. For this reason he has called you to his aid. This is why you are his advocate. He has entrusted his good name, his liberty, his very life to you. What a trust it is, what a frightening responsibility you have assumed for a fellow human being!

A good summation should be related not only to the facts of the case but to the atmosphere created as the trial progresses. I once had a case in which I represented the officers of a certain corporation who had filed income tax returns which understated the amount due the Government by some $1,800,000 or more. I admitted that this had been done and asserted that the defendants were not amenable to prosecution because they had made a "voluntary disclosure" to the Government.

There was then a policy, now no longer in existence, which permitted even a willful tax evader to escape prosecution if he repented in time. Fred Vinson, then Secretary of the Treasury, stated the policy in these words: "Monetary penalties may be imposed for delinquency, for negligence, and for fraud, but the man who makes a disclosure before investigation is under way protects himself and his family from the stigma of a felony conviction, and there is nothing complicated about going to a Collector or other revenue officer and simply saying, 'There is something wrong with my return and I want to straighten it out.'"

Now my clients had, I believed, complied with this voluntary disclosure policy. They had gone to the Collector at the Custom House in New York and had frankly admitted the understatements in their returns and had offered to pay whatever amount was due. The question litigated was whether or not they had made this disclosure before the investigation by the Government started. There was, I thought, a fair issue of fact on this point, but just before the summation, there was a ruling by the court that as a matter of law the Treasury Department was not bound by its disclosure policy. This ruling presented a real problem. The problem consisted of the fact that I had frankly admitted that the defendants' returns were wrong and that I now found myself with my only defense, namely, that of voluntary disclosure, taken away from me.

It seemed almost idle under these circumstances to sum up at all, but I nevertheless decided to do so. The Internal Revenue Department, as I viewed the evidence, had been guilty of nothing short of a fraud in inducing the defendants to make their disclosure and to present to the Government all of their many books and records which the agents were allowed to examine in defendants' offices for days and days. This did not seem fair to me, and I believed that it was possible that a jury might view it in the same light. I could not, however, any longer contend that there had been a voluntary disclosure since I was face to face with the judge's ruling that it was not a defense. What was I to do?

I thought of one of Lewis Carroll's poems that has delighted many generations of children familiar with *Alice in Wonderland* and *Through the Looking Glass*, and so I said to the jury: "I am going to ask you by your verdict to hold the Government to the ordinary standards of good faith and fair dealing that you would expect between man and man. I am going to ask you to take a different position here toward these defendants than the Walrus and the Carpenter took with the Oysters. Some of you will remember your *Through the Looking Glass.* You remember how the poem started:

> *"O Oysters, come and walk with us!"*
> *The Walrus did beseech.*
> *"A pleasant walk, a pleasant talk*
> *Along the briny beach;*
> *We cannot do with more than four,*
> *To give a hand to each."*

"Well, 'A pleasant walk,' you see, was the voluntary disclosure.

"And then, after their walk along the beach, the Walrus suggested that the time had come for a slight collation. You remember:

> *'A loaf of bread,' the Walrus said,*
> *'Is what we chiefly need:*
> *Pepper and vinegar besides*
> *Are very good indeed—*
> *Now, if you're ready, Oysters dear,*
> *We can begin to feed.'*

"Up to that point, the Oysters thought they were all right, you see—just having a nice walk like our walk down to the Custom House."

And I continued: "These books were given to the Government for the honest purpose of disclosure in reliance upon the good faith of the Government, just as the Oysters had relied upon the invitation of the Walrus, you see. And remember, ladies and gentlemen, how after a light refreshment was proposed, there was a dissent from the companions whom the Walrus and the Carpenter had invited for a stroll:

> *'But not on us!' the Oysters cried,*
> *Turning a little blue.*

The Closing Speech

'After such kindness, that would be
A dismal thing to do.'

"And then the double talk, you know, official double talk:

'The night is fine,' the Walrus said.
'Do you admire the view?'

"And then you remember how the Walrus and the Carpenter sat down and ate the little Oysters.

'It seems a shame,' the Walrus said,
'To play them such a trick.
After we've brought them out so far,
And made them trot so quick!'
The Carpenter said nothing but
'The butter's spread too thick!'

"And then the pity, you know, the sadness of the people who catch other people in a trap and then destroy them:

'I weep for you,' the Walrus said:
'I deeply sympathize.'
With sobs and tears he sorted out
Those of the largest size,
Holding his pocket handkerchief
Before his streaming eyes.

"They gave us a pleasant run with the Internal Revenue agents, and because my clients made all their books available to the Government, they are now in its clutches. It has been testified here that the Government agents were extremely polite and pleasant to the defendants as they gathered in the evidence which was furnished them. And now will you consent that the defendants be eaten alive even as the Oysters were? You remember the last phrase:

'Shall we be trotting home again?'
But answer came there none—

And this was scarcely odd, because
They'd eaten every one."

Some of the jurors smiled at my little excursion into literature. They all saw the point. They retired for their deliberations and returned with a verdict of guilty as they were bound to do under the court's charge, but they added a recommendation of clemency which the court considered in imposing sentence.

But for the direction of the court, which took the question of voluntary disclosure from the consideration of the jury, the defendants might have been acquitted because of the atmosphere created by Lewis Carroll's delightful commentary on entrapment.

A summing up, among other things, must be an argument, and the sole aim of that argument must be to convince twelve men. A good argument, however, will be concealed within the form and texture of your presentation, but it must have a core of solid reasoning and logic. It must be like the steel framework of a skyscraper; it not only supports but holds the structure, yet the girders are covered up by the exterior walls. A mathematical tyro can establish that when two parallel lines are crossed by a transversal, the diagonally opposite exterior and interior angles are equal. And when he is through doing so, there is no room left for doubt or cavil or debate. Such a demonstration should be the framework of the summation.

Like a good geometrician, you should, before you start discussion of your proof, clearly state the proposition you are intending to establish. At the very outset, you should define the issue, state explicitly the proposition in dispute and, in so doing, eliminate all those areas of fact which are not in controversy. A perfect example of how this should be done was Erskine's summation in the defense of Thomas Paine. "The first thing," he said, "which presents itself in the discussion of any subject is to state distinctly and with precision, what the question is, and when prejudice and misrepresentation have been exerted, to distinguish it accurately from what it is not." How well he did what he said ought to be done, I tried hard to record in my life of England's greatest advocate.

Having made the point at issue lucid, Erskine, with an inspired mixture of logic and eloquence, proceeded to the establishment of his main contention; and as he moved from point to point, it was clear that he had drafted out a skeleton of the main points of his argument. For although he used no notes and there were, therefore, no mechanical obstacles to his spontaneity, the arrangement of his arguments had been long preconceived and was, therefore, no haphazard performance. Although speaking always with apparent extemporaneity, what he said, even as we read it now, was evidently the extension of a well-considered plan.

There was nothing in it that was not well designed to bring about a favorable verdict. With candor and complete frankness, he discussed the pertinent evidence. He seemed to divine the thoughts of every juror, and to anticipate the questions which they might ask each other in the jury room. He did not talk *at* the jury; he reasoned *with* them, and as he reasoned, he was both accurate and fair. He allowed his adversary's evidence the fullest weight; he neither ignored, suppressed, nor misrepresented anything. He was a well-bred gentleman and everything he did and said comported with the high standards of such a man.

Never for an instant did he lose contact with the jury. He understood how large a part current feeling and opinion inevitably would play in their deliberations.

In his defense of John Frost, the solicitor, he showed how well he knew that his real antagonist was England's fear of France and her hatred of Jacobinism. Frost had come home from a trip to Paris and sat one night in the Percy coffeehouse. He was asked how he liked the French capital; and in his cups he was heard to exclaim: "I am for equality and no King. I mean no King, the Constitution of this country is a bad one." For these words he soon found himself under indictment, charged with disturbing the peace of the Kingdom and with having brought "our most sworn serene Sovereign into hatred and contempt."

In his opening for the Crown, Sir John Scott had compared the Constitution of England with that of France, much to the latter's disparagement, and so, when Erskine finally addressed the jury, he said that he:

" . . . had no notice from the record that the politics of Europe were to be the subject of discourse, yet experience ought to have taught me to expect it; for what act of Government has for a long time past been carried on by any other means? When or where has been the debate . . . in which the affairs of France have not taken the lead? The affairs of France have indeed become the common stalking-horse for all purposes . . . but I assert that neither the actual condition of France, nor the supposed condition of this country, are . . . before you . . . and that . . . the words must be judged of as if spoken by any man or woman in the kingdom, at any time from the Norman Conquest to the moment I am addressing you."

And then he added with great candor:

"Mr. Frost must forgive me if I take the liberty to say, that, with the best intentions in the world, he formerly pushed his observations and conduct respecting Government further than many would be disposed to follow him."

But had the time come, asked Erskine:

". . . when obedience to the law and correctness of conduct are not a sufficient protection to the subject, but that he must measure his steps, select his expressions, and adjust his very looks in the most common and private intercourse of life? Must an Englishman in future fill his wine by measure, lest in the openness of his soul, and whilst believing his neighbors are joining him in that happy relaxation and freedom of thought which is the prime blessing of life, he should find his character blasted, and his person in prison? Does any man put such restraint upon himself in the most private moments of his life, that he would be contented to have his loosest and lightest words recorded and set in array against him in a court of justice?"

And now for the final plea.

"If," said Erskine, "the defendant amongst others has judged too lightly of the advantages of our Government . . . let him feel its excellence today in its beneficence; let him compare in his trial the condition of an English subject with that of a citizen of France, which he is supposed to prefer. . . . But if you condemn the defendant upon this sort of evidence, depend upon it he must have his adherents, and, as far as that goes, I must be one of them."

Poor Frost was convicted and sentenced to six months in His Majesty's jail of Newgate. Twenty years had passed before the Prince Regent gave Frost a royal pardon. Fourteen months more ensued before he made an application to the King's Bench for restoration of his name to the attorneys' roll, but the court said: "Though the pardon releases him from all the effects of the sentence upon him, it does not follow that he must be replaced on the roll of attorneys; more particularly his want of practice and experience in the profession for one or two and twenty years must have induced a degree of unfitness for the employment, which could not be supposed to attach to an attorney on his first application to be placed on the rolls. Motion refused."

That evening at the coffeehouse back in 1793 had been a costly one—so costly that even Erskine's great advocacy could not save him.

On May 15, 1800, in the Drury Lane Theater, John Hatfield fired a pistol at King George III. Although indicted for murder and high treason, the defendant was accorded a fair British trial. Erskine was his counsel and now see how he not only touched the subject of prevailing sentiment but capitalized on it for his own use by dwelling upon English fairness and the excellence of the British administration of justice.

"Gentlemen of the jury," he began, "the scene in which we are engaged, and the duty which I am not merely privileged but appointed by the court to perform, exhibits to the whole civilized world a perpetual monument of our national justice. The transaction, indeed in every part of it, as it stands recorded in the evidence already before us, places our country and its Government upon the highest pinnacle of human elevation."

Like a strong, cool breeze that sweeps away the sultry skies of a mid-August afternoon, Erskine, in these two sentences, had cleared the atmosphere of a surcharged courtroom.

"It appears," he went on, "that upon the fifteenth of May last His Majesty after a reign of forty years, not merely in sovereign power but spontaneously in the very hearts of his people, was openly shot at (or to all appearances shot at) in a public theater in the center of his capital and amidst the loyal plaudits of his subjects. . . ."

And then, raising his voice and looking straight in turn at every juror in the box, he added: "Yet not a hair of the head of the supposed assassin was touched."

The case at last went to the jury and while an anxious courtroom watched, the twelve men finally returned to hear their foreman say: "We find the prisoner is not guilty, being under the influence of insanity at the time the act was committed."

The great masters of the past are worthy of unending study. They knew the law of their case, its philosophy and history, and had learned how to fit their facts into the legal principles. They well understood that if what they said was so presented that the presiding judge would be forced to echo it in his charge, they had multiplied their chances of success. You will be fascinated by their gift of understatement, their strong conviction that no point is ever better made than when not directly made at all but is so presented that the jury itself makes it. Men pride themselves on their own discoveries, and so a point which the jury are allowed to think their own ingenuity has discovered can put the advocate in a position where the jury begin to regard him as not only their spokesman but their colleague.

It is a fascinating thing to follow and to discover bright shafts of wit—with what discretion and restraint these valuable weapons are employed.

For each new case the lawyer has a special problem. He alone has seen and heard the witnesses. He, not some master of the past, has divined the feeling of *his* judge and jury; he alone has felt the atmosphere of his own courtroom and is, therefore, in a better position to decide upon his course of action than all the silent mentors of the printed page.

Imagination is of incalculable aid. An illustration of how it can be used was once given by a great Chicago lawyer, Weymouth Kirkland. He had been called upon to defend a group of insurance companies which were resisting claims based on the alleged death of an engineer named Peck. The plaintiff contended that Peck had fallen overboard from a steamer while crossing Lake Michigan. The defendants, on the other hand, were seeking to establish that Peck had never fallen overboard, that he had left his coat in his stateroom as a ruse, and that when the boat docked in the early morning, he had quietly slipped down the gangplank.

Much evidence was adduced by the plaintiff for the purpose of establishing that if Peck had in fact fallen overboard, the currents and the prevailing winds would have carried his body to a particular spot. One of the plaintiff's witnesses was a cook on another steamer whose ship, three days after Peck's disappearance, sailed past the exact spot where other witnesses had said the currents would have carried Peck's body. On his direct examination, the cook said that exactly at that spot he happened to glance out from his locker, saw the body, and recognized it as that of his old friend, Peck.

It was a nice opportunity for cross-examination, and Mr. Kirkland used it in this way:

Q. How long had you known Peck?
A. Fifteen years.

Q. You knew him well?

A. Yes, sir.

Q. How did you happen to see his body?

A. I looked out of the porthole.

Q. You recognized it beyond doubt as the body of Peck?

A. Yes, sir.

Q. Did you make any outcry when you saw the body?

A. No, sir.

Q. Did you ask the captain to stop the ship?

A. No, sir.

Q. What were you doing when you happened to look out of the window and saw the body?

A. I was peeling potatoes.

Q. And when the body of your old friend, Peck, floated by, you just kept on peeling potatoes?

A. Yes, sir.

It was a bit of cross-examination well done. And how was it used in the summing up? Did Mr. Kirkland tell the jury that the cook's testimony was palpably untrue? Did he denounce the absurdity of the answers? He handled it far more adroitly. As he stood before the jury for his final plea, he produced a potato from one pocket and a knife from another. Thus equipped, he rested one foot on a chair and proceeded to peel the potato, saying: "What ho! What have we here? Who is this floating past? As I live and breathe, if it isn't my old friend Peck! I shall tell the captain about this in the morning. In the meantime, I must go right on peeling my potatoes."

By innuendo he had destroyed all the cook's testimony. A little wit had accomplished far more than the finest rhetoric or the fiercest denunciation of this perjurer.

If I were asked to name the prerequisites of an advocate, I would mention imagination among the first. One seeking to persuade a court or jury which does not possess that quality would be a man impervious to all the overtones and subtle possibilities presented by the facts. Imagination for the trial lawyer is as essential as for the novelist, the artist, or the poet. Poetry and literature and painting are the products of a mental synthesis of ideas fused from many elements; and so it is that by the formation and expression of mental images that your true advocate brings before the jury the essence of his contention. In a single flood he dramatizes the real point and makes his hearers see a picture which their untrained senses had not yet discerned.

Whatever means you employ, you must lift your jury from mere logic to the springs of action that transcend cold reasoning, to the feelings and the emotions that govern, inspire, and produce the verdict. Never for an instant forget that it is a favorable verdict you are seeking.

The most impregnable of syllogisms will not secure it for you. Nothing will do it but the hearts and wills of twelve men whom you must capture. You must find a way to reach those hearts. How better can you do this than by such a systematic arrangement and presentation of the facts that each bit of evidence fits into the pattern of your theory and every circumstance advances your contention. But persuasion is far more than that—persuasion is effected only when you make those who hear you want to follow you, only when you have, as it were, so proselytized your listeners as to turn them into zealots for your cause.

If you had the finest Stradivarius, you would not possess a more glorious instrument than the hearts and souls of twelve men. And if you had all the skill of Paganini, Ysaye, or Zimbalist, if you had all of Mischa Elman's magic, you would not have too much with which to make your jurors' heartstrings vibrate. There ranged before you they court the inspired touch of a master's hand.

And yet all your artistry will fail if your listeners who hear and feel your art suspect that it is nothing else. Plain men like to think themselves above emotion, impervious to rhetoric and susceptible only to cold reason. Knowing this, it will be yours somehow to disguise your highest flights so that Pegasus seems only a rather well-built and serviceable draft horse.

You must be not only a musician but an actor. You must have studied your client so perceptively that you can understudy him. You must be him. You must not merely play Hamlet, you must be Hamlet himself. More than a musician or an actor, you must be a soldier and a leader. You must be a general and a humble platoon leader who knows how to gain compliance with the most potent of all military orders: "Follow me!" You must make your jury follow you even as they follow your eyes that search them through and through. The true advocate is even more than that; he is a conqueror whose will has brought about subjection and surrender. Is advocacy an art? Is there anywhere a greater one?

As we have learned from Cicero, fashions in public speaking change with the passing years, but have fashions changed so much that the day of great forensic effort has now passed? There are many now who think it has, but Emory Buckner once said: "Given a situation where there is widespread or great human interest, then the contagious effect of sincere indignation and the persuasive power of reasonableness and honesty in assembling compelling facts will remain, until some legislative body passes a law changing human nature."

Such a situation was created by the impeachment trial of

Andrew Johnson—the first and thus far the last impeachment trial of an American President. The greatest lawyers of the nation, Curtis, Evarts, Groesbeck, and Stanbery, were enlisted on the President's side and each in his way aided to destroy the trumped-up case concocted by the radical conspirators.

The articles of impeachment were laid against Lincoln's successor upon the alleged ground that he had violated the Tenure of Office Act. The real ground was that he was following Lincoln's plan of reconstruction for the South, and had refused to Robespierrize the late Confederate states, or to treat them as "conquered provinces." Because of this, Ben Butler and Thad Stevens and their malignant followers denounced President Johnson as a traitor, and it was a small town lawyer named Thomas Nelson who made the most telling speech for the defense. Hear him!

"An effort has been made," he said, "to draw a 'picture of the President's mind and heart'; he has been stigmatized as an 'usurper,' as a 'traitor to his party,' as 'disgracing the position held by some of the most illustrious in the land,' as a 'dangerous person, a criminal but not an ordinary one,' as 'encouraging murders, assassinations, and robberies all over the Southern states'; and finally by way of proving that there is one step between the sublime and the ridiculous, he has been charged with being a 'common scold,' and a 'ribald, a scurrilous blasphemer, bandying epithets and taunts with a jeering mob.' . . . I am willing to admit that if he is guilty of any of the charges . . . a whip should be put in every honest hand to lash him around the world. . . ."

It was a good beginning. "But," continued Nelson, "who is Andrew Johnson? Who is the man . . . to whom the gaze not of Delaware, but of the whole Union and of the civilized world is directed? . . . Who is Andrew Johnson? Go to the town of

Greeneville but a few short years ago . . . and you will see a poor boy entering that village a stranger without friends . . . scarcely able to read, unable to write . . . he enters the state of Tennessee an orphan, poor, penniless, without the favor of the great; but scarce had he set foot upon her generous soil, when he was seized and embraced with parental fondness, caressed as though he had been a favorite child. . . ."

With appealing simplicity Nelson then portrayed the astonishing career of his fellow townsman. And he went on: "Never since the days of Warren Hastings . . . has any man been stigmatized with more severe reprobation. . . . All the powers of invective . . . have been brought into requisition to fire your hearts and to prejudice your minds against him. . . . All the elements have been agitated. . . . The storm is playing around him, the pitiless rain is beating upon him, the lightnings are flashing around him; but . . . in the midst of it all he still stands firm, serene, unbent, unbroken, unsubdued, unawed, unterrified . . . threatening no civil war to deluge his country with blood; but, feeling a proud consciousness of his own integrity, appealing to heaven to witness the purity of his motives . . . and calling upon you, in the name of the living God . . . that you will do equal and impartial justice. . . ."

And his rhetorical questioning continued: "Who is Andrew Johnson? Are there not Senators here who are well acquainted with him? Are there not men here whose minds go back to . . . 1860 and 1861 . . . when men's faces turned pale? . . . Where was Andrew Johnson then? Standing almost within ten feet of the place where I stand now, solitary and alone . . . when 'bloody treason flourished over us,' his voice was heard arousing the nation. Some of you heard it. I only heard the echoes as they rolled along . . . to arouse the patriotism of our common country. . . . The only member of the South who was disposed to battle against treason then . . . now is called a traitor himself."

Nelson continued to inquire: "Who is Andrew Johnson? . . . When the battle of . . . Bull Run . . . was fought . . . when men's . . . hearts grew faint, where was Andrew Johnson then, this traitor, this usurper, this tyrant? Again he was heard . . . in the Senate . . . undismayed, unfaltering . . . and again the plaudits of hundreds and thousands shook the very walls of this capitol . . . when he . . . vindicated the American Constitution and proclaimed the determination of the Government to uphold and to maintain it."

Andrew Johnson was acquitted by one vote. It was Nelson's speech that, more than all else, contributed to that result. It is one of the best examples I have ever come upon of a truly great summation.

PART TWO

ADVOCACY IS INDEED AN ART

Present Low Estate
of Advocacy

T HE ART OF ADVOCACY! It is an art indeed, but one which in these latter days has fallen into neglect, judging by the lack of enthusiasm evinced for it in many of the law schools as well as in the forum where both its theory and its practice are of such vital moment to those who would essay it as well as to those for whom it is essayed.

Advocacy, indeed, in many quarters is looked upon with disfavor and with a feeling not far removed from contempt. At the Harvard Law School, for instance, the faculty not long ago caused a poll to be taken that would rank the "skills of a lawyer" in the order of their importance. And when the vote was in, it was found that the lowest rating by a fairly large margin was given to skill in advocacy. Even if this response simply means, said former Assistant United States Solicitor General Frederick Bernays Wiener, "that most Harvard alumni never get to court, but instead devote most of their energies to the office or to conferences or consultations with clients, the rating is amazingly wrong."

That Harvard should revise that rating was at least suggested by Mr. Justice Arthur T. Vanderbilt, the former Dean of the New York University Law School, when last January he spoke at the dedication of the Hall named in his honor.

"Advocacy," he said, "is not a gift of the gods. In its trial as well as in its appellate aspects it involves several distinct arts, each of which must be studied and mastered. Yet no law school in the country so far as I know pays the slightest attention to them. It is blithely assumed with disastrous results that every student is a born Webster or Choate."

That the art of advocacy of late years has been declining— indeed, that it has now reached its lowest point—is unquestionably the fact, a fact for the proof of which many witnesses might be called.

Speaking at the dedication of the new Stanford University Law School in July, 1950, Mr. Justice Robert Jackson observed that "the unsolved problem of legal education is how to equip the law student for work at the bar of the court. . . ." He told his audience that the greatest opportunity for improvement in the legal profession and where it is now most vulnerable on the score of performance is its work in the trial courtroom. "It seems to me," he said, "that, while the scholarship of the Bar has been improving, the art of advocacy has been declining." He was himself a product of the old apprentice system and knew well both its virtues and its flaws. But, he said, "if the weakness of the apprentice system was to produce advocates without scholarship, the weakness of the law school system is to turn out scholars with no skill at advocacy."

An indifference in many of the schools to this great subject undoubtedly accounts for the poor arguments now so generally heard in the appellate courts. "It is amazing," writes Mr. Wiener, "how few good arguments are presented and heard even in the highest state and Federal tribunals. Within the year I have been told by a justice of the Supreme Court that four out of five arguments to which he must listen are not good. And comments from judges of other appellate courts give me no reason to suppose that the percentage of good arguments is perceptibly higher elsewhere."

The nisi prius judges, as well as those of the appellate courts, have often told me the same story.

Now, what is this thing we call the "art of advocacy"? An art, Noah Webster tells us, is "skill in performance acquired by experience, study, and observation." Advocacy is a word derived from the Latin verb *advocare,* "to call to one's aid." An advocate is one who "pleads the cause of another before a tribunal," and in a larger sense, "one who defends or espouses any cause by argument." But no cause, I hope to show, was ever well espoused if it was done by argument alone. It was not argument alone that saved Great Britain just twelve years ago.

In June of 1940, through the lightnings and the raging storms, a startled England and a startled world could hear a deeper sound. Rumbling above the thunders of that fateful hour, the voice of Winston Churchill spoke of his countrymen and to the world: ". . . we shall fight on the beaches, . . . we shall fight in the hills. . . ." They did not have anything with which to fight—nothing but the invincible English character, unconquerable love of liberty and an undying resolution to defend it, come what might—a resolution strengthened and reborn from the courage that perhaps the greatest of all advocates instilled into the hearts of his distracted fellow countrymen.

Not since the days of Greece and Rome had the world seen or heard a greater advocate or more exalted orator. His eloquence possessed a timeless quality; it was that which has moved men from the dawn of time and will ever move them while men are still men. Springing, as it did, from his own profound emotion, an answering emotion was aroused in all who heard him.

Not since the days when Pericles had stood at Athens to commemorate the warriors who fell at Samos; not since Demosthenes spoke his Philippics against the father of Alexander; and those days of ancient Rome when Cicero thundered against Catiline or championed the cause of Sicily against Verus; not since that autumn day at Gettysburg when Abraham Lincoln dedicated the living to the great task still confronting them—not since then had any man ever ascended Churchill's high Olympus of persuasion.

In ancient Greece, as in the London of twelve years ago, so Plutarch informs us, all manner of distempered feelings had arisen. And it was Pericles alone, he writes, who, "knowing how to handle and deal fitly with each one of them, and in . . . making . . . use of hopes and fears . . . plainly showed . . . that rhetoric, or the art of speaking is . . . the government of the souls of men, and that her chief business is to address the affections and passions, which are as it were, the strings and keys to the soul, and require a skillful and careful touch to be played on as they should be."

In the dark summer of the year 1940, there stood before the world two advocates, Churchill and Hitler. One sought to persuade the world at any cost to defend human liberty, and the other to destroy it. Not since the debate in *Paradise Lost,* so finely imagined by the genius of John Milton when God and Lucifer contested for the world, had two such antagonists stood ranged against each other. Like Milton's adversaries, they were battling for the souls of men. Both recognized the affections and the passions as the strings and keys to the soul. Back of and permeating all that Churchill said were his character and his courage. He personified the courage and the character of the British people. Through all the tempest of the Hitler speeches, the world discerned that this evil man embodied all that was worst in his frightened dupes and that what he advocated was the debasement of mankind. Finally, and at long last, and by the grace of God, the exhausted jury of the world brought the great verdict in.

Like that of Pericles, Churchill's advocacy belongs now to the ages, and the historians of the future, if not of our generation, will with one voice, I think, proclaim that but for him the verdict might have gone the other way. There were not only character and courage in this great man—there was also the finest art. The two together turned the scale. He understood the art of advocacy as only the greatest advocates in the history of the world have understood it.

The art of advocacy, like any other art, is composed of many principles and consists of many parts. Like any other art—like poetry or music or painting or sculpture—it requires not only natural aptitude but long training. In painting there is not only the canvas but all the colors of the spectrum, the combination and the use of which determine the capacity of the artist. So, too, the composer and the musician must find their implements in the chromatic scales.

In advocacy, among the most important tools are English words, the study, the selection, and the use of which are not only essential to the advocate, but in large measure will determine what kind of an advocate he is. Language is the medium—it is the means by which he must convey his thought and through which his arguments are constructed and expressed. What will it profit you to know all the law and the prophets if you lack the power to make these clear to others?

"The spoken and the written word," said Lord MacMillan, "are the raw material of the lawyer's trade, and the possession of a good literary style which enables him to make effective use of that material is one of the most valuable of all professional equipments." "The one point," says Cicero, "in which we have an advantage over the brute creation is that we hold converse with one another, and can reproduce our thought in words."

Of course, the object of all advocacy, whether in the courts or elsewhere, is to persuade, and persuasion, says Aristotle, "is clearly a sort of demonstration, since we are most fully persuaded when we consider a thing to have been demonstrated. . . . Of the modes of persuasion furnished by the spoken word there are three kinds. The first depends upon the personal character of the speaker, the second on putting the audience into a certain frame of mind, the third on the proof or apparent proof provided by the words of the speech itself."

You will not, I am sure, have failed to notice that of these prerequisites to persuasion, Aristotle has placed "the personal character of the speaker" first. He thus enunciated a profound and penetrating truth. "Persuasion," he continued, "is achieved by the speaker's personal character when the speech is so spoken as to make us think him credible. We believe good men more fully and more readily than others; this is true generally whatever the question is, and absolutely true when exact certainty is impossible and opinions are divided."

This kind of persuasion, he continues, "like the others *should* be by what the speaker says, not by what people think of his character before he begins to speak." But he quickly adds: "It is not true, as some writers assume in their treatises on rhetoric, that the personal goodness revealed by the speaker contributes nothing to his power of persuasion; on the contrary his character may be called the most effective means of persuasion he possesses."

The art of advocacy is unlimited in its scope. It is a study large enough to attract the ablest and best of men. But when we consider to what low estate the word "oratory" has fallen in our times, it comes to us almost as a surprise to see in what esteem this word was held in ancient Greece and Rome. There oratory was an art for proficiency in which young men competed with the same zest that inspired their rivalries in the Olympic games. The law schools of that time were known as schools of oratory, and in such seats of learning great Greek and Roman advocates were trained.

In Rome, during the youth of Cicero, more opportunities for the study of eloquence were found than at any other period of history, save perhaps at Athens in the days of her great orators. The Roman republic imperatively required that those who sought high office must first be practiced speakers, and the only avenues to public fame were through the army and the bar. Even her military leaders were taught how to speak, and a deficiency in this field was as insuperable an obstacle to high command as inadequacy in purely military qualities.

From Rome, then, as well as Greece, it is not surprising that we may call her great men to witness that advocacy is indeed an art. They understood it, they practiced it, and they revered it as one of the admirable and most useful of all human undertakings. No study was too long, no effort too exacting for the attainment of proficiency, and they have left us models of the art that will endure as long as there is civilization.

Oratory, said Quintilian, is "the art of speaking well." It is an art acquired by study and by practice, dependent, however, as all arts must be, in large measure upon personal aptitude. "I hold," said Cicero, "that eloquence is dependent upon the trained skill of highly educated men, while you consider that it must be separated from the refinements of learning and made to depend on a sort of natural talent and practice."

To begin with, he wrote, "a knowledge of many subjects must be grasped, without which oratory is but an empty and ridiculous swirl of verbiage; and that a distinctive style has to be formed not only by the choice of words but also by the arrangement of the same; and all the mental emotions with which nature has endowed the human race are to be ultimately understood, because it is in the calming or kindling of the feelings of the audience that the full power and science of oratory are to be brought into play. To this there should be added a certain humor, flashes of wit, the culture befitting a gentleman, and readiness and terseness alike in repelling and delivering the attack, the whole being combined with a delicate charm and urbanity."

In another passage he illustrates the difficulties of the subject by calling attention to the small number of those who have succeeded in it. "Who," he asks, "in seeking to measure the understanding possessed by illustrious men, whether by the usefulness or the grandeur of their achievements, would not place the general above the orator? Yet who could doubt that from this country alone, we could cite almost innumerable examples of leaders in war of the greatest distinction, but of men excelling in oratory a mere handful? . . . The smallest number of distinguished men is found among orators and poets . . . and even in this small number . . . far fewer good orators will be found than poets."

But to those who press on in their ambition to become advocates, he says, "Let this then be my first counsel, that we show the student whom to copy, and to copy in such a way as to strive with all possible care to attain the most excellent qualities of his model."

Cicero's advice that the youthful lawyer set up before him some model of the past is as sound now as when he gave it. It applies not to lawyers only but to every calling. The young man who carries in his mind the picture of a master whom he would like to emulate may, in the course of time, begin to acquire some, at least, of the qualities of his hero. This applies to all fields—to the battlefields of war as well as to the battlefields of justice. In a searing moment of perplexity in the trial, there may flash before the lawyer's mind the recollection of how some master of the past once met a similar difficulty and was inspired to follow his example, even as a great naval commander once bethought himself of a model he had carried in his heart from the days of his graduation from the Naval Academy. On a May morning of the year 1898, Admiral Dewey stood on the bridge of the *Olympia,* trying to decide whether he would sail into Manila Bay. He had no radar; he knew nothing of the Spanish minefields; there was no aerial reconnaissance to reveal the exact location of the enemy's ships. Should he risk his fleet? He decided to sail in. The rest is history.

Years later, Elihu Root once asked him: "When you stood there on your bridge that day, what were you thinking of? How did you decide what to do?" "I was thinking," he replied, "what would Farragut do if he were here!"

And yet no model will ever serve every age. Modes and fashions change in advocacy as in all other fields. Why but for this, Cicero says, "do you suppose that nearly every age has produced its own distinctive style?"

A reading of Cicero's *De Oratore* is a thrilling adventure to any who are interested in the art of advocacy and who wish to learn the elements of this great calling. And here, perhaps, we may uncover a clue as to why advocacy has undergone such a decline in contemporary America, and why oratory has become a word of disparagement for any oral utterance that rises above a monotone.

All of us are furnished with a vocal organ of some kind, and unless we were born dumb, can express ourselves in more or less intelligible words. Many, therefore, feel that since they can open their mouths and talk, there must be no mystery about public speaking and that to call advocacy an art is utterly absurd; that all you need to do in court or elsewhere is to open your mouth and shout. It is not surprising, then, how often we have heard those essay to speak in public who have neither gifts nor training for the task.

While the subjects of other arts, says Cicero, spring as a rule from hidden and remote sources, "the whole art of oratory lies open to the view, and is concerned in some measure with the common practice and speaking of mankind, so that whereas in all other arts that is most excellent which is farthest removed from the understanding and mental capacity of the untrained, in oratory the very cardinal sin is to depart from the language of everyday life, and the usage approved by the sense of the community."

Though the language of everyday life is essential for persuasion, advocacy, as every page of the ancient writers will establish, is far indeed removed from a simple, everyday performance. There are, says Aristotle, "these three means of effecting persuasion. The man who is to command them, it is clear, must be able (1) to reason logically, (2) to understand human character and goodness in their various forms, and (3) to understand the emotions—that is, to name them and describe them, to know their causes and the way in which they are excited. Of the elements in speech making, speaker, subject, and person addressed, Aristotle says, "It is the last one, the hearer, that determines the speaker's end and object. . . . We must take into account the nature of our particular audience . . . for as Socrates used to say, it is not difficult to praise the Athenians to an Athenian audience. . . . That the orator's own character should look right is particularly important in political speaking; that the audience should be in the right frame of mind in lawsuits—when they are feeling friendly and placable, they think one sort of thing; when they are feeling angry or hostile, they think something either totally different or the same thing with a different intensity; when they feel friendly to the man who comes before them for judgment, they regard him as having done little wrong, if any; when they feel hostile, they take the opposite view."

And what, says our teacher, is it that inspires confidence in the advocate's character? "There are three things," he says, "that induce us to believe a thing apart from any proof of it: good sense, good moral character, and good will. . . . Good will and friendliness of disposition . . . form part of . . . the emotions. . . . The emotions are all those feelings that so change men as to affect their judgments and that are also attended by pain or pleasure."

After many further pages, the preceptor of Alexander comes at last to "the style of expression." For it is not enough, he says, "to know what we ought to say; we must also say as we ought; much help is thus afforded toward producing the right impression of a speech." The first question, he continues, is "how persuasion can be produced from the facts themselves. The second is how to set these facts out in language; a third would be the proper method of delivery; this is a thing that affects the success of a speech greatly, but hitherto the subject has been neglected. Indeed, it was long before it found a way into the acts of tragic drama and epic recitations: at first poets acted their tragedies themselves. It is plain that delivery has just as much to do with oratory as with poetry.

"Good delivery," he continued, "is essentially a matter of the right management of the voice to express the various emotions— of speaking loudly or softly or between the two; of high, low, or intermediate pitch; of the various rhythms that suit various subjects. These are the three things—volume of sound, modulation of pitch, and rhythm—that a speaker bears in mind." Whether we would or no, we must pay attention to the subject of delivery, "because we cannot do without it." And while we must fight our cases on the facts, we cannot be satisfied not to "annoy our hearers," but should bend every effort "to delight them." Nothing, he says, ought to matter but the facts. "Still," he adds, "other things affect the result considerably, owing to the defects of our hearers."

Who am I to add or subtract anything from Aristotle? And yet there is one point that he has not touched upon—to me, a vital point—and that is sincerity.

"It is my opinion," wrote Alexander Woollcott, "that the sincerity with which any article is written or any tale told imparts to it an accent which cannot be mistaken or which cannot be counterfeited, just as the sincerity with which a man speaks imparts to his voice a color of truth that no perjurer can feign." The success or failure of an advocate comes down at last to this: What manner of man is it who is speaking? This is what Emerson meant when he wrote: "What you are speaks so loudly I cannot hear what you say."

An advocate might obey every rule that Aristotle and Cicero have laid down, but if he is not sincere in what he says, he will not achieve persuasion. In persuasion, Emerson once wrote, "the essential thing is heat, and heat comes from sincerity." And Professor Hill, for many years a great teacher of rhetoric at Harvard, advises us that "without sincerity a man who has all other graces and gifts will be but 'sounding brass or a tinkling cymbal'; with it, a man who lacks everything else will prevail, for the spiritual fire that is in him will go from him to others, whatever the obstacles."

That Sir Edward Marshall Hall knew this as few men knew it is illustrated by a story he once told. "I well remember," he said, "listening in a case to a fine speech by a man who was a great speaker without being a great advocate. The speech was perfect in composition and logic, but it left one cold, whereas the speech in reply, badly as it might read in the reports, was a human speech on the level of its audience, and it won the verdict. A few days later I happened to meet one of the jury, and asked him how they failed to be convinced by the other speech. 'Oh,' said he, 'the speaker was right enough, but he didn't believe a word of it himself; he had his tongue in his cheek all the time.' "

How many and how varied are the innumerable components of the art of advocacy! First of all, the advocate must be, not merely appear to be, a man of character. He must be possessed of a compelling personality. He must have a shrewd, adroit, well-stored, and tutored mind. He must understand men and women and must have that sympathy which only comes from understanding. He must have courage. He must have tact. An intuitive conception of psychology must be his in order that he may unravel human motives and the passions they engender. He must have mastered at least the rudimentary principles of logic and have acquired the power to reason clearly. The mastery of his mother tongue is an absolute prerequisite, and wide reading in many fields, unrelated to the law, must have whetted his imagination, increased his vocabulary, and strengthened his mental powers.

Since words are his medium, he must know a great many of them and have the ability to use them well, and yet, as Aristotle admonishes us, not "depart from the language of everyday life." He must have learned how important is the choice of words best adapted to convey to those addressed the meaning he intended. Brevity is a great end, but though your true advocate will use no unnecessary words, he will not hesitate to employ as many as are needed to express his thought. It is not enough, wrote Quintilian, that he use language that may be understood; he should use language that *must* be understood. Above all, like a skilled general who understands just how to deploy his troops, he will have found out how important is the management of words in the order most likely to communicate ideas. Eloquence, said Emerson, "is the power to translate a truth into language perfectly intelligible to the person to whom you speak."

A speech must progress in order to move. It must press on from point to point. It must with each paragraph rise a little higher until at last, through an ever-ascending series of words and clauses, it mounts finally to the bright pinnacle of a climax.

In general and above all, the advocate must, through study of the law and many other subjects, have acquired a ready and a supple mind. His traversing of many fields must have given a facility for mastering others. In representing a banker he must have mastered accounting and finance. In appearing for a writer, he must know literature; for a soldier, tactics and strategy; for a doctor, a conception of anatomy and of the whole philosophy of the healing art. In short, to acquire all this ability and to do all these things takes a large man; nor can he hope to triumph except through long study, great experience, and a profound observation of the world we live in, of its history, its literature, and of the men and women who compose such civilization as we have.

"But why," some of you may ask, "have you gone to so much pain to establish that advocacy is indeed an art?" I have done so because so many now deny it.

Suppose it had become the general opinion that the mastery of the violin were no art at all; that anyone could play it without talent and without study; that it was unimportant whether you knew the difference between the E string and the A; that it was not essential that the instrument be in tune; that bowing was of no consequence; that anyone, whether he had ever played or not, could walk out onto the stage of Carnegie Hall and give a concert provided he had ten fingers and could walk. But such a supposition, you are saying, is absurd. It is absurd, but no more so than the contemporary opinion about persuasion and the means by which it is effected.

Yet oratory is a thing despised and advocacy a subject almost of ridicule. Why is this so? It was not so at the golden dawn of our Republic when gay, young Alexander Hamilton stormed the convention at Poughkeepsie and brought New York into the

Union. It was not so in the United States Senate when Daniel Webster replied to Hayne. It was not so when Lincoln spoke his great second inaugural address. Why is it so now?

I have often wondered. Perhaps the cheap bombast of Fourth of July orations contributed to this conclusion. Perhaps William Jennings Bryan turned us away from that which posed as oratory. Perhaps the abandonment of Greek and Latin as prerequisites for a classical education has weaned us from our admiration of the great orators of the ancient world.

In any case, within the last two or three decades, I have no doubt that the general disgust at the poor public speaking visited upon us at public dinners has made a large contribution to the widespread disfavor with which public utterance is generally received. In New York and in other great cities throughout America, in the Waldorf and in other gilded hostelries of the nation, expensive dinners are arranged and well attended. The feast at last concludes and we settle back, seeking such comfort as the small, straight-backed gilt chairs afford, and strengthen our patience for the inevitable boredom.

The mechanical loudspeakers wheeze and hum and the speaker's face is half concealed by the microphone in front of him—a modern contrivance that short-circuits the contact between audience and speaker, and thus destroys that most important element of public speaking. The relationship between those who speak and those who listen is thus broken, for a speech depends upon a kind of mutual thought transference—on waves that pass between the audience and the speaker and from him back again to his listeners. If this interchange is broken, the orator will be speaking at and not with his audience. He will be hammering on cold iron. He will be pounding upon unresponsive brass. And as if this were not enough, the person chosen for the address, nine times out of ten, will be one who does not know how to speak. Generally, he understands little of the use of voice or the shades of intonation and inflection. He usually is without wit, and often what he says is read from an ill-written speech.

Perhaps some day it may be understood that one who has not learned the art of speaking well has no more right to intrude himself upon an audience than would an untrained violinist to give a concert in an auditorium. "Do you play the violin?" a man was once asked. "I don't know," he said, "I never tried." If he tried, the audience would surely know.

But even more than public dinners, our recent political conventions at Chicago have shown the low estate to which advocacy has fallen in America. "If television has done nothing else," wrote Jack Gould in *The New York Times* of July 23, 1952, "it certainly has pointed up the drab state of the art of oratory in contemporary political life. The endless stream of rhetoric that has flowed first from the Republican meetings and now the Democratic convention suggests unmistakably that the technique of speech making is going to need re-examination."

The delivery of the Democratic keynote address, he wrote, by one who "had been heralded in advance as something of a spellbinder, capped what had been practically three weeks of astonishing lacklustre performances on the speaker's rostrum. With only a handful of exceptions, the basic qualifications for persuasive oratory—the originality of phrase, the freshness of the point of view, and the economy of words—have been noticeably lacking in both parties.

"While radio enabled oratory to be heard in the farthest corners of the country," he continued, "it also had a debilitating effect on its quality. The power of the microphone was a major factor in the rise of the professional ghost writers. The address was timed down to the split second and issued in advance as an accommodation to the various mass media. The effect of this 'canning' process was to rob oratory of its spontaneity.

"And now television," he declared, "is imposing new hardship and handicap on the political speakers. . . . Conscious that he is being seen, the political speaker is tempted to do what no professional orator in his right mind would ever try: give a convincing performance while reading from a script on stage.

"For it must be realized," he went on, "that the TV camera unerringly shows if what he is saying comes from his heart and his conviction or if he is merely reciting. As with the actor, he must prove that he is 'inside his part' and not just running through it."

But this was written before Governor Stevenson had spoken to the delegates. "His two speeches at the Chicago convention where he was nominated," wrote Arthur Krock on September 15, 1952, "restored the level of political oratory in this country to that which Woodrow Wilson occupied."

And in describing Governor Stevenson's appearance before the American Legion, Joseph Alsop said that while there was no grand oratorical flourishing and no rodomontade, one "could sense the passion when Stevenson solemnly declared that true patriotism 'is not short, frenzied bursts of emotion, but the tranquil and steady dedication of a lifetime'; and you could feel the passion also in his brief, almost poetic invocation of the beauty of this land of ours."

If Mr. Krock of the *Times* and Mr. Alsop of the *Tribune* can thus write without a charge of partisan leaning, perhaps I too may be absolved of political bias if I tell you that in my opinion Governor Stevenson's addresses not only rose to Wilson's level but approached that of Abraham Lincoln. They may well serve as models not only of English prose composition but of advocacy in its highest sense.

Cicero observed that an orator should be able not only to kindle the feelings of his audience, but said that to this there should be added "humor, flashes of wit, the culture befitting a gentleman." The Governor's speeches, to my mind, conform to this Ciceronian requirement. The great orator of Rome also observed that an advocate should have "readiness and terseness alike in repelling and delivering the attack," and that all of this should be combined "with a delicate charm and urbanity." Do you not find all these in the Governor's addresses? Cicero declared that "in oratory the very cardinal sin is to depart from the language of everyday life, and the usage approved by the sense of the community." There is no such departure in any of the Governor's speeches.

If advocacy is a thing worthy of renewed study, these speeches afford material for that purpose. That advocacy is still indispensable in the large affairs of men should be evident to anyone who reads the morning paper, and it is my firm belief that this art is even more important in the courts of justice. Without the best of advocacy justice would be more blind than she is conventionally depicted. "Justice," Daniel Webster once said, "is the most important interest of men on earth." He likened it to a temple, and the simile was not the product of a mere poetic license. But it is a temple still uncompleted.

On Morningside Heights for many years there stood the raw beginning of what finally became the Cathedral of St. John the Divine, one of the most dramatic structures of its kind in the whole world—a noble Gothic shrine for the worship of God. In it now the mighty voice of a great organ rolls. Advocacy in the temple of justice is like an organ.

A great ecclesiastical structure was in the making when one day a passer-by paused to observe the masons at their work and stopped to talk with them. "What are you doing, my man?" he asked the first. "I am earning my living," he answered. Advancing toward another, the stranger posed the same question, and the second mason answered, "Oh, I am cutting this stone to measure." "And what of you?" he asked the third. "What are you doing?" The man looked up and paused before he spoke, and then he answered, "I, sir, am building a cathedral."

VIII

A Great Advocate

THE GREATEST AMERICAN JURY LAWYER of his generation was Martin W. Littleton. His rise to fame and leadership at the bar is a saga of character and courage.

One of nineteen children, he was born in a little mountain town in eastern Tennessee in 1872, when that state, along with the rest of what had been the Confederacy, was still floundering in the backwash of the Civil War. His family, like all their neighbors, was poor, and while he was still a child, migrated to Texas. There were no child labor laws then; in his early teens, he became a section hand on a railroad.

In his whole life he had just nine months of formal schooling. He never saw an academy, a college, or a law school until years later when he became the recipient of innumerable honorary degrees. Littleton's poverty was the kind endured by Andrew

Johnson. Poverty is a hard and cruel master who teaches with hard knocks, sour looks, and long hours. I would not wish poverty on anyone; it is unpleasant, and yet if you will examine the lives of famous lawyers, you will find that many of them started as poor boys. In England, as in ancient Rome, as well as in the United States, among the brightest ornaments of the bar, living and dead, are men of humble origin. In our own times, I can think of few great lawyers who were not poor when they were young. Perhaps the goad of poverty spurred them on to battle with their fate and triumph over it.

When Martin was about seventeen, and as yet could barely read and write, he found time somehow one day to journey to the county seat, and in the courthouse—the one place of entertainment in those days—listened to the trial of a murder case. Stout Cortez on his peak in Darien, when he stared at the Pacific, did not find wider vistas stretching out before him. Littleton watched the black-haired young lawyer who was acting as the defendant's counsel and thought how glorious to be a lawyer. But for him, so poor and so untaught, it seemed a prospect impossible of attainment.

One day not much later, however, as he was walking along a dusty road, he heard the sound of an approaching horse harnessed to an old buggy. He turned and looked and there beheld the same young man he had watched in court—the defendant's lawyer, his hero. The driver reined to a stop, and asked Martin if he wanted a lift. He accepted; his fate had overtaken him.

The man asked him his name, where he lived, and what he was doing, and Martin told him. A few more questions elicited the story of young Littleton's visit to the courthouse, and with looks of shy admiration, he asked his host if it were not wonderful to be a lawyer. "Would you like to be one?" the young man asked. "That might not be as impossible as you think. Come to my office the next time you're in town and I'll lend you some books." Books! Martin had scarce read one. What might there be in books? What might there not be!

When Martin appeared at the lawyer's office a few days later, his new friend was as good as his word, and Martin went off carrying a copy of Blackstone, Kent's *Commentaries*, and Chitty's *Pleadings*. "Come back," his new friend called out as he was leaving. "When you have read these I will lend you more law books and others too, for if you would be a real lawyer, you must know much more than you will find in books of law." At home in his small room Martin sat down and read. He read all night. He went without dinner the next day and read until he fell asleep, as excited and enthralled as any of his contemporaries would have been with a new murder or detective story.

From then on, every waking hour not spent in toil was given up to reading—reading law. And as the occasion offered, he would go to town, return the books he had read, and bring back new ones: Greenleaf, Story on *Equity*, Bishop's *Criminal Law*, Perry on *Trusts*, Cooley on *Torts*, and many others. And then one day his benefactor asked him if he had ever heard of Shakespeare. He had not. The young advocate then told him that Shakespeare was worth knowing, and gave him Shakespeare's plays, a copy of Burns' poems and Plutarch's *Lives*, and as Martin left, he said: "You had better take this too; there is more in this than any other book," and handed him a copy of the King James Bible.

About this time, Martin succeeded in finding a new job—it was in a bakery. His duties required him to attend the ovens through the night. The loaves in those days were thrust in over the fires on a long shovel, and I shall never forget Martin's telling me how in the intervals between the turning of the loaves he lay before the oven doors, and with the light from the fires, pored over the Bible and Burns' poetry. Meanwhile, his acquaintance with the young lawyer ripened into a warm friendship, and Martin would go to his office as often as he could, to be catechized and questioned about his reading, to be told the meaning of the passages that were too hard for him.

There was a rule in Texas in those days that no one was eligible for admission to the Bar until he was twenty-one, but in Martin's case the rule was somehow waived and he appeared to take his Bar examinations before his twentieth birthday. The examinations were conducted in this wise: the applicant was placed in the witness chair before the judge and was interrogated by him as to his knowledge of the law. The lawyers present in the court were allowed and, indeed, invited to join in the interrogation. So keen did this youthful applicant appear, so impossible was it to trip him up, that the news spread, and presently all the lawyers in the courthouse gathered round, each vying with the others to see if they could stump him. But he could not be stumped, and so, with flying colors, at the age of nineteen, he became a full-fledged member of the Texas Bar. He began at once to try cases and soon his ability became the subject of discussion. He was so young and so strong, so serious and yet withal so gay. His knowledge of the law astounded both the judges and the lawyers, and his juries listened spellbound as he spoke to them. At twenty-three he was elected prosecuting attorney, and at twenty-eight, like Alexander, he was looking about him for new worlds to conquer.

He had had great training—training acquired by the reading of a few great books and the competition that his fellow lawyers gave him. By this time he had read much, and all he read was fresh and new and unspoiled for him. He got his education even as Lincoln had acquired his. But more than books, he had studied the most difficult of all volumes, the volume of human nature. He had come to know not only how men talked and acted but why they acted as they did, and he had learned to read character, to unravel motives, to know why some men were good and others bad, and in this process had developed and built up his own powerful personality.

"Can personality be taught?" Merle Crowell asked him many years later. "Yes," said Martin, "but to do this you must possess or create a consuming interest in your fellow beings. The man of compelling personality is the one who plays the searchlight of his soul upon others, who gives them the warmth and candor of his heart. Thus he sets them on fire. . . ."

But the horizons of Texas—yes, of Texas—had begun to seem too limited for him. New York City was the mecca of his dreams and so one day, about the turn of the century, with his young wife and two small boys, he left Dallas and brought his family with him to the city of Alexander Hamilton. His re-sources were little more than adequate for a one way trip. To a distinguished member of the New York Bar, whose interest in young men had become proverbial, he presented a letter of introduction from a Texas judge. The old lawyer studied the young Texan with kindly eyes, and finally said: "Young man, you cannot possibly survive in this city. You will be met by the finest products of our great eastern law schools, who bring with them not only the prestige of the great names of Yale, Harvard, and Columbia, but also a vastly superior legal training to that which you have had. If you have the funds for a return to Texas, I advise you at once to use them for that purpose; if not, I shall be glad to lend you money for your trip home."

Littleton thanked him both for his advice and his offer, and his dark eyes flashing, answered: "I have come to New York and, by God, there I will stay. Whatever the competition, I will speak my way into the notice of this city." He stayed and in due course more than made his promise good.

But the start was hard and painful. He took a small and inexpensive flat in an obscure upper part of Manhattan, and for reasons that I never understood, journeyed every day to Brooklyn. There he frequented the police courts, occasionally earning a five- or a ten-dollar fee if he had had a good day. Even in that unattractive forum, his talent for expressing himself, his skill in cross-examination, his appealing smile, his quick wit, and his unfailing courtesy to the magistrates began attracting general notice. And thus one day it came about that a country judge assigned him to the defense of an indigent prisoner charged with the crime of suicide—an unsuccessful crime, of course, since otherwise Martin would have had no client.

Knowing nothing of the nature or the history of this criminal offense, he betook himself to the public library where he spent long hours to learn what could be learned upon this subject. He read all he could find about it in the Bible, in the statutes, the decisions and the law reviews, and with his quick and self-trained mind, grasped the philosophy that underlay the crime that consists of an unsuccessful effort to take one's own life.

Finally, the great day came when he stood before the judge and jury in the County Court of Kings. It was his first jury trial in New York City, but that it would not be his last became evident at once. He had learned all that there was to learn about suicide, but what was far more important, he had found out, understood, and marshaled the facts of his own case. His defense was that this law was the heritage of the days "when a

man's body belonged to the king and his soul to the church."
But now since there was no king in the United States, a man's
body had ceased to be the property of any earthly ruler, and
since we have no state ecclesiastical authority, his soul belonged
no longer to the church but to God and God alone, and no human power had jurisdiction over that.

The judge and jury watched the young Texan with sympathy
and startled admiration as he sought to prevent a verdict that
would incarcerate a tired and hopeless man who had tried to
answer the great question Hamlet asked, but never seemed to
get around to answering. The defendant had indeed taken arms
against his sea of troubles and had decided not to be. He had
borne all he could of the slings and arrows of outrageous fortune,
and had concluded that he would no longer grunt and sweat
under a weary life. Martin, it appeared, had not read and reread and committed to memory his Shakespeare to poor advantage.

The jury seemed to find pleasure in bringing in a verdict of
not guilty, and when it was recorded, the kindly judge beckoned
the young lawyer to the bench. "Young man," he said, "how
long have you been practicing law in Brooklyn?" And Martin
told him that he had been there only for a few months. "Well,"
said the judge, "I have just listened to as brilliant a defense as I
have ever heard. How would you like to take a position on the
legal staff of the Brooklyn Rapid Transit Company? If you
would, I am giving you a letter to the general counsel whom
I know well."

The next day Martin found himself one of the assistant counsel for a great railroad. His progress here was rapid. Coming
from the South, he was, of course, a Democrat, and it was not
long before he began taking an interest in Brooklyn politics. A

year or two passed, and the District Attorney of Kings County, who had heard of the ability of this rapidly developing trial lawyer, made him an assistant on his staff. In the prosecutor's office, he showed his ever-growing power and conducted many difficult and important criminal prosecutions. His circle of friends widened, his reputation grew, and finally one autumn while he was still in his thirties, he was elected Borough President of Brooklyn, and after his term of office had expired, he was offered the general counselship of the railroad at the almost unheard of retainer of $50,000 a year. He declined it, saying that he wanted to practice law on his own account.

In Wall Street he opened up an office and almost immediately clients came. Soon he was being retained in many of the important cases of the day. His defense of Harry Thaw brought crowds to the old criminal branch of the Supreme Court such as had before never sought admission to that gloomy room. Winston Churchill was in town at the time and came one day to hear him, although his interest in the case became so marked and his comments so intensely vocal that he was ejected from the room.

Time passed and Littleton was elected to Congress, although, like Rufus Choate, he did not enjoy it and relinquished his seat after serving out one term. It was only a few years later that I first met him, and came one day to court to watch his conduct of the defense of Michael A. Rofrano, a deputy street cleaning commissioner under Mayor John Purroy Mitchel. Rofrano was being tried for murder in the first degree. Between the indictment and the trial, he had fled the jurisdiction and so finally when brought to trial, was confronted not only by the adverse opinion engendered by his flight but by some very difficult and awkward facts surrounding the death of the man who had been murdered; but whether Rofrano (who was not charged with the killing himself but with aiding and abetting it) had brought about this murder was the question that Littleton was now called upon to help solve.

I watched him in the conduct of this case as one aspiring to the operatic stage might have watched Caruso or a young sand-lot player have observed Babe Ruth at bat or a medical student looking down from the amphitheater to see Dr. Harvey Cushing removing a brain tumor. I watched his every move, his every gesture, his every intonation as he asked his questions. Here was a brilliant advocate still comparatively young, yet already famous, displaying all the gifts that nature had endowed him with and hard application had improved. There was a kind of magic in his language. He was master of what Justice Jackson has so finely called "the short Saxon word that pierces like a spear."

He spoke the mother tongue as he had found it in the King James Bible. He spoke with precision yet with rare charm, and although in deadly earnest, there was a friendly smile in his dark eyes and one often on his lips. But this smile was no mechanical contrivance, no mere muscular manipulation practiced before a mirror. Rather was it the look of a strong and resolute man with perfect confidence in the fact that what he was doing was worth doing.

And what a figure of a man he was! Of not better than medium height, his sturdy body gave evidence of having been accustomed to hard physical work, and as he talked, the sweat came down his face. And what a head he had! It was a large one, crowned by a profusion of black hair now turning gray. His dark eyes were wide apart, surmounted by shaggy eyebrows. His forehead was high and seemed somehow to convey that behind it a fine brain was working and had been working for these many years. He was a great figure of a man, and as I looked at him, I thought of the English navvy who pointed to Daniel Webster on the streets of Liverpool and said, "There goes a king." I thought too of Sydney Smith who, when he first saw Webster, exclaimed, "Good heavens, he is a small cathedral by himself!" I watched him, noting how his known reputation for high integrity and good faith was impressing itself upon the jury and the courtroom.

One of his most effective weapons was his voice, low pitched, well modulated, and very strong, and he had learned to use it well. As he passed up and down before the jury box, talking with them and not at them, I knew that I was watching a great artist. What he had learned he had learned by himself, without formal instruction, save the tutors furnished by a generation of opposing lawyers, and it was evident that he had made that most valuable of all studies, the study of himself. Knowing that he knew his Shakespeare as few men knew it, I have no doubt that he had learned by heart the finest of all elocutionary admonitions, namely, Hamlet's advice to the players.

Remember how they gathered round the young Prince when he told them: "Speak the speech, I pray you as I pronounced it to you, trippingly on the tongue; but if you mouth it, as many of your players do, I had as lief the town crier spoke my lines. Nor do not saw the air too much with your hand, thus; but use all gently; for in the very torrent, tempest, and—as I might say— whirlwind of passion, you must acquire and beget a temperance, that may give it smoothness. . . . Be not too tame neither, but let your own discretion be your tutor: suit the action to the word, the word to the action. . . ."

No one who ever heard Martin Littleton could doubt that he

had read and conned every syllable attributed to Hamlet, and no one could contend that he ever deviated from that advice. The jury no doubt did not have Hamlet's counsel in their minds, but they were listening to one who pronounced his words as Hamlet would have wished. They were, although they did not know it, listening to great art, and all they knew was that they were hearing a great man, one who had won their confidence, their esteem, and perhaps even their affections.

It was a difficult case, as all criminal cases are difficult. Politics, even as they were in Rome or Erskine's England, were heavily interwoven with the prosecution's case. The political party opposed to Mayor Mitchel was being courted by the District Attorney who believed that if he could convict one of Mitchell's cabinet he might receive the endorsement of that party in the next campaign. Mr. Littleton met these problems as a gladiator in the Roman arena met wild beasts crouched before him and snarling for his life. He admitted that the defendant indeed had fled, but argued that he had done so not to avoid prosecution but to enable time to pass until a hostile press might tire of its campaign against him. And he took a course with the District Attorney which nearly every lawyer of experience eschews—he attacked the prosecutor openly; he put him on trial and established facts that justified this course. It was not only a brilliant but a brave defense.

The hour came at last when he stood before his jury for the final plea. There was still a faint smile in his eyes; there was no smile on his lips. He was a witty man but he knew that this was no time for the display of humor. He began in slow and measured tones, choosing every word with care. The words he chose were short Saxon words, such as you might find in Shakespeare or Burns or the King James Version or Lincoln's messages and speeches, yet all the jury knew was that they were listening to language that was clear to them and to an argument appealing to their reason.

Lincoln, we are told, came in his youth to the conclusion that he did not understand the word "demonstrate," and so sat down and mastered the six books of Euclid. Thereafter, every argument he made possessed the strength of an unanswerable demonstration in geometry. Littleton, too, well understood the potency of clear logic, and so began his address with a quiet presentation of the evidence, intermingling with it a course of reasoning from which there flowed inevitable conclusions.

He had embarked upon a great effort of persuasion and he knew well that argument alone could not achieve it. He made a clear, logical, and lucid argument, but he lit his argument with the warm and glowing sympathy of his own heart. In expressing his own feelings and those of his client, he was spreading the contagion of sympathy in the jury box.

Having done this, he moved gradually forward, and as he advanced, what before had been only logic suddenly began to glow and burn until it became red and finally white-hot with his fervor. Watching every juryman, he played upon the heartstrings of their emotions. As some swarthy blacksmith heats an iron white-hot and swages it with mighty strokes, so Littleton smote the feelings of his jury.

His speech was a long one, yet never for one instant was it monotonous. It was not all on one key. He varied the tempo, the volume, and the tone. As in a great orchestration where sometimes the violins play alone and at another the flutes, then all the woodwinds until, rising to a vast crescendo, the tubas, the trombones, the French horns and the trumpets, abetted by the kettledrums and the cymbals, so Littleton played upon his facts and with them on his jury.

His eyes were flashing now. His voice grew louder and more resonant, until it seemed as though Heaven had let loose her lightnings and her thunders. The surge, the roar, of a veritable Niagara swept and rocked the courtroom and the twelve men before him. He was fighting. He was fighting for a human life. He was forging barriers that would block the way to the electric chair. He was forging them in the jurors' hearts. Watching him as he mounted up from pinnacle to pinnacle, I thought of Shelley's "Skylark":

> *"Higher still and higher*
> *From the earth thou springest*
> *Like a cloud of fire;*
> *The blue deep thou wingest,*
> *And singing still dost soar,*
> *And soaring ever singest."*

Worn and spent, he closed at last, and the District Attorney then summed up. The judge charged and finally the jury filed out for their deliberations. The hours dragged. Five hours and still they did not return; ten hours; eighteen went by while Rofrano's friends despaired and the defendant himself lost hope, but Littleton did not lose hope. Twenty hours, twenty-two and still no verdict. Finally, at the twenty-third, the jury filed back to their seats. "What is your verdict, gentlemen? Do you find the defendant guilty or not guilty?" "Not guilty," the foreman answered. A human life was spared and new laurels came to rest upon the brow of a great advocate. Spellbound and enthralled, I had watched a supreme work of art. I had seen the art of advocacy at its best. I had seen a master of the craft at work. It was enough to inspire any young and hopeful lawyer, but I had not only been inspired—I had added to my education.

All unwittingly I had followed in the trail that barristers of England and the great trial lawyers of America have ever trod. When the Dartmouth College case was being tried at Exeter in September, 1817, Rufus Choate, then a lad just under eighteen, came to hear Daniel Webster try it. The pathos of that great voice lit up his imagination and Webster then became and for the rest of his life continued as Choate's hero, his model, and his friend.

But next to watching a great advocate, perhaps equal or superior to this, is the opportunity really to come to know one. When I first saw Mr. Littleton at work, I had already met him. But I never dreamed that Martin Littleton would come to be my close friend—one of the truest friends I ever had.

My acquaintance with him, of course, at first was slight. He was a very great and famous man and I was young and utterly unknown. As time went on, however, I came to know him better and still better, and my admiration for him was such that I have no doubt that he was well aware of it. Even very great men are not indifferent to the esteem of youth. They would not be human otherwise, and I have never known a man more human than this lawyer. It was his human quality more than all else which contributed to making him the advocate he was. For an advocate, if he would be great, must understand men and women. He must know how and why they think and act. He must understand them —he must do more than that: he must really like them. How else could he have sympathy? How else could sympathy mature and grow and develop until it becomes at last compassion?

I heard his story from his own lips, not once but many times. He would tell me of his hard and underprivileged youth, his early struggles with obstacles seemingly insurmountable, the burden of stark poverty, and his painful and never-ending quest for that education which lack of formal schooling had forced him somehow to achieve himself. With all its hardships he never spoke of his grim youth with bitterness or complaint.

Often he recounted his experiences as a humble railroad worker, remembering the names of his fellow laborers and recalling their good points and their bad. From these he learned that good character, fine personal attributes, clear understanding, and innate ability to think straight and reason clearly are not to be sought for among college graduates alone. And from his early days in the Texas courts, he had found out that a man who really understood the law, even though that understanding had been acquired with no tutor but himself, could be a full match for any of the graduates of even the best law schools.

He knew that what the law deals with is human beings; that what they have done or left undone is the stuff on which the most recondite discussions in the courts are made. He knew that both judges and juries are but human, susceptible to, but seldom swayed by, reason only, and that it is upon their feelings, their emotions, even their prejudices, that an advocate must play, even as a cellist draws his bow across the strings. What he had learned was that there is a pathway to the human heart even if that heart through disuse or overeducation has grown hard. A lawyer who does not instinctively know, or who has not learned about human nature, though he may know all the law, could never adequately cross-examine a witness or sum up to a jury or argue to a judge.

In the late eighties, during the Assizes held at Lewes, a handsome young barrister named Marshall Hall came rushing into the barroom of the White Hart. "I've got a fifty guinea brief

for murder," he exclaimed to another young barrister named
Moresly who was seated there. "I wouldn't do it for a hundred
. . ." said Moresly. "I hate crime and wouldn't take the responsibility." Eyeing him with scorn, Marshall Hall replied, "I mean
to specialize in the two biggest gambles there are—life and death
—freedom and imprisonment. Facts, not principles, for me. I
don't know much law, but I can learn what there is to be known
about men and women."

Hall became a great and famous advocate. He had that indispensable quality for the role—stark courage. This, says Lord
Birkenhead, "was his outstanding characteristic. He was utterly
fearless in the service of what he conceived to be his duty, both
as an advocate and in other less vicarious paths of life." His in-
tention to learn all he could about men and women made him a
great barrister, but he would have been an even greater one
had he learned and known more law. A famous English chancellor, in describing the necessary qualifications for a judge, once
said: "First we try to find a gentleman, and if he knows a little
law, so much the better." This may be enough for a judge; for
the true advocate it most assuredly is not enough.

In the year 1819, an American Senator had placed a bet of
three dozen bottles of port that every judgment Erskine made as
Chancellor had been reversed. With a shade less than the finest
taste, he wrote to Lord Erskine to decide the wager. Erskine answered this unsolicited correspondent: "You have certainly lost
your bet on the subject of my decrees. None of them were appealed against, except one. . . . But it was affirmed without a
dissentient voice. . . . To save you from spending your money
on bets you are sure to lose, remember that no man can be a
great advocate who is no lawyer. The thing is impossible."

Martin Littleton was a lifelong, a sincere and close student of the law. He had been studying it ever since those long nights before the oven fires. Legal principles seemed a very part of him. He knew their history. He reveled in such books as Halsburry's *Laws of England*, Pollock and Maitland, Warren's *History of the Supreme Court*, Stephen's *History of the Criminal Law*, and I never ceased to wonder at his detailed knowledge of the decided cases.

His reading was anything but confined to law books. He had a veritable passion for history and literature, both prose and poetry, and he had read more than most men. He was one of the best educated men I had ever known. He knew his Plutarch and his Gibbon; he knew Mommsen and Ferrero. He knew England's long and glorious story, as he had gleaned it from Hume and Clarendon and Trevelyan, and it seemed to me that he knew Macaulay's history and his essays almost by heart. He found infinite delight in Carlyle. He knew Motley and Prescott, Bancroft and McMaster. Biography was his especial favorite and he never tired of reading Campbell's *Lives of the Chancellors and Chief Justices of England* or Beveridge's great life of John Marshall.

Martin's life, however, was not all work. He could play with the same zest, and after a hard game of golf, where his scores were usually in the low eighties, he would sit around in the bar of his club and tell good stories, stories that had wit and point and pith. I never heard him tell an off-color joke or evince pleasure when others did.

Littleton's interest in literature included not only history, biography, and the poets alone; he loved the great novelists as well. He told me once that he had had two lives—his own and that which Victor Hugo had enabled him to live in *Les Misérables*. He knew that the great novelists had plumbed the depths and scaled the heights of human nature, and that to know them was to learn more about men and women than ever could be possible in the tragically small span of threescore years and ten.

Charles Dickens had taught him much. He appraised the *Tale of Two Cities* as one of the world's great books. He found in *Oliver Twist*, as who has not, a true insight into the social ills with which society still suffers. He had smiled at the vagaries of Mr. Pickwick and found pleasure in the portrait of Serjeant Snubbin who appeared for the esteemed leader of the Pickwick Club in the great trial of Bardell against Pickwick, as well as in the portrayal of Mrs. Bardell's counsel, Serjeant Buzfuz, and had laughed with the great novelist in his depiction of the characters of Alfred Jingle, Job Trotter, Mr. Winkle, Samuel Weller, and Mr. Justice Stareleigh.

In *Vanity Fair* he had probed with Thackeray the depths of Becky Sharp's cold heart; and he knew the novels of Anthony Trollope well. Justly regarding *Orley Farm* as a masterpiece, he had studied there the character of Lady Mason and had appraised the talents of the immortal Mr. Chaffenbrass. The thousand pages of Warren's *Ten Thousand a Year* were not too long for him, and he learned there the depths to which corrupt solicitors could descend as he encountered the firm of Quirk, Gammon and Snapp and watched their devious espousal of the false claims of Tittlebat Titmouse in his struggle for a peerage.

He knew the long novels of Walter Scott (a knowledge increasingly uncommon now), and of these *Guy Mannering*, I think, appealed to him the most because of its portrayal of Counsellor Pleydell. He remembered how when Colonel Mannering one day called upon him in his chambers in High Street, the lawyer pointed to his shelves on which reposed so many fine editions of the classics, saying: "These are my tools of trade.

A lawyer without history or literature is a mechanic, a mere working mason; if he possesses some knowledge of these he may venture to call himself an architect."

In my innumerable talks with Martin Littleton, I had the opportunity to probe the treasures of a well-stored mind, and thus to reach a better understanding of what made him the greatest advocate of his day. Like Bacon, he had taken universal knowledge as his domain and in that enchanted commonwealth had found the soil for the development and growth of his own powers. His interest seemed to have no boundaries. He could discuss the beauties of Shelley's poems, or he could tell you about the Dow-Jones averages, the relative standing of the Giants and the Dodgers, the performance of a channel swimmer, or the transatlantic flight of Lindbergh. He could talk on an even footing with the learned professors of a college or a chief justice, or converse on equal terms with a bootblack or a taxi driver. Small wonder then that he could address juries as no man of his time could do, or press home his arguments with the most learned judge.

My luncheons with him, which for the last ten years of his life occurred at least once every week, were among the greatest pleasures I have ever known. At one of these, he told me of a caller (a Republican) who had looked up that morning at a picture of Andrew Johnson on his wall and had asked him how it was that he permitted so disreputable a character to hang there. I then broke in with a comment for which I was to pay with five years of hard labor. "I join your caller, Martin," I said. "Why do you have that drunken misfit on your wall?" His smile vanished and his eyes snapped as he asked how much I knew about that subject.

My answer was that I had then stated the sum total of my information about the seventeenth President of the United States, and that what I had said must have been the emanation of some lecture that I had heard in college, when the histories of the Civil War then studied had no doubt been written by Republicans. "Well," he said, "your education has been neglected. Let me tell you about the man who championed Lincoln's cause as few of his contemporaries championed it."

Enthralled, I listened as he told me what the poor tailor boy from eastern Tennessee had accomplished for his country. Martin's words came fast; they poured out like a torrent. He was talking to me alone, yet he spoke as he had talked to juries or as when so often he held great crowds spellbound in Madison Square Garden or in Carnegie Hall. His sentences burst forth in a tumult. He was arguing to me alone, yet it was advocacy in its very essence, and he had established for me once and for all that advocacy may be adapted to the persuasion of the smallest group, even of one man, as well as for the gaining of a jury's verdict or a decision from the Supreme Court of the United States.

Such was my humiliation for my ignorance displayed that I spent five years in hard contrition until I had written *Andrew Johnson—a Study in Courage*. Martin was kind enough to say he liked the book and told me that I had made full amends for the slander I had uttered years before.

There was such fire in this man that even his strong frame must ultimately be consumed by it. In the summer of 1934, his heart began to fail, and as the summer waned, it became evident to all of us that on this earth he could not much longer charm the hearts of friends and foes alike, or carry on the work which was his life. In the late autumn he died.

Wishing to do honor to his memory, I attended the funeral

services, hoping that I might hear said over all that was mortal
of a great friend, the glorious impersonal last rites of the Book
of Common Prayer with all its beauty and its august consolations.
But the services were held where the Prayer Book is unknown.
I still hoped, however, that if we must be treated to a funeral
oration, it might be a good one. It was not. It was the worst I
ever had endured.

The minister did not know Martin and so he chose for his
discourse a dreary topic, including an abstruse and controversial
theological point of little interest. One lawyer near me in the
church whispered that "the least you can say of this is that it is
irrelevant." But I listened on, smarting under the indignity that
was being visited upon a great man and a great friend. Finally,
however, I had heard all that I could bear of flat sentences and
unctuous phrases and I got up and left the church, trying to
forget that I had listened to the worst specimen of advocacy in
my life. And as I walked out, I bethought me of two lines from
Shakespeare's greatest play. Hamlet and his good friend, Horatio, after the appearance of the ghost, were discussing him whose
apparition they had seen. "I saw him once," Horatio said. "He
was a goodly king." And Hamlet answered, "He was a man,
take him for all in all. I shall not look upon his like again."

CHAPTER

IX

Some Portraits of
Great Lawyers

I N THE ROTUNDA of the Boston Courthouse there stands a
noble bronze. Wrought by the master hand of Daniel Chester
French with fine feeling and consummate art, the statue of
Rufus Choate looks down upon the hurrying throng of lawyers
who hardly pause to glance at the strong lineaments of a noble
face or the determined posture of a resolute and manly figure.
Here for all time is a glorious memorial that will commemorate
forever the greatest advocate of America.

Had I been a professor at the Harvard Law School when the
poll was taken that rated advocacy so low, I would have sus-
pended classes long enough to take my students for a look at
this great likeness of a great man, and when I got them back I
would have told them something of a career that stands unequaled in our American courts of justice, and would have tried

at least to stimulate an emulation of this American advocate. And had I been a teacher at any of the law schools near Washington, I would have taken my charges for a stroll beside the long lagoon that leads on to the Memorial of Abraham Lincoln, and would have made them look at the colossal statue of a colossal man—one of Plutarch's men. There he stands as a perennial reminder of the Olympian heights to which an advocate may rise—the symbol of what under liberty and freedom an American may become. There he stands gazing down on a posterity that well remembers how this country lawyer, who spent his prairie years in arguing petty cases before country juries, could finally become the advocate to persuade a reluctant North to save the Union, and yet, who with malice toward none and with charity for all, was dreaming even as he was struck down how he would one day bind up the nation's wounds.

The Lincoln literature is vast, the biographies almost innumerable, and the legends that surround his memory still grow. He will be remembered and revered as long as there is civilization on this earth, for he belongs now to the ages. Yet this incomparable man began his life in extreme poverty and was denied the rudiments of a formal education. In obscurity and dire need, he struggled with hardship until at last by dint of an unconquerable courage, unyielding resolution, and unremitting application, he conquered it. Flatboatman, surveyor, village postmaster, country storekeeper, then a lawyer, and in due course an incomparable debater with Stephen Douglas, and finally the President of the United States who saved the work of Washington, and at last martyrdom—such was the life of America's greatest man.

There is no evidence that he knew Aristotle or Cicero, and yet he divined all that they had taught. His hard struggle had given

him a deep understanding of life and human beings. He knew
men and women as few have, and, therefore, learned to reach
their hearts, their sympathies, and their emotions as well as
their cold reason. His juries listened to him spellbound and
nearly always followed him. "A stranger going into court when
he was trying a case," says Mr. Arnold, one of his constant associates, "would after a few minutes find himself instinctively on
Lincoln's side."

He made his juries feel that he and they were on the same
side, charting out the true course of justice. He took the "jurors
into his confidence," another contemporary writes, "and made
them feel that he and they were trying the case together," and
he illustrated as no other American lawyer has ever done better
the truth of Aristotle's dictum that the speaker's "character may
almost be called the most effective means of persuasion he possesses."

His character was incorruptible, his honesty a legend in Illi-
nois. Subterfuge and trickery were unknown to him. On the old
Eighth Circuit, a fellow lawyer, E. M. Prince, heard him try
more than one hundred cases of all kinds, and he has left this
comment: "Mr. Lincoln had a genius of seeing the real point in
a case at once, and aiming steadily at it from the beginning to
the end. The issue in most cases lies in a very narrow compass,
and the really great lawyer disregards everything not directly
tending to that issue. Mr. Lincoln saw the kernel of every case at
the outset, never lost sight of it, and never let it escape the jury.
That was the only trick I ever saw him play."

He never talked over the jury's heads, or sought to display
the learning, of which, as the years passed, he had much. His
logic, founded as it was on Euclid, was unassailable, but he
knew that a good story was more interesting than any logic and

far more apt to cause persuasion. In trying once to prove that a certain man's actions were far inferior to his words, he said that he was reminded of a steamboat he once saw that had a ten-horsepower engine and a twenty-horsepower whistle, so that every time the whistle blew they had to stop the boat. His stories were about ordinary men—about things familiar to his listener.

Every story that he told was a kind of parable, and the New Testament had taught him how effective parables can be. This was the way Christ taught when he was on earth; he illustrated his most profound doctrines by reminding those who heard him of the common things with which they were familiar. Do you not remember: "The kingdom of heaven is likened unto a man that soweth good seed in his field," and then the parable about a "certain rich man which was clothed in purple and fine linen and fared sumptuously every day." And that of the lost sheep: "What man of you having an hundred sheep if he lose one of them doth not leave the ninety and nine in the wilderness, and go after that which is lost until he find it?"

Lincoln knew these parables by heart. The Bible was one of the earliest books he read and he read it to the last. The language of the King James Version became his language. No lawyer, no man, has ever attained his mastery of the English tongue.

The advocate, says Lord Birkett, "must have the faculty of using the right words in the right order if he desires to be master of the art of persuasion. . . ." Lincoln was such a master, and because he was, he never used a polysyllable where a short Saxon word would serve better. No recourse to the dictionary is necessary for a perfect understanding of any utterance he ever made.

In the story of a great man's life you will find what made him great as well as what caused him to fall short. There will be found the qualities that gave him his persuasion. There can be studied the nature of his inherited capacity and the natural defects over which he triumphed. And as you search the records of men's lives, you will find that nearly every great man selected in his youth from the pages of biography a model on which he sought to found his own career.

Plutarch's lives of the great Greeks and Romans are a source of never-failing interest, and his narratives, abounding in incident and filled with the circumstances under which his heroes lived and wrought, give us a deep insight into many of the famous men of ancient times. He tells how Demosthenes, when still a child, was robbed by those entrusted with his estate, and how when he grew up, "he began to go to law with his guardians and to write orations against them," and how from this experience sprang his ambition to become an advocate. He had a sickly body to contend with, but he resolved to become strong and so trained for the great garland games until finally he became one of the fleetest runners in all Athens.

He had no natural gifts as a speaker and was at first "derided for his strange and uncouth style," to which was added "a weakness in his voice, a perplexed and indistinct utterance, and a shortness of breath," so that he failed utterly at first to find acceptance. Recognizing this, he decided to surmount these natural defects and so built himself a chamber underground to which for a long period he would every day retire to exercise his voice, varying this by walking on the seashore where he picked up pebbles from the beach and putting them in his mouth, declaimed until he was out of breath. And thus he labored on until he became at last the greatest orator and advocate of Greece.

Two and a half centuries later, in the year 103 B.C., at Arpium, in Italy, Marcus Tullius Cicero was born. At the age of twenty-two, he began his legal career at Rome and continued in it for thirty-eight years, until at last, at a place near Formiae, on a December day of the year 43 B.C., he was murdered on the orders of the Triumvirate, exclaiming, "Let me die in the country which I have often saved."

Interspersing his vast labors at the Bar and in the Senate house with the continuous study of the Greek masters, he devoted all his leisure time to literature. He was, said Plutarch, "the one man above all others who made the Romans feel how great a charm eloquence lends to what is good, and how invincible justice is if it be well spoken. . . ." In his youth he had ill health to contend with; his form was lean and meager, and his stomach was so weak that he could take nothing but a thin diet, and that not until the evening came.

His voice at first was loud and harsh and so unmanaged, his biographer has written, that "in vehemence and heat of speaking he always raised it to so high a tone that there seemed to be reason to fear about his health." But he triumphed over this and in later years would ridicule loud speakers, saying that they shouted because they could not speak. He was still young when he became the greatest advocate in Rome, and held a lofty view of his profession. "The perfect orator," he once said, "must be a perfect man." For nearly twoscore years, his was the greatest and most influential voice both in the law courts and the Senate house of the Roman capitol.

There is no more fascinating reading for the American of today than the study of the Roman republic. Her far-flung commerce, her transcendent mastery of the seas, her vast land legions, her cultivation of architecture and the arts, her vast influence in Europe, in Africa, in the Mediterranean and, indeed, the entire civilized world—all these fused with a kind of nervous energy, nay, a feverish impulse to progress, to push on—suggest many almost frightening parallels between the United States and the City of the Seven Hills. Ferrero, one of the most brilliant of modern historians, some forty years ago wrote a book which he entitled *Ancient Rome and Modern America*. Read this book and then read Toynbee and shudder.

It was in the most fateful years of Roman civilization when the republic was riding to its fall that Cicero's lot was cast. To take his part as an advocate in this troubled scene was the ambition by which his youth was fired. He recognized, as a young and eager student of the masterpieces of Athenian oratory, that it was only by a mastery of classical literature, as well as by observation, study, and emulation of contemporary Roman orators, that his hopes could know fulfillment, and he gave himself to this study with a passionate devotion.

In the Rome of his day, the house of the jurisconsult was visited not by suitors only, but by the many students who came to listen to his legal opinions which were called responses. And thus it was that Cicero attached himself to Scaevola, the augur, as a kind of pupil. He listened to his lectures and committed his maxims to memory, and he followed him to the law courts to hear him plead his cases and to the Rostra where he harangued the people, and thus received practical lessons both in eloquence and law.

We con the histories and biographies in an effort to restore the times and the man. But it is hard to make them live again. It was, then, with sheer delight that I came not long ago upon H. G. Haskell's fascinating *This Was Cicero—Modern Politics in a Roman Toga*. I had read about his first great triumph in the defense of Roscius when he was a young man of twenty-six, but in a flash the scene took life when Mr. Haskell wrote: "One late afternoon in the year 80, the dinner parties of the great houses on the Palatine were stirred by reports from the law courts. The young chap from the country, Marcus Tullius Cicero, had won the celebrated Sextus Roscius murder case about which Roman society had been gossiping. What interested those fashionable diners-out was not merely the verdict of acquittal. Everybody took it for granted that the accused man was innocent and the charges against him were a frame-up. What especially intrigued them was that this twenty-six-year-old lawyer had dared challenge a powerful member of the autocratic regime then ruling Rome under republican forms. In the entourage of the dictator Sulla was an unscrupulous Greek who was trying to railroad Roscius to death or exile in order to cover up a shady financial transaction. It was this man whose anger Cicero had braved by appearing in the case. Naturally the incident was the subject of dinner-table conversation."

Lawyers were as much discussed in Rome as in contemporary America, but it was difficult then, as it is now, to analyze the reasons for success or failure.

All the students of Cicero are agreed that no man ever touched the keys that control the cadences of Roman speech as Cicero could do, and yet how baffling it is to study an advocate's true art from the cold record of his speeches. Most of them are still extant, and yet as we read his great argument against Verus, for example, how impossible it is to grasp what made that oration memorable. To come near to a full understanding, one would have to understand the politics of the day and the nature, circumstances, and setting of the corruptions of that faithless Roman praetor.

In times far nearer to our own, the difficulty is equally great.

Although I read and reread Erskine's speeches in the treason trials of the last decade of the eighteenth century, I never came near grasping their real import until I had read and studied a half-dozen histories of the French Revolution and as many of Great Britain. From them I came to see how English fears of French Jacobinism had brought these treason trials about and the poisonous contemporary atmosphere with which Erskine must contend.

In the course of that study, I read most of the speeches of Charles James Fox whose fame as a parliamentary orator is still bright. Discouragement, however, met my attempt to understand why they were so effective, until I came upon the story of a man who had expressed to Pitt his difficulty in grasping the reasons for the great reputation of Mr. Fox. "Ah," replied Pitt, "but you have never been under the wand of the magician." The fact is that the most important element in advocacy is the man himself.

This is true not only of Roman lawyers but of the great advocates of England and America. The *Lives of the Chancellors and the Chief Justices of England,* if you can find the patience to read through the ponderous pages of Lord Campbell, tell the story and recount the exploits of many famous barristers who were later elevated to the bench. Each of these lawyers had won fame at the bar before judicial office claimed him.

The stories of these men reveal an almost unbroken pattern of integrity. Few among them might not serve as models to the young; few were there who did not elevate their calling by a lifelong contribution to the cause of justice.

Read the story of Thomas Erskine, of Brougham, of Denman. Study the kind of lawyer Lord Mansfield was before he mounted to the bench. Along with Campbell read Marjoribanks' life of Marshall Hall and his uncompleted biography of Carson. Read Sir Charles Russell's defense of Florence Maybrick and Abbington's defense of Steinie Morrison as they stand recorded in Edward Lustgarten's exciting *Verdict in Dispute*. Follow him in the same volume as he portrays the defense of Norman Thorne by J. D. Cassels, and that of Edith Thompson by Sir Henry Curtis Bennett as well as that of William Herbert Wallace by Roland Oliver.

And take at least a brief glance at two great Massachusetts lawyers, Daniel Webster and Rufus Choate, whose likeness in the Boston Courthouse I mentioned earlier. What men they were, and how their lights still shine as beacons of the Bar! There must be something inexplicable about a voice that brought the Supreme Court to tears when, in arguing the Dartmouth College case, Webster made this banal observation: "She is a small college, but there are those who love her."

Like so many Americans who later became famous, Webster started as a poor boy. Of himself he once wrote: "I read what I could get to read, went to school when I could and when not at school, was a farmer's boy, not good for much for want of health and strength but expected to do something." Books were scarce in those days but there was a small circulating library in the village. From this Webster borrowed all he could, and committed every book he read almost to memory.

One of his tasks, while still a farmer's boy, was the tending of a sawmill. But here, too, he found time for reading. He would set a log and while it was going through, devour a book. Like Lincoln, there came a time when he knew great books. And in the open fields he practiced public speaking. He loved the hills and the woods, and fished with gusto in the trout brooks. He loved the blue sky and the free air, but most of all he loved to stand beside the sea.

He went at last to Dartmouth where soon his gift of speech was duly noted. All of his contemporaries there took notice of his eloquence. The power of clear statement was born in him, as were the musical tones of voice that still echo down the years. His eloquence had no doubt been stimulated by his outdoor life as well as his tremendous passion for good reading. But to speak as he spoke requires more than books or a good vocal organ. It must come from the man himself. What made Webster a great advocate? God made him, but Webster co-operated to the best of his ability.

There is small wonder that such a man made so lasting an appeal to young Rufus Choate when he first saw him. The occasion was the Dartmouth commencement of the year 1819. Rufus, then just turned twenty, was the valedictorian. Being himself a natural orator, the youthful Choate in his valedictory brought tears not only to the eyes of pretty girls assembled there but to those of old trustees who are generally supposed to be exempt from such emotion.

On the platform that day sat Daniel Webster. From then on until his death, Webster was Choate's model, mentor, guide, and friend. Following his triumphal career at Dartmouth, Choate attended Harvard Law School under the aegis of the distinguished Chief Justice Joel Parker, who also was a Dartmouth graduate. Then he spent some months in Washington where he served for a time in the office of William Wirt who was President Monroe's Attorney General, varying his duties there by teaching in a girls' school (a course followed by Elihu Root a half century later), and he attended, when he could, at the Supreme Court, where he listened not only to the arguments of Daniel Webster but to other great lawyers of the day as they sought to persuade Chief Justice Marshall and his associates to follow them.

Yet despite these many occupations, he still found time, as throughout his life he found it, for the study of the classics.

Returning home to Massachusetts, he spent several months in the law office of Asa Andrews in Ipswich, and still more in Salem in that of Judge Cummins, well known for his caustic tongue. And in the September term of 1823, in the Court of Common Pleas, he was admitted to the Bar of Massachusetts.

And it was not long before he became known in Essex County as "the great criminal lawyer." He seemed to have a special talent with his juries and a veritable genius for transforming a commonplace defendant into an heroic figure. He had a power over juries akin to hypnotism and was at his best when the evidence was most against him.

He had, as every great advocate has had, a ready wit, and would appear solemn while he pronounced some absurdity that convulsed his listeners. "He came to Salem," writes Claude M. Fuess, "poor in purse, but with a reputation which already extended through Essex County—a young man of whom wagging tongues prophesied great things. He was even then a striking figure, nearly six feet in height, of brown complexion, with dark and gloomy eyes and a profusion of curly hair which he was at no pains to brush. He was careless in his dress, but not slovenly. Choate had what is called personality, an inexplicable and altogether indefinable factor, but one vitally essential to success." He was a frank, a generous, and a modest man; such men find little difficulty in attracting others to them. And so it is not surprising that only seven years after his admission to the Bar, he was in 1830 elected to Congress.

The national arena beckoned; wider vistas were opening up, and it was not long before his voice was being listened to in the House of Representatives. His fame as a speaker had preceded him to Washington. A description of his first effort on the floor of Congress has been left for us by Ben Hardin of Kentucky. As Hardin was preparing to retire to the cloakroom, he paused to listen for a moment. "That moment," he later wrote, "was fatal to my resolution. I became charmed by the music of his voice, and was captivated by the power of his eloquence, and found myself wholly unable to move until the last word of his beautiful speech had been delivered."

In the latter part of the year 1834, Choate moved with his small family to Boston where his ever-growing practice expanded even further. Though he never forsook literature, the law was his first love; politics held little attraction for him. "It is well enough," he once said, "for an American at some position of his life to go to Congress for a brief time, if opportunity offers, as a sort of recreation, but the great aim of a young man should be advocacy."

And what an advocate he was! The stories of his courtroom methods are still recounted by the Boston Bar. His voice, a good baritone, was controlled and musical, yet he filled the courtroom with his fervor. Once at Worcester in his enthusiasm he split his coat from the collar down. He had many strange and varied mannerisms fascinating to read about. We see him on the morning of a day in court. He arrives worn and spent from the previous night's preparation. His tired eyes are surrounded by the bluish circles of fatigue. He arrives without fanfare at the counsel table, and removing the many documents from his green bag, arranges them before him. Although there has been no rain, his feet are shod in heavy rubber overshoes, and despite the fact that it is summer, he has wrapped about his neck a fleecelike muffler. His body is encased in several overcoats of varying hue. He clasps and unclasps his hands. The jury is already in the box; his keen eyes scrutinize the entire courtroom but come finally back to the jurymen before him. The crier opens court, and as he does so, Choate removes his outer overcoat; and as tense excitement permeates the court, still another coat is taken off. Presently we hear him say: "May it please your Honor, and gentlemen of the jury." The day's work has begun.

His energy never flags and his body throbs with almost convulsive jerks, and as he raises his arm it trembles with emotion. His head thrown back like that of a thoroughbred horse, his breath comes through his nostrils with a noise which no one in the courtroom can fail to heed. And as he reaches the high point, perspiration flows down his face.

Difficult, nay, impossible as it is to appraise by reading it in cold print, in his case there comes through to us somehow why it was that juries followed him. He loved plain people, even as Lincoln did, and, like Lincoln, he had wit. Once in defending a divorce case wherein he sought, of course, to dispel all thought of guilt in the husband's flirtations with the corespondent, he said: "They were playful, gentlemen of the jury, not culpable. After mowing toil, they sat down on the haymow for refreshment, not for crime. There may have been a little youthful fondling—playful, not amorous. They only wished to soften the asperities of hay making."

Despite his disinclination for public office and his strong predilection for the law, on February 22, 1841, he was elected to the Senate and here his reputation as a speaker, already great, was immeasurably enhanced. In support of a measure the result of which was the Congressional Library, he made a speech which

Calhoun pronounced as "the most beautiful that ever fell from human lips." And as he listened, the old South Carolinian exclaimed to those near him: "Massachusetts sent us Webster, but in the name of Heaven who have they sent us now?"

Retiring finally from the Senate, having liked it not much better than the House, Choate returned to Boston and the practice of the law, until finally his exertions as an advocate impaired his health. In 1855, a friend told him that if he continued with his labors without rest or a vacation, he would undermine his constitution. "Sir," replied Choate, "the constitution was destroyed long ago; I am now living under the by-laws." But even these could not support his failing strength much longer. In July, three years later, a European trip was planned, but they took him off the boat at Halifax, and at twenty minutes before two, on the morning of July 13, 1858, he died.

Nine days later, a great concourse of Boston citizens filed slowly into Faneuil Hall. Here where he had so often spoken eulogies of others, Edward Everett arose to speak the final words: "He reaped little but fame, when he ought to have reaped both fame and fortune. . . . His work is done—nobly, worthily done."

From the Boston of Rufus Choate in the late fifties to the little community of Jamestown, N. Y., in the year 1913, is in every way a far cry, yet that the chain of advocacy had not been broken was made clear when in that year the future American prosecutor of the Nuremberg trials was admitted to the Bar. It was there that there grew up perhaps the last example of a lawyer trained by the apprentice system. Robert H. Jackson, for these thirteen years a Justice of the United States Supreme Court, has given us a most appealing narrative of the Jamestown law practice as he knew it in his most formative years.

In the June, 1950, issue of the American Bar *Journal*, he

wrote: "The county seat lawyer, counselor to railroads and to Negroes, to bankers and poor whites, who always gave to each the best there was in him . . . has been an American institution. . . . Such a man understands the structure of society, and how its groups interlock and interact because he lives in a community so small that he can keep it all in view. . . . He sees how this society lives and works under the law and adjusts its conflicts by its procedures. He knows how disordered and hopelessly unstable it would be without law. He knows that in this country the administration of justice is based on law practice."

Paper rights, he went on, "are worth when threatened just what some lawyer makes them worth. Civil liberties are those which some lawyer respected by his neighbors will stand up to defend. Any legal doctrine which fails to enlist the support of well-regarded lawyers will have no real sway in this country. . . . The experience that gave life to our judge-made and statutory law, at least until the last few years, was this type of country life. From such homes came the lawyers, the judges, and the legislators of the nineteenth century. Their way of living generated independence and amazing energy, and these country boys went to the cities and dominated the professions and business as well. . . . Much of the changing trend of law and of political and social policy is due to the declining number of men who have shared this experience."

As American as a hooked rug, a pine chest, or maple sugar, these observations have a refreshing quality about them, but there is a somewhat sad, nostalgic note as well. "The county seat lawyer and the small-town advocate," says Justice Jackson, "are pretty much gone, and the small city lawyer has to struggle to keep his head above water. . . . The lawsuit has declined in public interest before the tough competition of movie and radio. . . . Much controversy has now shifted to the administrative tribunal and the country lawyer hates it and all its works.

"But," he went on, "this vanishing country lawyer left his mark on his times, and he was worth knowing. He 'read law' in the *Commentaries* of Blackstone and Kent and not by the case system. He resolved problems by what he called 'first principles.' He did not specialize, nor did he pick and choose clients. He rarely declined service to worthy ones because of inability to pay. Once enlisted for a client, he took his obligation seriously. He insisted on complete control of the litigation—he was no mere hired hand. But he gave every power and resource to the cause."

This county seat lawyer and small-town advocate "identified himself with the client's cause fully, sometimes too fully. He would fight the adverse party, and fight his counsel, fight every hostile witness, and fight the court, fight public sentiment, fight any obstacle to his client's success. He never quit. . . . The law to him was like a religion, and its practice was more than a means of support. It was a mission."

Two months later he wrote: "I am a vestigial remnant of the system which permitted one to come to the Bar by way of apprenticeship in a law office. Except for one term at law school, I availed myself of that method which was already causing uneasiness—to which feeling I must have added, for the system was almost immediately abolished. You may be comforted to realize that I am the last relic of that method likely to find a niche in the Supreme Court."

By whatever method Robert Jackson received his training, the result was a great advocate and finally a great judge. He started as a country lawyer of the kind he so graphically described. He came by his advocacy in the hard contests of the courts.

Like all the good lawyers I have ever known, Bob Jackson is a good storyteller, and he has often described to me his early contests before local justices of the peace, conducted in some old cow barn under the dim light of a kerosene lantern swinging from a cobwebbed beam. And it was here that he learned his first unforgettable lessons. On one of these occasions, the old farmer who served also as justice of the peace consistently had ruled against him. Hoping to persuade him of his error, young Jackson with a flourish one day handed the great jurist the latest case just published in the *Advance Sheets*. Gazing at it and noting that it was not bound either in law calf or in canvas covers, the learned justice handed it back with the brief comment: "I don't take no law from no magazines."

In his recent brilliant book, *Trial Judge*, Mr. Justice Bernard Botein has written: "I know of no child prodigies among trial lawyers. A certain seasoning of actual experience is a necessary ingredient in the trial advocate. He can learn a good deal from books, and should of course have the rules of evidence at his finger tips, and be well grounded in the law affecting his case. But to develop beyond the point of adequacy, he must learn from his own mistakes and successes and from watching other lawyers in action."

Robert Jackson, I am sure, would have resented being called a child prodigy. He learned his advocacy the hard way—by practice, observation, and experience. How is an advocate made? That is the best of all ways. Can advocacy be taught by a formal instructor? I do not think so, although there is no doubt much valuable instruction could be given as to what should be avoided. But no tutor ever lived who could surely make a great advocate.

God alone can make one, even as he makes poets and artists by bestowing on them something of the divine fire; yet even this demands the co-operation of the recipient.

Well, I have used many words and still have not given you the certain specifications for the making of an advocate—a living advocate—but I can tell you how one of the greatest advocates of fiction, Mr. Tutt, was created.

When I was a young prosecutor, there was a great criminal lawyer famous in the old Criminal Courthouse. His name was Abe Levy; he was the father of the distinguished author, playwright, and lawyer, Newman Levy. Abe Levy held the respect and affection of all the young assistants whom he treated with consummate tact and courtesy—and usually worsted. He was the defender of the famous Nan Patterson and so many others equally celebrated in their day. He was a fine man and a great lawyer, but he was more than that; there was something within him that made juries want to follow him.

But to return to Mr. Tutt. Some years ago, I was appointed one of three arbitrators to help decide a difficult case. One of the other two was Arthur Train whom I knew well. Walking up town one day with him after the hearing, I said: "Arthur, how did you come upon the character of Mr. Tutt? From what sources, from what materials did you make him up?" He thought a moment, and then with no possible trace of irreverence answered: "I compounded Mr. Tutt out of three characters—Abe Levy, Abraham Lincoln, and Jesus Christ."

PART THREE

GOOD ADVOCACY–
A CRYING NEED

X

Advocacy and the Criminal Law

O N A MAY MORNING of the year 1938, a tired man stood before the Court of General Sessions of the Peace in New York City to hear a jury of his peers pronounce him guilty.

It was springtime, the season of hope and promise, but there was no hope that day in the heart of Bertram Campbell. After a hurried trial, he had been found guilty of forging four checks totaling $10,000 drawn on the Hanover Bank and Trust Company, and he was now being denounced by the Assistant District Attorney as the tool of a notorious band of forgers. The judge who had presided at the trial remanded him to the Tombs for sentence the next week, remarking to the jury as he did so, "I may say that I have not the slightest doubt in my mind that your verdict is correct."

In *The New York Times* the next morning, there was this

headline: EX-BROKER IS GUILTY IN $10,000 FORGERY. *Accused of Being "Front" for Operators as Yet Undetected.*

One week later, the defendant was brought before the same judge again. Pale and gaunt, he stood before the spokesman of society, the holder of the scales of justice, to hear the sentence: five to ten years in State prison, and then the judge denounced him as a brazen liar and called him lucky "not to be in the dock for perjury."

Lord Hategood at the Fair was not more eloquent. The minions of the law did not, as in Faithful's case, scourge him with whips or lance his flesh with knives or burn him to ashes at the stake though these torments might have seemed preferable to Campbell's sentence, for death would have brought his sufferings to an end. Twenty-four hours later, the headline in *The New York Times* blared out: EX-SALESMAN JAILED IN FORGERY PLOT. *Receives Five-Year Term—Refuses to Reveal Accomplices.*

Held for a time in the old Tombs prison preparatory to his handcuffed journey up to Sing Sing, he was subjected to every indignity for which that old bastille was famous. His cell was filthy and he was forced to sleep on bare steel. He was fed the worst of food on a tin plate pushed under his cell door. His nights were made hideous by the cries and screams of a fellow prisoner whom he believed a raving maniac. But more than all this was the agony of despair with which he thought of his poor wife and children suffering the indignity and pain of having a good husband and loving father referred to as a convicted felon.

In due course, they brought him manacled to the old fortress on the Hudson. Here every insult that the State is capable of inflicting on a prisoner was meted out. He ceased to have a name now; he had become a number, one of the vast army of convicts without a country, for he was no longer a citizen of the United States. He was now no better than an animal, a caged animal, while back in the little home in Freeport a tired woman wept and prayed. Tears flowed as she tried to sleep at night; tears filled her eyes as she went each day about her sad appointed tasks. The Campbell family was in ruins. Their hopes were gone; despair, cold, bleak despair, filled all their aching hearts. Was there no God, was there no justice in the world?

Bertram H. Campbell was an obscure man. He was one of the anonymous and inconspicuous mass of little men who walk the *via dolorosa* of this life unnoticed and alone. He had few friends, no powerful backers and no acquaintances with power to help him.

He had been a customer's man in Wall Street and had held many unimportant small posts in the financial world. He had lived in a small house in one of the dreary little suburbs of Long Island, and daily could be seen among the anonymous mass of bored commuters going to the city every morning and returning every evening to the dubious tranquillity of identical little homes. The world lets such as these pass by and little cares nor long remembers what befalls them.

And so, when he stood trial that day in General Sessions, his was an unimportant case—unimportant to the prosecutor except as an opportunity to add a small new scalp to his belt, unimportant to the press whose delight is in the downfall of a great and powerful man, unimportant to the few spectators in the courtroom, unimportant to a tired judge, unimportant to everyone save the accused. To him it was his liberty—his life.

To everyone save Campbell it was a drab, run-of-the-mill affair. To him it was everything. And so they had hurried through his trial in a routine manner. In an atmosphere created by the police and prosecuting staff who assume that every man arrested must be guilty, he had listened as five witnesses positively identified him as the one whom they had seen deposit two forged checks. They were, to quote the report of the Parole Board seven years later, "employees of banks, all of good reputation and superior intelligence."

There had been no defense except Campbell's own denial and the testimony of a few character witnesses who came in fear to speak of his good reputation. During the trial, his lawyer had become ill, but the defendant said he wanted no mistrial, and so next day new counsel appeared announcing that he was ready to proceed, and the judge observed that the change of counsel had been to Campbell's benefit. But of just what that benefit consisted, the jury's prompt verdict against him renders it at this distance not easy to detect.

When the jury returned with smug looks of righteous indignation and were commended by the judge for their fine work, an indifferent courtroom watched as the officers of the law closed in to lead him away.

And so convict Campbell became a felon and a prisoner. All was lost—everything! The headlines of the next morning, as I have said, crunched their sadistic morsel, and a case which fell far short of a *cause célèbre* was soon forgotten, but the man convicted did not forget as he looked forward to five years of a felon's life. Five years! How the pen of Victor Hugo would have described this tragedy! With what a masterpiece of suffering and despair would he have caused the tears of a hard world to flow? How Zola would have roused the sympathy of people hitherto unmoved, but there were no Victor Hugo and no Zola to describe his plight; there was no one left to speak for him.

Abandoned and proscribed, the prisoner began the long days,

the endless nights, of his imprisonment. Slowly the days grew into weeks, and then, with aching steps, the months crawled by —endless, dreary, hopeless months. One year passed, and then two, and finally three, but Campbell's "debt to society" was not yet paid. Another month went by, then two, then three. Finally, at the end of three years and four months, the State, in its infinite generosity, granted him a parole.

It was October, 1941; he had been in jail since that May day of 1938, when a jury had pronounced him guilty and had been heartily thanked by the judge for doing so. Back in Freeport, Campbell found such work as he could get, but no one wants much to do with an ex-convict on parole. For another three years and ten months, he was forced to report at regular intervals, and it was not until August, 1945, that this surveillance came at last to an end. For seven years he had been the plaything of the State. His days were filled with agonizing misery, and nightmares tortured all his sleep, nightmares in which he lived again his prison years.

But why have I dwelt so long on Bertram Campbell? I have done so because he was convicted of a crime he had not committed—a crime of which he was totally, wholly, and completely innocent. That there was no doubt as to his innocence was fully proved when in July, 1945, a professional bogus checkwriter by the name of Alexander Thiel came forward and confessed that it was not Campbell who had forged and passed the checks, but he. And so, after seven tortured years, the rusty, creaking wheels of justice began at last to turn.

The witnesses who had identified him at the trial came forward to retract their previous identifications. An inquiry by one of the bar associations, ably conducted by Mr. Robert Daru, revealed much. The private detectives of the surety companies, it seemed, had been helpful, very helpful in amassing the evidence against Campbell. Wesley Irvine, a former bank teller, one of the identifying witnesses at the trial, now told how a photograph of the defendant had been shown to him before the police asked him to observe Campbell in the flesh. But for this picture, he said, he never would have made the identification which he now retracted, and there was a curious circumstance about that picture. Campbell wore a mustache, but whether the picture originally shown the retracting witness had revealed a mustache, he was not sure; he swore positively however that when he later saw the photograph, it then had "a mustache superimposed or dubbed in."

Much work had been done with these identifying witnesses before the trial, it seems. One of the methods employed was to impress them with the "unimportance" of their testimony—this, no doubt, to quiet their consciences in making the identification. Two other witnesses now asserted that they never would have identified Campbell had not pictures of him first been shown them.

Governor Dewey now acted with commendable dispatch and granted a full pardon, "based not on mercy but justice," and presently another judge did what he could to remove the black stain from the records by dismissing all the indictments against a man who though innocent had been convicted. The Legislature now took a hand and enlarged the defendant's right to sue the State for false imprisonment, and on June 17, 1946, the New York State Court of Claims awarded him a judgment of $115,-000.

But this pitiable victim of the State's injustice was not destined to enjoy this financial retribution long. His spirit and his health had been broken by his long ordeal and his strength began to fail. He tried to rest quietly at home and limited his activities, but it was of no avail. On the seventh of September, just eighty-two days after the Court of Claims awarded its ironic compensation, Bertram H. Campbell died a martyr to the cause of justice—a victim of the law.

The newspapers referred to the matter for a day or two. A *New York Times* editorial somewhat sententiously declared: "The moral of the case seems to be the very old one that it is better to let a guilty man go free than to convict an innocent man. Courts, prosecuting attorneys, and juries ought to give that moral some study. Respect for the law suffers when criminal procedure becomes a matter of taking as many scalps as possible." But it has always been so, and so it will continue.

I despair of a changed attitude to which the *Times* looked forward, but I do not despair of sometime having a trained corps of advocates, as in England, from whose ranks at least one man, when the occasion calls, will step forward to throw the whole weight of his character, his ability, his courage, and his strength between an unjustly accused citizen and the onrushing juggernaut of the State.

Cases of mistaken identity are always difficult, and yet I believe that had a great advocate been there, he would have cross-examined those identifying witnesses so as to search their consciences and even their souls. He would have shaken them as a terrier throws fear into a rat. Their smug assurance would have vanished; their complacent certainty would have weakened, and perhaps, who knows, they might have been forced to recant their false identification on the witness stand, even as they did seven years later.

I cannot read about this case without my gorge rising, to think that in modern free America so evil a thing could happen, such a shambles of injustice could be tolerated, and so hideous an abattoir of slaughter be allowed. Society can do no more evil thing than to deprive an innocent man of his liberty; and as you think about it, will you not all agree that there is no finer, nobler act on earth than to defend an innocent man? The Campbell case established as nothing else has the need of good advocacy in this country and the danger always confronting an accused without it.

But there are those who say that cases of this kind are rare. The thought that an innocent man could be found guilty seems to them as fantastic and remote from probability as premature burial. Some judges seem to share that view. Judge Learned Hand, for instance, in one case spoke of the "phantom of the innocent man convicted," as though the idea were a kind of specter brought forth by adolescents to frighten little children on Halloween.

To such I would say, read the Campbell case, and unless your sympathies have dried up from malnutrition or overly sophisticated education, you must pale at that dreadful and iniquitous disaster and shudderingly whisper to yourself, "There but for the grace of God go I"—as indeed you do. But if this judicial abortion has not persuaded you that it can happen here again and perhaps, God forbid, to you, take down from the shelf a book written by the late Edwin M. Borchard, a distinguished professor of law in the Yale Law School. He called the book *Convicting the Innocent*.

The four hundred and seven pages of this authoritative volume set forth with meticulous accuracy the stories of sixty-five persons who, within recent years, have been convicted of crimes they did not commit—crimes of which they were as innocent as Campbell and whose innocence was as conclusively and unanswerably proved. Fifteen of these cases were based upon mistaken identification. Eleven involved circumstantial evidence in which perjury was an ingredient. Fifteen occurred where the perjury of prosecuting or other witnesses occurred in a setting of circumstantial evidence, honest or manufactured. Four of them were convictions for murder in which the "murdered" person later turned up alive and well. Fourteen dealt with prosecutions in which the victim was "framed" by hostile witnesses. In several of the cases cited, a third degree or other undue influence was used to procure "confessions" by duress. Professor Borchard's book is one of my favorites. I commend it to you.

Man's inhumanity to man is a story without an ending. Down through the echoing dark corridors of time come the screams of those who suffered on the rack or cried aloud to God to save them from the flames. History in no small part is made up of the records of the thousand times ten thousand Bertram Campbells.

Throughout the ages, man's inhumanity to man has been manifested in false charges brought against the innocent. That this still goes on, the Campbell case attests. Can anyone then deny that now more than ever there is a crying need for trained advocates, strong, able, willing, and unafraid to stand between the accused citizen and the legions of society ranged against him— between the defendant and the embattled press, between the man under indictment and the public clamor of the moment. We have had such advocates in the past—men like John Adams, Daniel Webster, Rufus Choate, Abraham Lincoln, Martin Littleton, and a host of others. Are we still breeding them or are they a dying race?

If advocacy in the criminal courts is being now eschewed by those who think it not respectable to be seen there, why is this so? There are several reasons: First, because there is a vast confusion in the public mind about the duties and the functions of an advocate—an ignorance of our legal and constitutional safeguards that guarantee every accused person a fair trial, the right to procure the compulsory attendance of witnesses in his behalf, the privilege of enjoying the assistance of counsel, and the presumption of innocence. Second, in the past thirty or forty years, there have grown up organized bands of criminals operating what are known as rackets, whose crimes have been so flagrant and so foul that an impatient public would not take it amiss if they were shot down without a trial. Third, the understandable and well-founded fear of Russia and all her dark conspiracies arouses feelings akin to lynch law.

Justice is a flame that often flickers in the headwinds of an aroused public sentiment; but it is a fire that must be kept alight if we are to escape such trials as are daily witnessed in the Kremlin and if we are to avoid the lawless sway of a Gestapo. If lawyers do not do their part to keep the fire of justice lighted, who will lead our people back to the civilized conception that every man, no matter how we hate the crime of which he stands accused, has nonetheless a right to be defended, to the end that all that can rightfully be said for him is well said? If we can no longer convince our people that this is an ideal worth fighting for, liberty as we know it is at an end. If there should come a time when there are none left to cry out when the Bertram Campbells are made to suffer tortures, the America that we know would then follow the republics of the past down the long road to oblivion.

A true understanding, then, of the criminal law and an enlightened conception of the role of advocates needs a reawakening. George Orwell in *1984* has pictured what it would be like to live in a world without liberty, a land where a knock at the door cannot be answered by a habeas corpus, where trial by jury is no more and advocacy is dead. He paints a dreadful scene, the ingredients of which lie all about us.

For there is today a cynicism about human rights. Witchcraft is no longer found as once it was in Salem only two and a half short centuries ago when poor George Burroughs was, on the confession of witnesses induced by torture, put to death. But now only the nomenclature has been changed. For "witchcraft" substitute the word "Communism" and all the passions of those early Massachusetts days, so brilliantly described by Bancroft, are awake again.

To hate crime is just and laudable, but to condemn in advance of trial a man who as yet is only accused is to adopt the philosophy of a lynching party. To condemn and pillory and ex-ecrate the lawyer who stands forth to defend a man still presumed to be innocent is no less than an attempt to destroy sacred rights embodied in our Constitution and specifically guaranteed by our Bill of Rights.

Yet all these things are now done, done openly, flagrantly, and without shame; and as long as such attacks are countenanced and applauded by large segments of the press, the threat of our fundamental liberties increases.

Many persons so despise the crime that they no longer can distinguish between it and the question whether the indicted man is in fact guilty. Such persons either openly oppose his right to counsel, or if they grudgingly admit it, feel that if he is to have counsel, he should not have a very good one.

The long and tragic story of man's inhumanity to man is darkened by the recollection that the most flagrant miscarriages of justice were those in which the prisoner had no one to speak for him. Such was the case of Mary, Queen of Scots, who, with no counsel at her side, was forced to listen while alleged copies of inculpating letters were read out, without accounting for the absence of the originals and without proof of the authenticity of the copies. On these alone, and without any witnesses offered by the prosecution, she was convicted. Her two secretaries in London could have helped her; she asked for their appearances, but the tools of Elizabeth laughed at her demand, and so, as many other innocent victims have, she met her death at the hands of the executioner.

In Gilbert's *Yeomen of the Guard*, there is a beautiful and tragic song set to the lovely music of Sir Arthur Sullivan. This is the refrain:

> *The screws may twist,*
> *And the rack may turn,*
> *And men may bleed,*
> *And men may burn.*

They often have and they will again if the philosophy of certain demagogues is finally adopted. There was no thumbscrew and no rack for Bertram Campbell, but he was struck down just as cruelly and just as wantonly, and was just as effectually tortured and destroyed.

But public clamor against giving an accused a fair trial is not new, as anyone may see who glances back at Boston in the year 1770. Two regiments of British soldiers had been for some time garrisoned in the little Massachusetts capitol. His Majesty's Fourteenth and Twenty-ninth Regiments of Foot were something less than welcomed by the populace. Patrolling along the streets in their red coats, small boys had often pelted them and called out in derision, "Who buys lobsters?" The sentries had been ordered to bear almost anything rather than provoke a riot, but as the snow deepened in the streets, tension mounted, and on February twenty-second (no one then took note that it was George Washington's birthday) the explosion came.

On the afternoon of that day Ebenezer Richardson, a customs informer, came home from work. A crowd of boys surrounded his abode, and as they pelted it with snowballs, in an upper window Richardson appeared with loaded musket. "By God," he shouted, "I'll make a lane through you," and fired, killing one of the boys. Five days later, there was a great funeral procession. Starting at the Liberty Tree and marching north to the Town House, it arrived finally at the burying ground by the Common. The Congregational clergy were out in force. John Adams marched behind the coffin and there, too, in the procession, dressed in sober black, was John Hancock.

The town, though tense, was quiet for another week, and then, at a little after nine on the evening of March fifth, near the Custom House, a file of nine British soldiers was sent out by Captain Preston to protect a sentinel then undergoing an assault from the mob. There was a rattle of musketry, and when the smoke cleared, five citizens of Boston lay prone upon the dirty snow; three of them were dead and the other two were about to die. Thus occurred what is known to history as the Boston Massacre.

The crowd surged forward to drag their dead to cover; while British drums began to beat, two platoons marched out from the barracks to form cover for the main guard, and still a third took up its position at the corner by the State House, and at the word of command, dropped to one knee in position for street firing.

And now from all the steeples bells were tolling and men

rushed through the streets with knives and cudgels. Boston had gone mad.

Captain Preston and the nine soldiers who had fired were now made safe in jail—safer, it was believed, than they would have been within their barracks.

A few hours later, a friend of the British officers was knocking at John Adams' door. "As God is my witness," he said, "Preston is an innocent man. His soldiers were defending their lives from the mob. . . . He has no one to defend him. Mr. Adams, would you consider—will you take his case?" Three of the Crown lawyers already approached, he said, had peremptorily declined to defend him but Josiah Quincy, Jr., had accepted if John Adams would act with him.

It was the most unpopular case in America; it was thrice unpopular in Boston. To take it would arouse the hatred of the city and the contempt and loathing of the Liberty Boys. John Adams was at this time not only a rising lawyer; he was rapidly becoming one of the political leaders of America. To defend a British officer might spell his ruin. The Declaration of Independence was still five years in the future and no prophet could have forecast that he would one day become the second President of the United States. But had there been a seer to cast his horoscope, he would have taken a dim view, indeed, of Adams' future political career if he accepted this retainer.

With the full knowledge of how this case would affect his political career, Adams replied to his caller: "I will take this case, I will defend Preston if it is the last thing I do," whereupon a retaining fee of one guinea was handed him.

The news soon spread. A member of the Sons of Liberty stopped him on the street, asking him if it could be true that he had "undertaken to defend these murderers." John Adams answered, saying that he was about to defend men who as yet were presumed innocent.

The Sons of Liberty were pressing for an immediate trial, but he succeeded in postponing it until October when he hoped that tempers would have had time to cool.

Meanwhile, on March twenty-second from Braintree, old Josiah Quincy wrote his son in alarm that he had heard Josiah had "become an advocate for these criminals who are charged with the murder of their fellow citizens. Good God! Is it possible?" Nor did his letter omit telling young Josiah of the "bitterest reproaches" that were being uttered against him.

A few days later, the son wrote his aged and infirm parent: "I have little leisure, and less inclination, either to know or take notice of these ignorant slanderers who have dared to utter their 'bitter reproaches' in your hearing against me. . . . Let such be told, sir, that these criminals charged with murder are not yet legally proved such, and therefore, however criminal, are entitled by the laws of God and man to all legal counsel and aid; and that my duty as a man obliged me to undertake the defense; that my duty as a lawyer strengthened the obligation."

Newspapers now were happily discussing Moses and the laws of God, and ministers were thundering from their pulpits: "Who so sheddeth man's blood, by man shall his blood be shed." Small boys were hurling stones through the windows of John Adams' house. Meanwhile, however, he sat quietly in his office reading a new volume he had just obtained from London. It was the Marquess di Beccaria's *Crimes and Punishments*.

And as he thought of the grave burden he had now assumed and the injury he would suffer, he read in his Beccaria: "If by supporting the rights of mankind and of inviolable truths, I shall contribute to save from the agonies of death one unfor-

tunate victim of tyranny, or of ignorance equally fatal, his blessing and tears of transport will be sufficient consolation to me
for the contempt of all mankind."

How Adams and young Quincy defended Captain Preston and
the British soldiers has been too often told to justify a repetition.
But that these two American patriots in the heat of an aroused
colony extracted a verdict of acquittal for Captain Preston and
six of the eight private soldiers from a Boston jury within six
months after the "massacre," and less than five years before the
Battle of Bunker Hill, is a monument to the courage and independence of the American Bar.

Today, I wonder if a lawyer who had conducted such a defense could become President of the United States? Could he do
so if he had only acted as a character witness? For there is
today, I think, a stronger public feeling of intolerance for any
who have in any way participated in an unpopular cause than
this country has ever known before. There is less understanding
of the true nature of our American system than ever has been
seen in our whole history.

The hue and cry, lynch law and trial by newspaper have
gravely threatened the impartiality of our administration of justice. Trial by newspaper is one of the worst evils of our day.
The only place for the trial of a case is in the courtroom, and
yet how often do we see the newspapers trying the defendant
on their own, independent of the court and jury. What is printed
in the press is ultimately seen by the jury, no matter what judicial
injunctions may have been given.

In trial by newspaper, the defendant has no right to compel
the attendance of witnesses or to cross-examine the sources quoted
by the newspaper. In trial by newspaper, alleged evidence is
presented which has either been directly rejected by a court or

which, under no circumstances, could be admitted. The statements of alleged witnesses are set forth, but there is, of course, no opportunity to cross-examine them. A trial by newspaper is in every way an ex parte, one-sided affair in which all the safeguards of justice which the courts of the United States and England have worked out through the centuries are ignored. An erroneous conviction can be set aside on appeal if there have been errors by the trial court, but against false or prejudicial evidence introduced by publicity, whether planted by prosecutors or the police or published through the industry of the reporters, the appellate courts can give no redress and, thus, the defendant's right to a fair trial is destroyed. Here is an evil against which no advocate can contend.

When we think of bloody Jeffreys and his persecution of poor Alice Lisle, we preen ourselves upon the favorable comparison which our times make with his, and yet is it possible to imagine our contemporaries dealing with a culprit as leniently as James I dealt with a bribe taker by the name of Francis Bacon? His sentence was hardly rendered before it was commuted. Sending him to the Tower proved a mere form, for in two days he was at liberty again. He had not only been sentenced to the Tower but required to pay a fine of 40,000 pounds and been adjudged incapable of ever again holding public office. But within three years of the pronouncement of the sentence, this fine was remitted. Is it possible to imagine such leniency today?

We live in troublous, dangerous years, and with all our vaunted progress in the improvement of our social conscience, real tolerance and magnanimity are less evident now than in less hectic periods. Our attitude toward the criminal law has hardened, and the disapproval of those who may defend indicted persons, though similar to the views expressed by the elder

Quincy to his son, if anything, are more severe today than in an aroused Boston of the year 1770.

There is immediate acknowledgement of a doctor's right and duty to administer to every patient regardless of his moral character or previous life, but in the United States there is no such liberal attitude toward lawyers; and this, no doubt, is one reason why great advocacy in the criminal courts is passing or has passed.

Advocacy and the criminal law—the two are inseparable. No jury of twelve men could ever send a prisoner to the electric chair unless the prosecutor had aroused their feelings and their passions to the fever pitch; nor could any man escape without an advocate to lead the jury to the side of justice, and yet the critics of the criminal law and those who practice it level all their sharpest barbs against the conduct of the average criminal trial. They demand that it should be conducted in the manner of a scientific inquiry.

But the truth is, said Sir James Fitzjames Stephen, that "litigation of all sorts and especially litigation which assumes the form of a criminal trial is a substitute for private war, and is and must be conducted in a spirit which is often fervent, and even passionate. No man will allow himself to be deprived of character or liberty or possibly of life without offering the most strenuous resistance in his power, or without seeking, in many cases, to retaliate on his opponent and his opponent's supporters. A trial of any importance is always more or less of a battle. . . ."

But if it is warfare, why are not the warriors on this battlefield entitled to as much esteem as that traditionally accorded to brave soldiers? That this is not so, the letter of the elder Quincy to his son attests.

How wrong this attitude unquestionably is was never better

stated than by the President of the United States when he wrote
to a delegate of the American Bar Association in September,
1951: "The Bar has a notable tradition of willingness to protect
the rights of the accused. It seems to me that if this tradition is
to be meaningful today it must extend to all defendants, including persons accused of such abhorrent crimes as conspiracy to
overthrow the Government by force, espionage, and sabotage."

Yet, he continued, "undoubtedly some uninformed persons
will always identify the lawyer with the client. But I believe that
most American citizens recognize how important it is to our
tradition of fair trials that there be adequate representation by
competent counsel. Lawyers in the past have risked obloquy of
the uninformed to protect the rights of the most degraded. Unless
they continue to do so in the future an important part of our
rights will be gone."

Judge Harold Medina, when he saw that letter, said that it
"contains one of the finest statements of the fundamental principles of American democracy it has been my privilege to read."

Demosthenes and Cicero, Erskine and Brougham, Webster,
Choate, and Lincoln—all made their reputation in the criminal courts. Their skill in advocacy has lighted them down in
honor to our times. The Bar of England still seeks out the graduates of the Old Bailey for advancement to the bench. Yet if
you go out to a dinner party in New York, you may meet a member of some great law firm who will speak with raised eyebrows
of contempt of the criminal courts and those who, on occasion,
practice there.

Yet the greatest advocates which either England or America
has produced have been those brave enough and able to stand
forth as the champions of men accused of crime. It is a noble
calling. Two years ago Quentin Reynolds wrote a biography of

Samuel Leibowitz. Appropriately he selected *Courtroom* as the title of this arrestingly narrated story. But more interesting even than his cases were the conversations Quentin Reynolds had with Leibowitz after he became a judge of the Kings County Court and, finally, its senior jurist. "For the most part," the judge told him, "the public has a sham idea of what goes on in the course of a criminal trial. They are constantly exposed to portrayals of phony trial scenes in our motion pictures and more of the same on the radio and television."

But, he added, "I am fully convinced that our criminal courts offer the cleanest and most challenging battleground for the testing of legal knowledge and wisdom."

When the book was written, Mr. Reynolds again called upon the subject of his pages and asked him whether he thought that law students should be encouraged to practice criminal law. "I do, indeed," the judge replied, "and the law schools could certainly do a better job for training students for life in the courtroom. Remember that a trial, especially in a criminal court, is more of a fact suit than a lawsuit. The troublesome problem confronting the court and jury is not so much what *the law is, as what happened*. Did he steal? Did he assault? Did he commit arson? Did he kill, and under what circumstances?"

In the August, 1952, American Bar Association *Journal*, there is an article by Roscoe Pound, Dean Emeritus of Harvard Law School. He begins it with this sentence: "Mr. Justice Holmes put it as the function of the law school of a university to teach law in the grand manner."

But what is the "grand manner"? Does it lie in encouraging students to sneer at advocacy? Does it lie in the breeding of contempt for those who would prevent the Bertram Campbells of this world from being convicted and destroyed though innocent?

Does it lie in the encouragement of law students to avoid any contact with that part of the law which has to deal with the protection of liberty through the defense of unjustly accused men? Does teaching law "in the grand manner" involve the discouragement of those who would prevent the rusty thumbscrew and the rack from being used, whatever modern forms these instruments may take?

The university law school, said Dean Pound, "has taken over from the apprentice system of our frontier era and . . . substantially the whole training of the American lawyer." Reading this, I am emboldened to inquire how many Robert Jacksons has it given us? How many Nathan Millers? How many Martin Littletons?

The thinking of so many persons is today obscured by ignorance and sometimes by sheer hypocrisy, by class feeling, by the belief that only those residing on the wrong side of the tracks should be concerned with the penal statutes. With incredulity the respectable stand aghast when one of their own members suddenly is caught up in the meshes of the law. "Poor Dick," I heard many persons exclaim when a prominent banker was finally exposed as an embezzler and a thief. But those who commiserated with him I am sure gave little thought to the hundreds of anonymous and friendless men awaiting trial in the innumerable criminal courts of a great city. The Bertram Campbells of this world excite small interest.

As long, however, as there are Bertram Campbells—and there always will be—the need for advocacy remains, for the long category of innocent men convicted is constantly expanding. New chapters constantly are added to Professor Borchard's book. A daily reading of the morning papers will establish this. In *The New York Times* of August 8, 1952, for example, I noted, on an inside page, a little article of three short paragraphs tucked away among other news "more important." The headline read: INNOCENT MAN PARDONED AFTER 6 YEARS IN PRISON.

This particular outrage occurred in Maine. In the opening paragraph of this obscure story we read: "Edward A. Hodson of Presque Isle, in prison for nearly six years for another man's crime, was pardoned today by Gov. Frederick C. Payne." Hodson it seems was convicted back in 1946 for an assault on a woman taxi driver. He was sentenced to fifteen years in State prison. At long last, a laborer by the name of Kennison confessed that it was he who had committed the assault. Hodson and Kennison were about the same height and weight. Both were wearing old clothes at the time of the attack, and a boot with which the assailant beat the woman fitted both men. On this evidence, a man completely innocent was struck down by the State and was tortured with six years of penal servitude.

In November, 1952, another judicial outrage was righted in the County Court of Queens County. Louis Hoffner had spent the last twelve years of his life in prison. On August 11, 1940, he was arrested in connection with the shooting of a bartender named Trifon Proestes in the holdup of a bar and restaurant occurring three days earlier. Of two witnesses, only one identified him as the killer. He did so only after having failed on several previous occasions. The stenographic report of the early failures disclosed the clearest contradiction of the sole identifying witness. It contained the minutes taken at the line-up, which were in the possession of the former District Attorney. Yet this startling contradiction was not produced at the trial, and Hoffner went to jail for twelve long, bitter years. For one hundred and forty-four agonizing months he languished there until at last, at long, long last the New York *World-Tele-*

gram set the rusty wheels of justice in motion, and District Attorney T. Vincent Quinn moved for a dismissal of the indictment and Hoffner, an innocent man, finally went free.

"There are members of the bar," Judge Leibowitz told Quentin Reynolds, "who either never see the inside of a courtroom, or who practice in the rarefied atmosphere of the civil courtroom, and who peer down their noses at the criminal lawyer with that deprecating look that a parent usually reserves for the errant child." Such lawyers (and I have known many such), would no doubt have turned that deprecating look on Bertram Campbell, Edward Hodson, and Louis Hoffner.

Is advocacy needed in the criminal courts? Is there a need for great engineers and great surgeons? Is there still a need for able generals? Then there is indeed a place for good advocates who who are unafraid, and who know how to stand their ground on all the battlefields of justice, including that most bloody one that every day is found within our criminal courtrooms. When that day comes, as in a declining Rome and in Revolutionary France it came, when there are none left able or brave enough to engage in this unending warfare, the liberties of American citizens will perish, and tyranny will reign supreme even as it now reigns in Moscow and in every dastard totalitarian outpost.

XI

Advocacy in the Appellate Courts

THE AMERICAN PUBLIC knows less about the appellate courts than any of the others. Appellate courts are seldom thronged with lay spectators, and what happens there is far less publicized than are the trials in the lower courts before judge and jury. No witnesses appear to be examined or cross-examined; there is none of the excitement or the human interest that are always found in the courts below. Here, however, jury verdicts may be upset and the rulings of the trial judge reversed. Here the real law is written. Here is spoken the last word in the case. Not till here is the issue finally determined.

Whatever his lack of interest in the appellate courts, who that has ever mounted the long granite steps leading to the vast cool corridors of the Supreme Court of the United States has not ex-

perienced a sense of awe? Who that has entered the great chamber where the judges sit has not felt a deep respect for our system
of administering justice? But who as he stares at the august pro-
portions of this dramatic room has not smiled at the recollection
of Chief Justice Stone's suggestion that when the judges enter,
they should be mounted upon elephants? It is only in America
that humor could be mixed with the deadly serious business of
a court that has no parallel in history.

Here in this tribunal for more than a century and a half great
chapters in our national story have been written. Here the laws
of Congress and of the several states have been arraigned at the
bar of justice, and if they contravened the Constitution, have been
struck down by nine men. Here the highest officers of the Government, including Presidents, have been told, "Thus far shalt thou
go and no further." And it was here on a spring day of the year
1952 that the high judges in their black robes sat in solemn con-
clave to listen to the great debate on the extent of Presidential
power to seize private property in peacetime without the judgment of a court.

With one accord the vast steel companies agreed upon one man
as their spokesman. His very presence seemed to lend an added
dignity to the cause he was espousing. Judges and lawyers, and
those who crowded in to watch, looked upon the figure of the
most celebrated appellate advocate of our times. Silence fell
upon the entire assembly as John W. Davis began to speak.

Trailing with him a national and international reputation as a
speaker of rare charm, the possessor of one of the clearest and
best stored legal minds, the prestige of a notable career both in
public life and at the bar, fortified by the strength of a compelling personality, possessed of a singularly gifted power of words,
rare charm, and subtle humor, he gained at once the ear of every

judge and the enthralled admiration of every listener in the courtroom. Here was an advocate worthy of a great cause.

For though in essence all forensic persuasion, whether before juries or a bench of judges, is directed toward the same end, there are many differences in method and approach; many arguments appealing to twelve laymen might not be suited to the more tutored ears and minds of judges. And yet it would be a cardinal mistake for one moment to forget that for all their learning and austere dignity, judges are only men. If you can make your argument come alive, appellate judges will follow you with as much interest as any jury.

I once proved this to my own satisfaction in a case I argued in the Appellate Division of the Third Department of the New York Supreme Court. The appeal involved the correctness of a determination by the Board of Regents of the University of the State of New York that had decided to revoke the license of my doctor client on the ground that he had committed a "fraud in the practice of medicine." As the director of a private clinic, he had permitted an unlicensed physician to serve upon his staff for about three months. There was no doubt whatever of the fact, but the evidence also showed that my client had engaged this man after a brother doctor of unquestionably good standing had recommended him most highly as a physician. My client believed him to be such, and as such had engaged him.

A few weeks before the argument, I received the Attorney General's brief in which a certain case decided by the same Appellate Division was cited at some length, and upon which his principal argument was founded. The case cited was dead against me. I rushed to the library to examine it, and after I had done so, said to my associates: "We will say nothing about this case in our brief; I shall handle it on the argument."

When at last I stood before the appellate court, after explaining the point of the appeal, I said, "Your Honors, I think that here at the outset I should frankly say that the Attorney General has cited a decision of this very court which is on all fours against my contention. It is a well-written opinion, and my adversary has founded a very fair and logical argument on the basis of that case. This authority and his argument would seem to put me completely out of court."

And as the five judges looked at me as though to say, "Then what are you doing here?"—I quickly added: "But, your Honors, there is one further statement that I feel it my duty to make about this authority, and it is this: the Court of Appeals has since unanimously reversed it."

The judges stared at the Attorney General as I went on: "Now my client here has been convicted of fraud in the practice of medicine. Fraud in the practice of medicine! But there is, I believe, such a thing as fraud in the practice of law, and I have always understood that to file a grossly misleading and deceptive brief constituted such a fraud. Now had I not resorted to the simple expedient of examining Shepard's *Citations*, it might well be that my opponent's brief would have misled you into the making of an erroneous decision."

In a silent courtroom I then continued: "But let me at once acquit the Attorney General of fraud in the practice of law by filing a deceptive brief. He has been guilty of no fraud, and if anyone ever charges him with that, I volunteer my services to defend him. Satisfied then, as I am, that he has been guilty of no fraud, I have nonetheless been searching for the right category into which to place his citing a reversed decision without informing you that it had been reversed. What shall I call his act? 'Gross negligence' perhaps? No, on reflection that term seems far too harsh. Searching for the right designation of what he has done, I think at last that I have come upon the correct answer: He is guilty of an 'honest oversight.'

"Of course," I continued, "the slightest effort on his part (through the use of Shepard, for instance) would have revealed to him that this authority had been reversed. An exertion on my client's part (by looking in the *Medical Directory*, for instance) would have disclosed that his unlicensed assistant was in fact unlicensed. Now there is an ancient doctrine of the common law which may be thus stated: What's sauce for the goose is sauce for the gander. And if it is fair, as I think it is, to describe the Attorney General's act as an 'honest oversight,' why is not a similar charity to be extended to my equally honest client?" By this time the judges were smiling, and I sat down. I won that appeal. I remember arguing an appeal from a judgment founded on a jury verdict against a doctor client. The case was this: A well-known and exceptionally able surgeon was once called in the middle of the night to attend a pregnant woman. It was not far from the time when the child might normally be expected. She complained of severe pain in the right lower quadrant of her abdomen in the general vicinity of the appendix. Now, it seems that the symptoms of an inflamed appendix and those of an ectopic gestation (conception in the Fallopian tube, instead of in the uterus) are so similar as to be indistinguishable. Diagnostically, all that the doctor could conclude was that the lady needed either the removal of her appendix or the Fallopian tube, but which he could not tell.

She was rushed to the hospital—a charitable hospital where the nurses were the agents of the hospital, not of the doctor. Instructions were given to prepare the operating room for immediate surgery. Now, since it was impossible for the doctor to determine what he would finally encounter when he made the incision, he directed that sterile dressings (pack-offs) be prepared for either contingency. The pack-offs for an ectopic gestation were wider than those used for an appendectomy, but both were several feet in length, tapering down to a V shape, to which there was attached a tape which, in turn, held fast a steel buckle. The purpose of the steel buckle was to attach it to an artery clamp so that the pack-off would not be lost in the patient's abdomen.

Both sets of pack-offs were placed in the same sterile pan. When the abdomen was opened, the doctor at once saw that what he was dealing with was a conception in the Fallopian tube. During the course of his operation, which was well and skillfully performed, he called from time to time for a pack-off to be used in the abdomen for stanching the surplus blood. As the pack-offs were handed to him, the nurses gave a "sponge count," that is to say, the nurse would count "one in," "two in," "three in," etc. The operation was uneventful and the woman made a prompt and satisfactory recovery—indeed, so satisfactory that she soon became pregnant a second time.

Not long after her second pregnancy, the doctor was again called to her home where she complained of sharp pains in the general vicinity of the operative scar. He could not account for this and, therefore, ordered an X ray. The X ray revealed, all too clearly, the presence of a foreign body, namely, a steel buckle. Now, no patient should be left with a steel buckle inside of her after the operation is completed—or indeed at any time. The doctor, in order not to alarm the lady, did not tell her of his findings, but promptly reported it to her husband and showed him the X ray. Shortly thereafter he performed a second operation in which he removed the buckle and about two yards of the pack-off. Again, she made an uneventful recovery, but she none-theless instituted suit. In this, I had one fact strongly in my fa-vor, namely, that the surgeon had not practiced deception but had been frank and honorable in his dealings with the patient's husband.

My theory of the case was that in the course of the opera-tion, two pack-offs (one of each type) had been inadvertently rolled together as one, so that when the nurse counted "one in," unbeknown to her and, of course, to the doctor, in fact two pack-offs had been inserted, one with the steel buckle attached. The one to which it was affixed was an appendectomy pack-off, and, as will be recalled, the patient was not being operated on for appendicitis; this pack-off therefore, had the nurse not been care-less, should not have been used at all. There were no definite facts to support this theory. It was, therefore, only a theory, and one unsubstantiated by the evidence. I had advanced this theory to the best of my ability before the jury, but without avail. The jury found against me, rendering a substantial verdict for the plaintiff. It was the appeal from this judgment which I am now endeavoring to describe.

The original pack-offs, of course, had long since disappeared, but I had facsimiles (frankly stated to be such) which I took with me to the appellate court. In explaining my theory to the five judges, I took these two samples, rolled them together as I thought must have been done during the operation, and told the court that while I could not prove that it had happened in this way, it seemed to me that the evidence supported this as the only logical theory. I pointed out to the court that a surgeon has only two hands and that in the course of any operation he must rely upon the assistance of nurses, and must trust the sponge count which they give him. Then I remarked that, of course, there was one thing that the doctor could have done which he did not do, and that was to open her abdomen from the pelvis to the neck, take out all of her organs, including her heart and lungs, place them on the operating table, and that in so doing he would undoubtedly have discovered the foreign body. There was, however, this objection to such a course; that had he done so, he would have been guilty of manslaughter, if not murder.

Several weeks following my argument, the court clerk notified me that the judges wanted to see the pack-off exhibits which I had used in the argument. I promptly sent them. After a month or two of additional deliberation, the court accepted my theory and reversed the judgment, and this reversal was sustained by the Court of Appeals.

You may recall my mentioning in a previous chapter the Carnavalle case. When I argued the appeal from that conviction in the Appellate Division, First Department, I had only one legal point of any merit. That point arose at the trial in this way: One of the questions at issue was whether the revolver placed in evidence by the District Attorney belonged to the defendant. The District Attorney wanted badly to prove this fact. To do so, he called the defendant's former mistress and asked her if, when she slept with him, he kept the revolver in question under the pillow. She said that he did keep a revolver under the pillow but was utterly unable to identify the pistol in evidence as the revolver in question.

From being a star witness for the prosecution, she became a considerable witness for the defense. On the redirect examination, the District Attorney then proceeded to assail her character (which, I must admit, was not impeccable). He asked her if she had not been a professional streetwalker. When this question was propounded, I objected and Judge Vernon Davis (one of the finest trial judges I have ever known) asked me the grounds of my objection. I first said that I objected on the ground that the question was irrelevant, incompetent, and immaterial, and as the judge was about to overrule that objection, I added: "And also upon the ground that the District Attorney is seeking to impeach his own witness." Both objections were promptly overruled and a conviction followed.

On the appeal, as I have said, I had only one good legal point, namely, the prosecutor's impeachment of his own witness. Laymen, I am sure, and no doubt many lawyers would regard this as a rather technical legal point. I was afraid that the court might so regard it and, therefore, I told the judges that in order to understand the nature of my overruled objection, I would have to place the point in its proper setting. This gave me an opportunity to discuss the prosecution's witnesses, many of whom had long criminal records and two of whom were brought from Sing Sing to testify. I set forth their characters in as clear and convincing terms as I was capable of doing. The fact that they were of bad character alone would not have brought about a reversal, but no one, judges least of all, likes a man who has spent his life in criminal pursuits. In setting forth the nature of the prosecution's witnesses, I omitted nothing that would add to the disfavor in which I thought they should be regarded, and in the course of my argument resorted to, I am afraid, something of a jury speech. The court reversed the conviction, placing the reversal upon the single point which was the basis of my appeal. But I am sure that my discussion of the other parts of the evidence had brought the court toward a desire to reverse, and having before them a point on which they could reverse, they did so. This reversal was sustained by the Court of Appeals.

The opposite side of this coin was presented to me in an appeal which I once had before the Court of Appeals. The action was for specific performance which, in turn, involved the question of whether or not there had been a contract, performance of which could be compelled. I contended that there was no such contract. There was a judgment in the trial court against my client, which I succeeded in reversing in the Appellate Division.

When the case came on in the Court of Appeals, my opponent, a very able lawyer, made a most vociferous argument in which he attempted to paint my client in a most unattractive light. His argument was eloquent and persuasive and I could see that it was having a considerable effect upon the judges. I turned to my associate as I waited for my opportunity to reply, and said: "If I even start to argue our side in the same way, please kick me in the shin." When finally I stood up, I presented, almost in a monotone, a cold statement of the facts and a short and simple statement of the governing legal principles. As I walked out of court, my client, who had come to hear, evinced obvious disappointment that I had not replied to his assailant in kind. I was sure, however, that I was right in my decision, and the Court of Appeals confirmed my view by sustaining the reversal which I had won below.

The best advice ever given about advocacy in the appellate courts was set forth in an address once delivered before the Association of the Bar by John W. Davis. "Supposing," he said, "fishes had the gift of speech, who would listen to a fisherman's weary discourse on fly-casting . . . if the fish himself could be induced to give his views on the most effective methods of approach? For after all, it is the fish that the angler is after, and all his recondite learning is but the hopeful means to that end."

It is true, is it not, he asked, that "in the argument of an appeal the advocate is angling, conspicuously and deliberately angling for the judicial mind? Whatever tends to attract judicial favor to the advocate's claim may be useful. Whatever repels is useless or worse. The whole art of the advocate consists in choosing the one and avoiding the other. Why otherwise have argument at all?"

With evident appreciation of the decline of advocacy in the appellate courts, he added: "Argument, of course, may be written as well as oral, and under our modern American practice the written argument has certainly become the more extended if not the weightier of the two. As our colleague Joseph Choate, Jr., recently remarked, 'We have now reached the point where we file our arguments in writing, and deliver our briefs orally.'"

Having cast so tempting a bait before the fish, it is not surprising to find them promptly rising to it. John T. Loughran, our beloved late Chief Judge of the New York Court of Appeals, was among the first to come to the surface. In an address delivered before the same association as that which Mr. Davis had so recently delighted, Judge Loughran took note of Mr. Davis' simile of the legal fisherman deliberately angling for the judicial mind and proceeded to provide hints as to how the angler best could make his catch. "I give you as a final word," he said, "the blunt but kindly admonition of Chief Judge Pound to a young lawyer on his first appearance in our court: 'Don't forget that you are talking to seven ordinary men like myself.'"

With so great a volume of work as comes before his court, he said, it must be clear that "the judges approach every case with a strong feeling of the necessity for prompt and exact grasp of the issues to be determined at the consultation table." And then he added: "Note this one point if no other! The chief end—

nay, the sole end of every argument is to equip the judges for the work of their conferences. The main facts are the pivot on which most cases turn, and it is not in the power of man to state them too clearly. In truth it is a personal confession that the charm of a lucid fact presentation seems one of the best arguments of all."

I have often heard office lawyers assert that oral argument in an appellate court is of no importance. But hear what the Chief Judge of the New York Court of Appeals has to say about that. "I know," he said, "that I experience a feeling of distinct disappointment when on the call of a case that falls to me, I hear the clerk say 'Submitted.' When the briefs of a submitted case are picked up at the end of a day that has told heavily, they are dead things. Under those circumstances it is hard for a judge not to feel a diminution of his ardor. The printed word of the ablest advocate, to me at least, falls far short of the same argument when heard face to face through his living voice."

He told about a lawyer's argument in a murder case. Every transition of his thought, said the Chief Judge, was introduced by the phrase, "Now, gentlemen, I expect to show . . ." After the repetition of that phrase a dozen times, he pulled himself up and humbly said to the court, "I beg your Honors' pardon. This is my first time in this court. You see I am used to talking to juries." Thereupon Chief Judge Crain broke in: "Why did you tell us that? We would never have known you were not here before. You talk like an old-timer, and if you want to call us gentlemen, it's all right with us. I hope we are." And when the lawyer had concluded, the Chief Judge said to him, "When you come here again, may you be fortunate to make as good an argument as you did today; and the best part of it is that you were yourself."

He spoke of the intimacy which an oral address breeds be-tween advocate and judge that no printed page can ever bring about. "Even an expression lacking in grace," he said, "often conveys a hidden appeal to the feelings of the court." And then he added: "I shall never forget the counsel who, just before our tired closing hour, half complainingly but with grave earnest-ness said this: 'Now, your Honors, before I sit down, I want to say a word about a brief that has been filed against us by an *ami-cus curiae.* I have to talk about that brief, because if the man who wrote it was a friend of the court, he certainly is no friend of mine.' Instantly," said Judge Loughran, "he had the attention of the whole court."

Still another fish (to use Mr. Davis' phrase) who rose to his bait was the late lamented Bernard Shientag, an extraordi-narily able Justice of the Appellate Division of the First De-partment. In an address before the same bar association two years ago, he said, "The presentation of a good oral argument is an art in itself entirely apart from the preparation of the brief. . . ."

He dwelt on "the importance of the speaking voice," telling us that "its wonderful powers cannot be overestimated. The natural full rich voice, neither too loud nor too low, neither too rapid nor too slow, varying in tone with an occasional lift, an appropri-ate pause, a quiet insistence on a word or a phrase—that type of voice so employed is calculated to hold the attention of the court."

And now for another judge—this time a Justice of the Supreme Court of the United States, Robert H. Jackson. Referring to the piscatorial invitation of Mr. Davis, Justice Jackson began his address before the State Bar Association of California, by saying, "I can only offer some meditations of one of the fish."

As to the value of oral argument, which some lawyers question, he said: "I think the justices would answer unanimously that now, as traditionally, they rely heavily on oral presentations. Most of them form at least a tentative conclusion from it in a large percentage of the cases.

"The very purpose of a hearing," he went on, "is that the court may learn what it does not know, and it knows least about the facts. It may sound paradoxical, but more cases are won or lost on the facts. A large part of the time of conference is given to discussion of facts, to determine under what rule of law they fall."

Like every judge with whom I have ever talked, Justice Jackson stresses the importance of oral argument. "The manner of delivery," he said, "must express the talents and habits of the advocate. No one method is indispensable and practice varies widely. But," he added, "if one's oral argument is simply reading his printed brief aloud, he could as well stay home. If you have confidence to address the court only by reading to it, you really should not argue there."

For the argument of an appeal, preparation is as essential as for the summation to a jury. "Do not think it beneath you," said Justice Jackson, "to rehearse for an argument. Not even Caruso at the height of his artistic career felt above rehearsing for a hundredth performance, although he and his whole staff were guided and confined by a libretto and a score. Of course I do not suggest that you should declaim and gesture before a mirror. But if you have an associate, try out different approaches and thrash out every point with him."

Every busy lawyer relies in part at least on others. But, he adds, "by all means leave at home the associate who feels constantly impelled to tug at your coattails, to push briefs in front of you, or to pass up unasked-for suggestions while you are speaking. These well-meant but ill-conceived offerings distract the attention of the Court, but they are even more embarrassing and confusing to counsel. The offender is an unmitigated pest, and even if he is the attorney who employed you, suppress him."

Through every sentence of Justice Jackson's address we sense his deep conviction as to the high import of the art of advocacy. "So long as controversies between men have to be settled by judges," he said, "proficiency in the art of forensic persuasion will assure one of first rank in our calling."

But, he continued, "if not a lost art, advocacy is an exacting one. When he rises to speak at the bar, the advocate stands intellectually naked and alone. Habits of thought and speech cannot be borrowed like garments for the event. What an advocate gives to a case is himself; he can bring to the bar only what is within him. A part written for him will never be convincing."

And the "most persuasive quality in an advocate," he said, "is personal sincerity. By that I do not mean that he believes in his case as the Mohammedan does in the Koran. But he must believe that under our advisory system, both sides of every controversy should be worthily presented with vigor—even with partisan zeal—so that all material for judgment will be before the Court, and its judgment will suffer no distortion. He must believe with all the intensity of his being in law as a framework of society, in the independent judicial function as the means for applying the law, and in the nobility of his profession as an aid to the judicial process."

Interspersed between his most serious admonitions there runs a vein of humor, and his wit flashes like the mica in granite. Even how the advocate should dress in the Supreme Court was not beneath his notice. He refers to the legend that "Chief Justice Taft once refused admission to the Bar to a candidate who appeared without necktie or waistcoat, with the suggestion that he renew his application when properly attired."

Now the Marshal's office, said Justice Jackson, "kept in active service, and still keeps in moth balls, one or two cutaway coats to lend to counsel in need." You will not be stopped from arguing, he said, "if you wear a race-track suit or sport a rainbow necktie. You will just create a first impression that you have strayed in at the wrong bar."

Let us turn now from Washington to the Supreme Court of New Jersey where Arthur T. Vanderbilt holds undisputed sway as Chief Justice. In 1950, he delivered a series of brilliant lectures at Washington and Lee University on the subject of "Forensic Persuasion." Famed as the former dean of a great law school, as an able advocate in his own day, and latterly as the reorganizer of the whole judicial system of a great state, and finally as the Chief Justice of its highest court, what he said was doubly important, and he said it with grace and humor. He too had some comments to make on the advocate's appearance.

"The court sees counsel," he said, "before it hears him. If he is dressed for the race track rather than the courtroom, the judges will form an impression that even a silver voice and the concourse of sweet sounds will never be able to blot out."

But subjects far more fundamental were considered by the learned Jersey jurist. In the argument of an appeal, he said, there are four factors: (1) the statement of the question, (2) the statement of the facts, (3) the argument of law, and (4) the speaker and his audience.

The four elements, he tells us, must be considered in preparing a brief, "but the written brief, save in the rarest instances, cannot hope to move its readers. It achieves its objective if it convinces. The aim of the oral argument, however, is to persuade. The human presence, and particularly the human voice, can convey meanings, can produce reactions, both favorable and unfavorable, far beyond the power of the printed page. More often than most counsel imagine, the oral argument may change the judge's mind, no matter how carefully he may have studied the briefs in advance."

Counsel, he especially admonished, "should never read from his brief except perhaps the shortest quotation from the most pertinent authorities. His argument should be delivered seemingly extemporaneously, preferably with nothing intervening between him and the court except a one-page outline of his argument which he should keep before him, so as to be sure not to skip any important point due to any interruption from the Bench."

And how important the opening of the argument is, let this experienced judge explain. "Much depends on a good opening," he said. "Counsel should plan and replan his first few sentences until he knows them by heart, without ever having gone through the conscious process of memorizing them. If he can get his airplane off the ground in the first minute or two, the battle of delivery will be half won. Throughout the entire argument counsel must give the impression of complete intellectual earnestness and drive, while at the same time exercising restraint in word and manner."

The ideal opening for an oral argument, he said, "is the plain statement in a simple sentence or two of how the case came to the court, its jurisdiction over the case, and what question or questions are to be argued."

And the greatest art in the argument of an appeal, he went

on, "lies in the statement of the facts of the case. Counsel should know every fact in all its ramifications, and be able to turn to it in the record without fumbling. Heaven forbid, however, that he should attempt in the statement of facts to tell all that he knows of what he should know! He must be able to extract from the record the relatively few facts that are significant and controlling, and to state them in language and in a manner that will capture the attention of the court. It was said of William Murray, better known as Lord Mansfield, the greatest of the English judges, that when he finished the statement of facts in a case, it seemed quite unnecessary to argue the law."

But success in oral argument depends, he said, "to a large extent on the advocate's appearance and bearing, the shades of meaning revealed by a cultivated voice and his style. Intellectual vitality and buoyancy, too, regardless of physical age, is an indispensable quality of great oral argument. Holmes has expressed the thought magnificently in speaking of Sidney Bartlett: 'His manner was no less sturdy than his language. There was in it a dramatic intensity of interest which made him seem the youngest man in the room when he spoke.' "

Stating what I have previously tried to say, but stating it far better, Justice Vanderbilt admonishes us that "the advocate should keep in mind at all times that judges are not really bookish fellows, who have lost their touch with the actualities of life. In their work on the bench they have to deal with everyday problems very much as they did when they were practicing lawyers."

Well, the fish have well responded. They are on the receiving end of counsel's argument; they ought to know what they like and what displeases them. The words of the four judges whom

I have quoted constitute a chart and compass for the course that should light us on our way to the achievement of good advocacy in the appellate courts. They have surely lifted the horizon on at least one field of the vast scene that I have been trying to describe.

CHAPTER

XII

Appellate Advocacy—
The Precepts of a
Master Craftsman

A s we have now heard from the fish, let us turn to watch
our fisherman as he casts his skillful fly—the performance of Mr. Davis was one that Izaak Walton himself might well
have envied.

He confined his address entirely to the oral argument. "I begin," he said, "after the briefs have all been filed, timely filed, of
course, for in this matter lawyers are never—hardly ever—be-
lated. I shall assume that these briefs are marvels of brevity, are
properly indexed, and march with orderly logic from point to
point; not too little nor yet too much on any topic, even though
in a painful last moment of proofreading many an appealing
paragraph has been offered as a reluctant sacrifice on the altar
of condensation."

He noted how in his early years appellate courts seemed to

welcome the announcement: "Submitted on brief"—an attitude, he says, that has now passed away; and you will recall the deep disappointment always felt by Judge Loughran when an advocate before him submitted without oral argument.

In support of his own strong belief in oral argument, Mr. Davis calls two witnesses, one from early England and another from our own times. Lord Coke, he tells us, once declared: "No man alone with all his uttermost labors, nor all the actors in themselves by themselves out of a court of justice, can attain unto a right decision, nor in a court without solemn argument where I am persuaded Almighty God openeth and enlargeth the understanding of those desirous of justice and right."

From our own times he quotes Chief Justice Hughes to the effect that "the desirability of a full exposition by oral argument in the highest court is not to be gainsaid. It is a great saving of time of the court in the examination of extended records and briefs, to obtain the grasp of the case that is made possible by oral discussion and to be able more quickly to separate the wheat from the chaff."

With this introduction, Mr. Davis embarked upon the topic he had chosen by announcing that he had ventured to frame a decalogue by which appellate arguments should be governed, adding with characteristic wit: "There is no mystical significance in the number ten, although it has respectable precedent, and those who think the number short and who wish to add to the roll when I have finished, have my full permission to do so."

I, for one, acknowledge my total inability to accept that invitation, or to attempt any addition to his decalogue. Far abler men than I might well be equally discouraged from an essay so bold.

For his first rule, Mr. Davis gives us this:

(1) "Change places, in your imagination of course, with the court."

In doing this he cautions us to remember that demigods do not people our appellate courts; that some judges are learned, some are less so; some are keen and perspicacious, some have more plodding minds. "In short," he says, "they are men and lawyers just like the rest of us. They know nothing of the facts, and hope that the advocate will furnish them the implements of decision." Your mere presence before the court constitutes an implied promise to furnish them, and you must try to think what it is if you were a judge that you would first want to know about the case. "How and in what order," asks Mr. Davis, "would you want the story told? How would you want the skein unraveled?"

For his second rule he gives us this:

(2) "State the nature of the case and briefly its prior history."

Since the procession of cases before appellate courts covers many and diverse fields, "Why not," asks Mr. Davis, "tell the Court at the outset, to which of these fields its attention is about to be called?" Your case may involve some profound question of constitutional law or perhaps the construction of a will or it may be some question arising in the settlement of a partnership. Whatever it may be, if the general nature of the case is mentioned, the judge may at once "call to his aid, consciously or unconsciously, his general knowledge and experience with that particular subject. It brings what is to follow into immediate focus."

Having done this, he says, "for the greater ease of the Court in listening, it is well to give at once the history of the case in so far as it bears on the Court's jurisdiction," and sometimes, he rather whimsically adds, "there may be, I am sure, a certain anxiety to know just whose judicial work it is that the Court is called upon to review. For judges, like other men, judge each other as well as the law."

But if you mention the trial judge, may I add, be sure that your approach is as deft and subtle as the suggestion just made. No matter what your sense of outrage at the rulings of the court below, do not show your anger, especially in your voice. "There is no record," writes Justice Vanderbilt, "of any appeal having been won by being ill-tempered."

Nor, says the Chief Justice of the Supreme Court of New Jersey, "does it ever pay to attack the trial judge, whose opinion is being reviewed. I have heard counsel start his argument by saying, 'This is an appeal from a judgment by Judge A. but there are numerous other good reasons for reversal.' This is good for a smile from the lawyers in the courtroom, or maybe from the court, but it never pays. Reviewing courts, in particular, dislike personalities. They have their own way of taking care of blundering trial judges, if counsel by his ineptness does not make it impossible."

Continuing this digression with Justice Vanderbilt, he drew on his own experience, saying: "I remember a case in which I argued the appeal, when the court below had done almost everything that it should not have done. In the first draft of my brief, I dealt with the trial judge without mercy, but in my second draft and in my oral argument, I treated the offender with urbane respect. My restraint was rewarded with an opinion of reversal which started: 'The case is so curiously replete with error that our only difficulty is to decide on what ground we ought to put the necessary reversal.'"

And now returning to Mr. Davis, let us attend to his third commandment. It is this:

(3) "State the facts."

There is, he said, a sentence of Daniel Webster's "which should be written on the walls of every law school, courtroom, and law office: 'The power of clear statement is the great power of the bar.' Purple passages can never supply its absence. And of course I must add that no statement of the facts can be considered as complete, unless it has been so framed and delivered as to show forth the essential merit, in justice and in right, of your client's cause."

It cannot be too much emphasized, he said, that "in an appellate court, the statement of the facts is not merely a part of the argument, it is more often than not the argument itself. A case well stated is far more than half argued. Yet how many advocates fail to realize that the ignorance of the court concerning the facts of the case is complete, even where their knowledge of the law may adequately satisfy the proverbial presumption. The court wants above all things to learn what are the facts which give rise to the call upon its energies; for in many, probably in most cases, when the facts are clear there is no trouble about the law."

How should the facts be presented? "Of course," he says, "there are statements and statements. No two men probably would adopt an identical method of approach. Uniformity is impossible, probably undesirable. Safe guides, however, are to be found in the three C's—chronology, candor, and clarity. Chronology, because that is the natural way of telling any story, stringing the events on the chain of time just as all human life itself proceeds; candor, the telling of the worst as well as the best, since the court has the right to expect it, and since any lack of candor, real or apparent, will wholly destroy the most careful argument; and clarity, because that is the supreme virtue in any effort to communicate thought from man to man. It admits of no substitute."

And now watch as more fish are rising to the fly of our master fisherman. "The main facts," says Chief Judge Loughran, "are the pivot on which most cases turn. And it is not in the power of man to state them too clearly. Unless the case is before the court by its own leave, the judges will probably know very little about the controversy before the argument begins. Let the main facts be brought forward, and they will vitalize the whole discussion as it proceeds thereafter. Let the main facts be clouded by a slipshod statement of them, and the rest of the argument is as good as lost. In truth it is a personal confession that the charm of a lucid fact presentation seems one of the best arguments of all."

And from Mr. Justice Jackson we hear this: "The purpose of the hearing is that the court may learn what it does not know, and it knows least about the facts. It may sound paradoxical, but most contentions of law are won or lost on the facts."

And now for Mr. Davis' fourth commandment:

(4) "State next the applicable rules of law on which you rely."

If a statement of facts has been properly done, he says, "the mind of the court will already have sensed the legal questions at issue, indeed they may have been hinted at as you proceed. These may be so elementary and well established that a mere allusion to them is sufficient. On the other hand, they may be in the field of divided opinion where it is necessary to expound them at greater length and to dwell on the underlying reasons that support one or the other view."

It may be, he went on, that "in these days of what is apparently waning health of our old friend *stare decisis,* one can rely less than heretofore upon the assertion that the case at bar is governed by such and such a case, volume and page. Even the shadow of a long succession of governing cases may not be adequate shelter. In any event the advocate must be prepared to meet any challenge to the doctrine of the cases on which he relies and to support it by original reasoning. Barren citation is a broken reed. What virtue it retains can be left for the brief."

Echoing somewhat the same thought, Justice Jackson said that "if the authority for your contention is a decision, of course you must make clear its meaning and application. But if one or two best precedents will not convince, a score of weaker ones will only reveal the weakness of your argument. I always look with suspicion upon a proposition with a page full of citations in its support. . . . If the overruling of a decision is all that will save you, go about asking it directly and candidly. But if your case can be supported by court decisions, it will not be wise to confuse it with even a good quotation from a dissent."

And now let us consider the fifth commandment which Mr. Davis has laid down:

(5) "Always 'go for the jugular vein.' "

The phrase is a familiar one, although Mr. Davis tells us that he does not know from what source he quoted it. "More often than not," he says, "there is in every case a cardinal point around which lesser points revolve like planets around the sun, or even as dead moons around a planet; a central fortress which if strongly held will make the loss of all the outworks immaterial.

The temptation is always present to 'let no guilty point escape' in the hope that if one hook breaks, another may hold. Yielding to this temptation is pardonable in a brief, of which the court may read as much or as little as it chooses. There minor points can be inserted to form 'a moat defensive to a house.' But there is no time and rarely any occasion in oral argument for such diversions."

Mr. Davis cited the late John G. Johnson, of Philadelphia, as an excellent example of this fifth commandment. "He was a man of commanding physical presence and of an intellect equally robust. Before appellate courts he addressed himself customarily to but a single point, often speaking for not more than twenty minutes, but with compelling force. When he had concluded, it was difficult for his adversary to persuade the court that there was anything else worthy to be considered. This is the quintessence of the advocate's art."

And now for the sixth commandment in our decalogue:

(6) "Rejoice when the court asks questions."

As though he were speaking from a pulpit, which in many senses was the case, Mr. Davis exclaims: "And again I say unto you, rejoice! If the question does nothing more, it gives you assurance that the court is not comatose and that you have awakened at least a vestigial interest. Moreover a question affords you your only chance to penetrate the mind of the court, unless you are an expert in face reading, and to dispel a doubt as soon as it arises. This you should be able to do if you know your case and have a sound position. . . . Nothing I should think would be more irritating to an inquiring court than to have refuge taken in the familiar evasion 'I am coming to that' and then to have the argument end with the promise unfulfilled. If you are really coming to it, indicate what your answer will be when it is reached and never, never sit down until it is made."

"Do not," he said, "get into your head that there is a deliberate design on the part of any judge to embarrass counsel by questions. His mind is seeking help, that is all, although it may be that he calls for help before he really needs it."

And then he adds this word of encouragement: "Judges are more annoyed by each other's questions than counsel, I have observed. I remember a former justice of the Supreme Court much given to interrogation, who engaged counsel in a long colloquy of question and answer at the very threshold of the argument. In a stage whisper audible within the bar Chief Justice White was heard to moan, 'I want to hear the argument.' 'So do I, damn him,' growled his neighbor, Justice Holmes. Yet questions fairly put and frankly answered give to oral argument a vitality and spice that nothing else will supply."

This was his seventh commandment:

(7) "Read sparingly and only from necessity."

"The eye is the window of the mind," he said, "and the speaker does not live who can long hold the attention of any audience without looking it in the face. There is something about a sheet of paper interposed between speaker and listener that walls off the mind of the latter as if it were boiler plate. It obstructs the passage of thought as the lead plate bars the X rays.

"I realize," said Mr. Davis, "that I am taking just this risk at present, but this is not a speech or an argument, only, God save the mark, a lecture."

And now for his eighth commandment:

(8) "Avoid personalities."

"This," he said, "is a hard saying especially when one's feelings are ruffled by a lower court or by opposing counsel, but nonetheless it is worthy of all acceptation, both in oral argument and in brief. I am not speaking merely of the laws of courtesy that must always govern an honorable profession, but rather of the sheer inutility of personalities as a method of argument in a judicial forum. Nor am I excluding proper comment on things that deserve reprobation. I am thinking psychologically again. It is a question of keeping the mind of the court on the issues in hand without distraction from without."

Mr. Davis' ninth commandment is:

(9) "Know your record from cover to cover."

This commandment, he said, "might properly have headed the list for it is the *sine qua non* of all effective argument. You have now reached a point in the litigation where you can no longer hope to supply the want of preparation by lucky accidents or mental agility. You will encounter no more unexpected surprises. You have your last chance to win for your client. It is clear therefore that the field tactics of the trial table will no longer serve and the time has come for major strategy based upon an accurate knowledge of all that has occurred. At any moment you may be called on to correct some misstatement of your adversary and at any moment you may confront a question from the court which, if you are able to answer by an apt reference to the record or with a firm reliance on a well-furnished memory, will increase the confidence with which the court will listen to what else you have to say. Many an argument otherwise admirable has been destroyed because of counsel's inability to make just such a response."

And now in two short words comes the tenth and last commandment:

(10) "Sit down."

When you have run through your outline previously prepared, he says, "and are satisfied that the court has fully grasped
your contentions, what else is there left for you to do?" The
mere fact that you have been allotted an hour more or less, does
not "constitute a contract with the court to listen for that length
of time."

On the contrary, he observes, "when you round out your argument and sit down before your time has expired, a benevolent
smile overspreads the faces on the bench and a sigh of relief and
gratification arises from your brethren at the bar who have been
impatiently waiting for the moment when the angel might again
trouble the waters of the healing pool and permit them to step
in. Earn these exhibitions of gratitude therefore whenever you
decently can, and leave the rest to Zeus and his colleagues, that
is to say, to the judges on high Olympus."

With his permission, I have given you a good part of what
Mr. Davis told the Association of the Bar in his justly celebrated
lecture. I have done so because nowhere else has the subject been
so well, so fully, and so brilliantly presented. In that address you
will find all that usefully could be said about arguing an appeal.
Of all he ever said or wrote, this address, I think, will be remembered longest. Yet only after many years of experience will
lawyers fully realize and appreciate the wisdom of his admonitions.

Perhaps a little of his warm and glowing personality has
come through to you from his words which I have quoted. But
you would have to know him well to appreciate the rare quality

of this man, for he is *sui generis*. There is nothing like him any-where. Why, when it takes so long to make a man like that, why all of God's handiwork must be one day struck down, is a question particularly difficult to answer in his case.

Some day, many years hence let us hope, when he can speak no more, the sculptor will take over, and even as the figure of Rufus Choate looks out upon the generations of Boston lawyers, so in the rotunda of the Supreme Court in Washington, a noble bronze will eloquently portray the face and form of the most brilliant advocate who ever argued there.

XIII

Barristers and Solicitors—
A Plea for a
Divided Bar

A N INTELLIGENT DIVISION of labor is the most certain means of assuring labor well performed. From the dawn of time some men have been fitted for some tasks, other men for other tasks. The earliest proof of this that I have ever come upon is found in the Book of Exodus.

You will recall how it is there recorded that the Lord commanded Moses to go to Pharaoh and tell him to set free the Children of Israel, and that he give the same message to Pharaoh's slaves. Moses demurred, and after offering excuses, finally said: "O my Lord, I am not eloquent. . . . I am of slow speech and of a slow tongue." And the Lord then sought to reason with him, saying: "Now therefore go, and I will be with thy mouth and tell thee what to say." But when Moses still expressed unwillingness to go, the Lord said: "Is not Aaron the Levite thy brother? I know he can speak well . . . thou shalt speak unto him and put words into his mouth; and I will be with thy mouth and shall teach you what you shall do. And he shall be thy spokesman unto the people; and he shall be, even he shall be to thee instead of a mouth, and thou shalt be to him instead of God."

The Lord himself thus recognized that an unwilling or an incapable speaker was no one to send upon a mission of persuasion. He recognized too the importance of good briefing, and the need of giving even a good advocate all possible help by putting the right words into his mouth. He saw that good advocacy was a special art to be practiced only by one previously equipped for it, and that the man who was not eloquent but slow of speech still had a most important role, namely, that of suggesting to the advocate the line of approach that he should follow.

If the separate professions of barristers and solicitors were not then born, the nature of the two professions, the difference between them, and the respective and complementary roles that they must play were clearly discerned by the most attentive of all observers. I shall not be irreverent enough to suggest that the sobriquet of "mouthpiece" was also born of that interview.

Of all that I have been able to read about English lawyers, I have never seen it suggested that the difference between barristers and solicitors is traceable to the Book of Exodus, yet it is clear that the origin of English advocacy is found in the Church. The story of the Inns of Court goes back to the Crusades, which we all know were inspired by religious motives. And today as at all times during the eight centuries of recorded legal history, the barristers (the near equivalent of our American trial lawyers) and the solicitors (who perform the work done by our office lawyers in America) stand poles apart. Only the barrister may be heard in the courts of record; the solicitor pre-pares the case which some barrister will present.

Both barristers and solicitors are concerned with the admin-istration of justice; both serve litigants, but they serve them in different ways. An English citizen with a case that must be handled does not go directly to the barrister; a solicitor is first engaged, and it is he who finds and interviews the witnesses, pre-pares the papers and the brief, and attends to the whole work of preparation. And then when finally all the routine work is done, it is the solicitor rather than the client who chooses which among the barristers is the best fitted for the conduct of the particular case in hand. Having made the choice, he walks one day down the Strand and turns up Chancery Lane, or perhaps on through Holborn and into Gray's Inn Road, until he comes to the par-ticular Inn where the advocate of his choice maintains his cham-bers. He brings with him a brief on which the retaining fee is marked.

The brief is much like our trial briefs here, but is better done, and it contains detailed advice (called "instructions") which serves not only as a guide to the theory on which the case should be conducted but something close to a directive as to how the particular witnesses should be examined or cross-examined. Now, the barrister may differ with the solicitor's "instructions," in which case he will discuss the matter with the solicitor, and will, if possible, arrive at some acceptable solution, or, if not, will decline the brief. With regard to the fee, however, there is no room for bargaining at all. He may accept it or reject it as he chooses, but he may not argue about it. And if thereafter the promised fee is not paid, he has no cause of action to compel its payment, for the payment of a barrister is not regarded as a matter of contract at all; it is still considered as something in the nature of a gratuity.

Now, when the barrister accepts the case, from that time on he assumes the whole conduct of the lawsuit. It is he alone, of course, who is authorized or permitted to plead the case in court, to examine and cross-examine the witnesses, address the jury and the judge. In doing this he will not forget the "instructions" his solicitor has given him, although under the exigencies of the moment he may deviate widely from the brief that has been handed him. But at no time during the trial does the solicitor (who, though present, is seated on a lower bench) participate in any way, except by the handing up of an occasional note to the barrister.

Nothing could be sharper, then, than the line which divides and separates the two callings. And there always was, and I believe still is, something like a social barrier between them: the same sort of thing perhaps that separates the proprietor of a retail store from the master of a great wholesale emporium, a difference similar to that which divides officers from enlisted men, for barristers in the early days were recruited solely from the upper classes. A barrister was supposed to be a gentleman, an esquire, whereas solicitors came from a lower social order; they were not expected to be "gentlemen" or the sons of "gentlemen."

In America we speak of ourselves as belonging to the "legal profession," a category that includes every duly licensed practitioner. In England, however, any barrister would strenuously object to being included in that category; only solicitors are spoken of as belonging to the "legal profession." A barrister is not a member of a profession, he is "a member of the bar," a man given the right of audience in court. Yet no barrister could be found who would not gladly be called a "great lawyer."

A barrister must stand aloof from the commercial aspects of law. He does not have a law office in the City; he maintains "chambers" in one of the four Inns of Court situated in a kind of park ending in the Temple Gardens that slope down to the Victoria Embankment. In this restricted and highly isolated area, once far removed from the heart of the City but now almost in the center of roaring London, is the birthplace of English law, the nursery of English advocacy, and the cradle of all English legal institutions. And among all of her traditions there is none more impervious to change than the gulf that divides her barristers from the solicitors or "attorneys," as they are sometimes called.

An old rule of one of the Inns of Court referred to an "attorney" as "an immaterial person of an inferior character." Indeed, within the memory of men still living, there was a side door of an old house fronting on Lincoln's Inn Fields, on which there was a brass plate with this legend: TRADESMEN AND ATTORNEYS—the owner evidently regarding them with equal repugnance.

But nothing that I have read has impressed on me the lowly status of the attorneys in Great Britain so much as the comment once made by Dr. Samuel Johnson. He was attending an evening party with a group of friends back in the year 1770. One of the gentlemen present left before the others. A discussion then arose as to who this man might be. At this point, Dr. Johnson observed: "I do not care to speak ill of any man behind his back, but I believe the gentleman was an attorney."

Why is it that in England the barrister has so separate a status, and one so respected? The answer, as with all English institutions, is imbedded deep in English history. It harks back to the twelfth century and the Crusades. Returning from the Holy

Wars, the Knights Templar, in the year 1180, acquired a large meadow that sloped down to the River Thames and stretched from Whitefriars on the east to Essex Street on the west. Here they made a lordly dwelling place, and in this area they built the Round Church which stood as their memorial until Hitler's airmen finally destroyed it.

At the beginning of the fourteenth century, this land passed into the possession of two societies of lawyers. From these societies arose the four Inns of Court: the Inner and the Middle Temple, Gray's Inn and Lincoln's Inn. Chaucer, in his *Canterbury Tales,* takes note of the Temple as an abode of lawyers. Long before the reign of Queen Elizabeth, the Inns of Court had come to be one of the leading universities of England, called by Ben Jonson "the noblest nurseries of humanity and liberty in the Kingdom." Here the apprentices of the law took up their quarters, and here in the Inns of Court the English profession was born. And here where Christianity was fostered and protected, monastic traditions lingered on to permeate the customs and the attitudes of these great law training schools.

Here too the echoes of chivalry reverberated between Holborn and the Strand, Kingsway and Chancery Lane. From this source the title of "serjeant-at-law" was derived. The badge of these high-ranking officers of the law was the coif, reminiscent of the pads worn by the armored knights between their helmets and their heads. These serjeants were at the top of the bar, and their order, Pollock and Maitland tell us, was well known before the year 1275. From their ranks alone were judges chosen. These serjeants-at-law, *servientes ad legem,* as they were called, lost most of their prerogatives in the year 1846, and the last serjeant-at-law died in the year 1921.

It was in the days of Edward the First that a new rank of lawyers known as *apprecenti-ad-legem* was apprenticed to the ser-jeants-at-law, the graduate journeymen of their profession, for the Inns of Court were, among other things, lawyers' guilds. These apprentices were called barristers. In due course, the barrister superseded the old serjeants, and the barristers were in turn divided between King's Counsel (the highest rank) and ordinary barristers. The King's Counsel wore (and still wear) silk gowns—hence a rise to this rank was known as "taking silk." The junior or ordinary barristers wore the humble stuff gowns. No barrister could become a King's Counsel—a K.C.—until he had been at the bar for at least five years.

But all barristers wear gowns (whether silk or stuff) when they appear in court, set off by a wig and white cravat. The costume gives them a sense of belonging to an elite corps, as well as maintaining a steady continuity with the past. The robed barristers in their pewlike seats facing the jury tier on tier and the judge in his full-bottomed wig and scarlet gown seated high upon the bench present to the onlooker an atmosphere almost ecclesiastical. To the visiting American lawyer, the scene appears at first almost theatrical. But as he hears and watches, he soon sees how well adapted are the costumes of all who participate in the work of high import that is taking place before him and he becomes aware of the glorious and brilliant past, of which both judges and barristers are the proud heirs.

They were all trained in the Inns of Court and are all members of one of the four Inns: Gray's Inn, Lincoln's Inn, the Inner, or the Middle Temple—though the judges perforce have severed their connection on mounting to the bench. In those Inns they had all been trained under the guidance and instruction of some senior barrister whom they served as student apprentices. Through the ages the apprentice system has been as rigorously applied there as in the guilds where master craftsmen passed on to their apprentices all that they had learned through a laborious life-time of hard application. From the masters of the law the neo-phytes not only acquired a sound knowledge of legal principles but went to court with them to watch their seniors applying them in innumerable cases.

In the Inns and in the courts the aspiring would-be advocates acquired not only a training in the difficult vocation they had chosen but an acquaintance with the great traditions of the bar, its history, its true function, and its indispensable position in the administration of justice. Under the guiding hands of special-ists they too at last became specialists themselves.

The story of the Inns of Court is one of the noble and impor-tant chapters of English history, a record of the growth of English law, an explanation of the exalted place it occupies in English thinking. Here in these Inns the great traditions of Eng-lish law were handed down from generation to generation. Young men aspiring to be advocates were here taught the purpose and the possibilities of advocacy.

The student was finally not "admitted to the bar" as in America by the court; he was "called to the bar" by one of the Inns. And from the beginning, a strange prerequisite was that he should have "kept twelve terms" in some one of the Inns. There were four terms in each year; the keeping of twelve terms, there-fore, embraced a period of three years. The terms were kept by dining in the Great Hall. Each novitiate, therefore, had met and conversed with many barristers and benchers before his twelve terms had been completed. So that barristers and benchers too—the governing members of the Inn—had thus been afforded the fullest opportunity for appraising not only the intellectual but the personal and social qualifications of the candidate. And this appraisal was no idle thing, for the sole and exclusive power of accepting or rejecting a candidate, with or without stated cause, rested with the benchers.

The benchers are indeed important; with them, not with the court (as in America), rests all disciplinary power over those who have been called to the bar; and from their determinations there is no judicial appeal of any kind.

The Inns of Court were a combination of law school, private club, lawyers' trade guild, and dormitory for their members. It is not strange then that a peculiar romance and glamor, through the centuries, has surrounded them. Nor is it to be wondered at that English barristers are a kind of homogeneous race apart, as proud of their traditions, their standards, and their history as the officers, let us say, of the Coldstream Guards. They are an elite corps, of which there is no parallel in the United States or elsewhere.

Like so many American lawyers before me, my first visit to these Inns of Court (back in the good days before Hitler's bombs had wrought havoc there) was like wandering in a kind of golden dream—a sort of premature admittance to the Promised Land. I stood between the polished Purbeck marble pillars and gazed at the oblong nave of the Round Church of the Order of Knights Templar, and saw there the tomb of the ancient "warriors of Christ," and as I came out, I looked with fascination at the eighteenth-century architectural beauty of the Master's House.

I walked along the Victoria Embankment to take in the loveliness of the Temple Gardens. Coming finally upon the Middle Temple, I dreamt of the days when Chaucer lived and wrote there, and of that later century when Oliver Goldsmith made this his abode, and Blackstone penned his *Commentaries*, and of that far distant evening when Shakespeare produced his *Twelfth Night* before the admiring gaze of Queen Elizabeth.

Enthralled, I took in the beauty of Fountain Court, and standing in admiration before Middle Temple Hall, I thought of the way in which Thackeray in his *Pendennis* and Dickens in his *Martin Chuzzlewit* had described this place. Middle Temple Lane brought me at last to Fleet Street and the Middle Temple Gate House which the genius of Sir Christopher Wren had put there, back in the days of James the Second. Passing thence across Fleet Street, I walked up Chancery Lane and gazed almost with rapture through Old Square at Lincoln's Inn. And as I entered the Benchers' Room, my eyes fell upon the great portrait of William Pitt that Gainsborough so long ago had put there. Turning, I looked into the face of Thomas Erskine of Lawrence's incomparable canvas.

Up at the eastern wing, I thought of the Drill Hall of the Inns of Court Volunteers, and the days of the Spanish Armada, when the barristers made themselves into an armed force for the defense of their country, and I thought of the reign of King Charles the First, when students and benchers, too, were given royal encouragement to perfect themselves in horsemanship and the handling of arms, little dreaming that a majority of them would follow an old graduate of Lincoln's Inn, named Oliver Cromwell.

I thought too of the days a century and a half later, when Napoleon was assembling his flatboats at Boulogne, preparatory to an invasion of Great Britain, when the barristers had formed themselves into companies to repel the invasion.

The Temple companies were commanded by Thomas Erskine. And there came a memorable day when a Grand Review of all volunteers was held in Hyde Park. King George the Third reviewed them. Erskine and his men came finally abreast of the reviewing stand, and as they did so, the King noticed the famed advocate, and called him. "What are these men?" he asked. "They are all lawyers, sir," said Erskine. "What, what," the King exclaimed—"all lawyers? Then call them the Devil's Own!"

Many stories, some no doubt apocryphal, have come down to us about the Temple Companies. One recounts how Lord Eldon and Lord Ellenborough were dismissed because they found it impossible to keep step. Another tells us how when the command "Charge!" was given, every member of the corps whipped out his notebook and wrote down six and eightpence; while still another recounts the proposal that there be inscribed upon their banners: "Retained for the Defense."

From Holborn I passed up Gray's Inn Road where, with quadrangle upon quadrangle enclosing a large greensward, stood beautiful Gray's Inn. "Nothing else in England," wrote our own Nathaniel Hawthorne, "is so like the effect of a spell, as to pass under one of these archways and find yourself transported from the jumble, rush, tumult, uproar, as of an age of weekdays condensed into the present hour, into what seems an eternal Sabbath. It is very strange to find so much of ancient quietude right in the monster city's very jaws. . . ."

Now, alas, however, little of all these glorious ancient monuments remains. Lincoln's Inn alone escaped the ruin of Hitler's bombs. Grievous damage was done the Middle and the Inner Temple, and Gray's Inn was almost totally destroyed, while the ancient Temple Church was left a weak and shaky structure. "But," says Justice Jackson, "perhaps the scars in the shrines and temples of the Bar are symbolic, for no intellectual force more consistently and uncompromisingly resisted the lawlessness and absolutism of Hitler than the spirit of the common law which radiated from these ancient landmarks."

But no physical landmarks, however durable, could in the matter of indestructibility compare with the spirit of the English Bar. Is it any wonder then that we American lawyers look with admiration, and perhaps no little envy, at the calling of the advocate as it is recognized and practiced in Great Britain?

From the long roll of England's barristers have come great and distinguished advocates, gifted counselors, incomparable leaders of public opinion, leaders in the House of Commons and in the Cabinet, Prime Ministers, and, of course, judges of a kind that seldom are vouchsafed to other lands. There is nothing to compare with them anywhere else on earth.

Why are English judges so uniformly excellent? One reason must be that they are appointed from the roll of those who have devoted a lifetime to the conduct of litigation in court—that is, from the barristers. An English judge, therefore, is a man who has been an advocate, and through advocacy has learned how a case should be conducted before a court and jury. A solicitor could no more be made a judge than he could be made an admiral of the fleet. A law teacher or writer would have as much chance of mounting to the bench as he would of becoming the chief surgeon of a great hospital.

In dividing through the centuries all lawyers into advocates and those who are not allowed to plead in court, it is plain that the English have been satisfied that this division of labor is a wise one. It was the choice between Aaron who could "speak well," and Moses who was "slow of speech and of a slow tongue." It was a choice between those who were and those who were not, either by training, inclination, or ability, adapted to the role of advocacy. It was a natural and intelligent choice. Like most English institutions, it was founded upon common sense, upon a deep perception of reality rather than upon cold logic. The French are logical, the Irish are logical, the English are essentially not a logical people, yet they have made a greater contribution to the cause of human liberty than all the rest of civilization. And no one unaware of this can ever understand the growth of the common law and the development of the principles of equity.

Since our law and all our legal principles were taken by us from Great Britain, why is it, one may ask, that we did not also accept their division of lawyers into the separate rolls of barrister and solicitor? The reason in part lies, I think, in the early American jealousy of courts and lawyers, considering them both as unpleasant reminders of what we regarded as the tyranny of the mother country. Nor were our early courts, manned as they were by nonprofessional judges, before whom a Bar indifferently prepared, and with whom law practice was a part-time avocation, well calculated to allay hostility toward both Bench and Bar.

Moreover, in the days before the Revolution, royal governors did little to encourage the colonial lawyers whom they regarded as a race of troublemakers. During the Revolution, the hostility toward lawyers that is always found in times of great convulsions was particularly manifest. After Yorktown the wave of egalitarian philosophy did not subside, and a generation that had been told that all men are created equal regarded it as a logical corollary that all careers are open to every man regardless of his education, fitness, or ability. They strongly believed that experts and specialists of any kind were worthy only of the scorn of a boisterous democracy. To such a generation, the idea of robed and bewigged barristers being alone given audience in court smacked of sheer class distinction to which our forefathers, and we their descendants, are constitutionally opposed.

Yet before Bunker Hill, there were young men in the colonies who wished to learn what English barristers could teach, and then to follow in their footsteps. Between 1760 and the Revolution, a hundred and fifteen American students were educated at the Inns of Court. Five signers of the Declaration of Independence, five delegates to the Continental Congress which adopted the Articles of Confederation, and six of the signatories of the United States Constitution were graduates of the Middle Temple.

These graduates, however, were not numerous enough to change a young democracy's distrust of both courts and lawyers. In John Adams' time, the practice of the law was largely in the hands of deputy sheriffs, and even constables. Hoping to change all this, he tells us of a meeting called to pass regulations "for confining the practice of law to those who were educated to it and sworn to fidelity in it," and to introduce among those who were practicing "more regularity, candor, and politeness as well as honor." These aims were not greatly forwarded, he feared.

But there was a growing struggle to introduce some orderly study of law in the colleges. To this end, William and Mary established the first regular law professorship in America. Eleven years later, James Wilson, an Associate Justice of the Supreme Court, became a professor of law at the College of Philadelphia. Lack of interest, however, compelled the abandonment of his courses in 1793, in which latter year James Kent began his lectures at Columbia, only to meet the same fate that had befallen Justice Wilson. Up in the beautiful village of Litchfield, Connecticut, the little school of law that Judge Tapping Reeve began proved more successful.

Yet neither in these schools nor elsewhere from the Revolution to this day do I find the record of any concentrated effort to adopt along with English law, the institution of a separate barrister class, of dividing the barristers from the solicitors—a program that has worked well in England for eight centuries.

That it still works well, will, I think, be acknowledged by any lawyer who has spent busman's holiday, as I often have, in the Old Bailey or in the Law Courts on the Strand. The unaccustomed setting may seem strange to you at first: the judge in his scarlet gown and full-bottomed wig, the bewigged barristers in their gowns. But you will forget all this as you observe the skill with which these specialists conduct their work. Objections to the evidence are few, and the colloquies are conducted in a polite tone and with well-modulated voices. Through them the beauty and the compass of the English language make it seem almost a different tongue. The direct examinations are short and to the point, the cross-examinations models of brevity and pith. Small wonder then that the English public looks with awe almost akin to reverence upon the proceedings in their courts.

Returning to the United States, while the memory of your visit is still fresh, if you visit almost any American court, you cannot fail to be impressed by the difference between what you see and hear there and that which you have so lately witnessed in Great Britain. The lawyers here will seem almost like amateurs compared with their English brothers. The sure touch of the specialist is lacking. What you will see nine times out of ten is a performance infinitely inferior to that of the trained English barrister. Here, what in England would be a solicitor may be seen struggling with a task for which he is unequipped either by training, temperament, or ability.

Is it impossible or too late in this country to create a special group of lawyers similar to the barristers of England? If it could be done, would it be desirable? I think it is neither impossible nor too late, and I am certain that it would be desirable.

We could not import the century-old traditions that have come down from the days of the Crusades. We have nothing like the Inns of Court nor any of the ancient glory that surrounds them. We have no Temple Gardens, no Pump Court, no Fountain Court, no Chancery Lane nor Lincoln's Inn. We have nothing like the Inner or the Middle Temple, no Gray's Inn nor any of the romance that haunts these noble palaces, yet in the history of the American Bar, comparatively brief as it is, we have had many advocates the full equal of England's best in any age.

No graduate of any of the Inns of Court ever surpassed our own Alexander Hamilton or John Adams or Daniel Webster, and the long roll supplies many others. There stands Abraham Lincoln! The voices of William Evarts, Henry Stanbery, William Groesbeck, and Thomas Nelson of Tennessee echo down the years from their great defense of President Andrew Johnson. In our times we have had Joseph Choate and Delancy Nicoll, Elihu Root and John G. Johnson, Martin Littleton and William Travers Jerome, and John W. Davis, who, thank God, is still with us.

All of these were the full equals of the finest English barrister. But with the exception of Mr. Davis, there are few heirs indeed of America's great advocates of the past. Not only are our greatest advocates all dead; advocacy has died with them—or nearly died. I do not believe that it has died; I propose that it be revived. Most of the law schools are indifferent to the subject, with the consequent indifference on the part of nearly all their students.

This may account for the Bar's loss of leadership in the United States, a loss so eloquently deplored by Chief Justice Harlan F. Stone in a famous article published in the Harvard *Law Review*. The practice of the law has been greatly altered by the advent of enormous law firms wherein few or no trial lawyers may be found. The offices of these firms have no resemblance to the chambers of a London barrister. In these are collected eighty or more lawyers who are in reality solicitors who for the most part perform the work done by the solicitor in Great Britain. "In my own city," Judge Learned Hand has written, "the best minds of the profession are scarcely lawyers at all. They may be something much better, or much worse; but they are not that. With courts they have no dealings whatever, and would hardly know what to do in one if they came there. Indeed, the situation has become such that I cannot quite see how a system of jurisprudence dependent upon precedent is permanently to get on at all with its best talent steadily drawn away from the precedent makers."

Great though my admiration for the English system is, in one respect, I think, our own has an advantage. An English barrister does not, as a rule, interview his client; it is done for him by the solicitor. This detachment, it seems to me, deprives the barrister of that very first-hand knowledge of the case and of the man he represents, the importance of which cannot be exaggerated. But this detachment is not an essential or necessary part of the English system.

My proposal is that we here in America create and recognize the separate roles of barristers and solicitors, and divide them one from the other as in England. I plead then for a divided bar, to the end that those best fitted for either branch of the profession be definitely placed there. In the process, advocacy (because performed by those most capable of performing it) is bound to improve, perhaps in time to equal that of our departed masters. And by this process, is it too much to hope that there may come a day when American barristers may justly be regarded as the equals of their English counterparts?

The proposal, if not a new one, has been little discussed hitherto; it has never, so far as I know, been actively advanced. It is an idea to which so far little attention has been given. Indeed it was only after a prolonged search through the literature that I came finally upon an article in the October, 1935, issue of the *Journal* of the American Judicature Society, entitled: "Should Advocacy Be Restricted to Experts?"

The American Bar Association in 1935, it seems, in trying to find a subject for that year's essay contest, chose this: "The Barrister and Solicitor in British Practice; the Desirability of a Similar Distinction in the United States." But, wrote the Judicature *Journal*, "It no longer appears that this was a timely subject. The contestants apparently found very little opinion, if any, concerning the advisability of so restricting the right to advocacy."

From the point of view of the public, the author of this article declared the advantages were that "specialization furnishes a service test for candidates for judgeships, since judges would be for the most part selected from those who specialize in the handling of contentious business in the courts; . . . the court's work would be expedited when it is done by experts; . . . false claims would be less likely to be pressed by those of special standing, since they have that standing to protect with the court; greater knowledge of the rules of the courts by the Bar would be developed, and the criticism and scrutiny of the judge's work would hold the judge much more in check than in the present system; there would be better service to the client in that legal business would be better attended to, and more quickly reached and disposed of.

"It requires," the author of this article went on to say, "some stretch of the imagination, but it is not impossible to think of the time, perhaps not very far distant, when in a number of the more populous states advocates will have proved the worth of their ideals and standards by their services; when they will have convinced novitiates that the only way to learn how to try cases is to give up every other activity for a time sufficient to get training under a recognized advocate; when they will have proved to the average office practitioner that he cannot afford to continue to go into court because he can get his cases tried better and at less expense by retaining an advocate."

We have in this country no divided bar, and yet, this article observes, "for two centuries we have had lawyers who were barristers in all but title, and they have been the glory of our profession. Any lawyer can name a number of such *de facto* barristers, some dead, some living. Such an advocate is one of exceptional endowments who reaches the stage of being able to take only the cases he chooses to take. Cases reach them just as they reach the English barristers, fully prepared by competent lawyers."

The need of a trained barrister class was recognized half a century ago when Francis Wellman wrote: "In the United States we recognize no distinction between barrister and solicitor; we are all barristers and solicitors by turn. One has but to frequent the courts to become convinced that so long as the more than ten thousand members of the New York County Bar all avail themselves of their privilege to appear in court and try their clients' cases, the great majority of the trials will be poorly conducted, and much valuable time will be wasted."

And then he went on to say that "in our local courts there is an ever-increasing coterie of trial lawyers who are devoting the principal part of their time to trial practice. . . . We are thus beginning to appreciate in this country what the English courts have so long recognized: that the only way to insure speedily and intelligently conducted litigation is to inaugurate a custom of confining court practice to a comparatively limited number of trained trial lawyers."

There is then a kind of natural evolution toward the English system. A sudden revolution would no doubt arouse much professional opposition, especially from our American solicitors, who now untrammeled, may play the part of advocates if they so desire. . . . While it is true that a gradual evolution may ultimately accomplish the same end without formal sanctions, it is also true that the division of barristers and solicitors, as in England, by the slow process of evolution, may delay too long a meritorious and much needed change.

XIV

The Ethics of Advocacy

O N A LOVELY MAY MORNING in Long Island a week or two before the start of a much publicized trial, I was making my way toward the little church which has meant much to me. The Sunday bells were ringing as I walked up the steps and there encountered a charming lady whom I knew well.

Her face was a little flushed as she hurriedly exclaimed to me, "I don't like what you're doing." "What am I doing?" I asked. "You are going to defend that awful, guilty man," she answered. "But how do you know he is guilty?" I somewhat diffidently inquired. "How do I know he is guilty? How silly, of course I do! Haven't I been reading every word in all the papers?" "But haven't you discovered that newspapers are not always right? Don't you remember what the Paris press said about Dreyfus before his trial, and how they had to retract all they had said after his terrible ordeal at Devil's Island, and his ultimate though long-deferred, complete exoneration? God, whose church we are now entering, alone knows whether my client is guilty."

By this time, the choir, preceded by the Cross and the flag of our country, was about to march up to their appointed places. I found my pew and prayed that morning as I had never prayed before for strength, for courage, and for guidance, and as I prayed, I thought of the old hymn that my father loved and had taught me to love too: "In the hour of trial, Jesus, plead for me." I thought too of the many references in the Prayer Book to Christ as our mediator and advocate—an advocate who would help both the righteous and the sinner. I remembered the words of the Holy Communion: "If any man sin we have an advocate with the Father Jesus Christ the righteous."

With all my heart I believed that my client had not sinned, but if he had, I knew he had a far, far better advocate than I. If such an advocate would plead for him, who was I to decline?

And now the choir had finished the last note and we were exhorted: "Let us humbly confess our sins to Almighty God." Sins? Did these respectable people have sins? And as I reflected again upon this, we were on our knees, and as the Rector intoned, we followed in that most glorious of prayers: "Almighty and most merciful Father, we have erred and strayed from thy ways like lost sheep. We have followed too much the devices and desires of our own hearts. We have offended against thy holy laws. We have left undone those things which we ought to have done; and we have done those things which we ought not to have done; and there is no health in us. But thou, O God, have mercy upon us miserable offenders. Spare thou, O God, those who confess their faults. Restore thou those who are penitent."

Lost sheep! Offenders against God's holy laws! Miserable offenders! Even these, it seems, could look to God for restoration. Nice people—bankers and stockbrokers and lawyers and doctors—were these sinners? So it appeared, for there they were upon their knees, making confession of their sins. There was not, then, that sharp division between the righteous and the sinners, it seemed, for we had all strayed like lost sheep, and there was no health in any of us—even in attractive and beautiful women one meets at a dinner party, or in their healthy, tanned, and handsome husbands. God did not divide the world between the right and the wrong side of the tracks. We have all done those things which we ought not to have done, and left undone those things which we ought to have done, and there is no health in any of us. We are all criminals before God—offenders against His holy laws.

But my friend who criticized me at the church is not alone. From time immemorial, laymen have misunderstood the lawyer's role, have failed to grasp the true nature of his duty, and have never comprehended why a man accused, generally disliked and prejudged by the press, was nonetheless entitled to the defense of honest counsel. Few have read, and those who have care less about, the plain words of the United States Constitution, the Sixth Amendment to which commands that in every criminal prosecution the accused "shall enjoy . . . the assistance of counsel for his defense."

When a heinous crime has been committed, and the public, stirred to frenzy by the newspapers, has settled down on the belief that the accused is guilty, many otherwise fair-minded persons become enraged to see a respected lawyer undertaking the defense. They have never read, and if they had, would not agree with the Fifth Canon of Ethics which declares that "it is the *right* of the lawyer to undertake the defense of a person accused of crime, *regardless of his personal opinion* as to the guilt of the accused; otherwise, innocent persons, victims only of suspicious circumstances, might be denied proper defense. Having undertaken such defense, the lawyer is bound by all fair and honorable means to present every defense that the law of the land permits, to the end that no person may be deprived of life or liberty but by due process of law."

This rule of justice has obtained in England from the beginning; it still obtains there. "It is perhaps strange," writes Sir Patrick Hastings in his charming autobiography, "that the duties and obligations of a barrister are so little understood by the lay mind. So often the comment has been made, 'How can honest counsel defend or represent a cause in which he cannot possibly believe?' The answer is very simple. Counsel has no right to believe or disbelieve either his client or his case; he has a duty to perform; he must perform it. He alone has the right of audience in the superior courts of justice, and such right carries with it obligations that are well defined. He has been likened to a cabman on the rank. He is not entitled to refuse a fare, and he has no right to arrogate to himself the task of forming an opinion as to whether his client is innocent or guilty, truthful or a liar. His duty is quite simple. He is entitled to rely upon his solicitor's instructions, and within the conduct of those instructions to fight his cause to the best of his ability. There is only one rule of conduct that he ever need consider, that is to be just as honest and straightforward in his practice as he would be in his own private life. Then he cannot possibly go wrong."

More than a century and a half before Sir Patrick wrote these words in defense of his right and duty to represent an unpopular client, Erskine was saying to a London jury: "From the moment that any advocate can be permitted to say that he will or will not stand between the Crown and the subject arraigned in the court where he daily sits to practice, from that moment the liberties of England are at an end. If the advocate refuses to defend from what he may think of the charge or of the defense, he assumes the character of the judge; nay, he assumes it before the hour of judgment; and in proportion to his rank and reputation, puts the heavy influence of perhaps a mistaken opinion into the scale against the accused, in whose favor the benevolent principle of English law makes all presumptions, and which commands the very judge to be his counsel."

But perhaps the most classical statement on this subject was uttered by Dr. Samuel Johnson. You remember how Boswell one day asked him: "But what do you think of supporting a cause which you know to be bad?"—and how the author of the great dictionary answered him: "Sir, you do not know it to be good or bad, till the judge determines it. I have said that you are to state facts fairly; so that your thinking on what you call knowing a cause to be bad, must be from reasoning, must be from supposing your arguments to be weak and inconclusive. But, sir, that is not enough. An argument which does not convince yourself may convince the judge, to whom you urge it; and *if it does convince him*, sir, you are wrong, and he is right. It is his business to judge; and you are not to be confident in your own opinion that a cause is bad, but *to say all you can for your client*, and then hear the judge's opinion."

However, the most debated, and I think the most debatable, view of this subject was expressed by Brougham in his defense of Queen Caroline. Of all the cases about which I have ever read, including even those of Erskine, his defense of that much abused

royal lady was the best conceived and the most brilliantly conducted; yet in his great final plea to the House of Lords there
was an assertion, the correctness of which has ever since been
debated.

In the midst of his summation, Brougham told the Peers that
an advocate by the sacred duty which he owes his client knows,
in the discharge of that office, but one person in the world, *that
client and none other.* To save that client by all expedient means,
to protect that client at all hazards and costs to all others, and
among others to himself, is the highest and most unquestioned of
his duties. And he must not regard the alarm, the suffering, the
torment, the destruction which he may bring upon any
other. Nay, separating the duties of a patriot from those of an
advocate, and casting them if need be to the wind, he must go
on reckless of the consequences, if his part it should unhappily
be to involve his country in confusion for his client's protection."

What Brougham said there has been the subject of controversy ever since. I certainly do not agree that the duty of counsel
is such as to override his duty to his country. "That is a proposition," said Sir Norman Birkett (later Lord Justice of Appeal)
speaking before the Canadian Bar Association a few years ago,
"to which the Bar of Canada would not agree." Neither would
the Bar of the United States. It was, indeed, a proposition with
which Brougham himself did not thoroughly agree, as he revealed many years after he enunciated it.

But to understand what Brougham wrote to Sir William Forsythe in 1859—nearly four decades after the Queen's trial—
we must recall that King George IV was pressing for a divorce,
although he himself had previously married Mrs. FitzHerbert, a
Catholic, which marriage, if proved, under the Act of Settlement, would have deprived the King of his throne.

Referring to his celebrated speech, Brougham wrote Forsythe: "The real truth is, that the statement was anything rather than a deliberate and well-considered opinion. It was a menace, and it was addressed chiefly to George IV, but also to wiser men, such as Castlereagh and Wellington. I was prepared, *in case of necessity*, that is, in case the Bill passed the Lords, to do two things—first, to resist it in the Commons *with the country at my back*, but next, if need be, to dispute the King's title, to show he had forfeited the crown by marrying a Catholic, in the words of the Act, 'as if he were naturally dead.' What I said was fully understood by Geo. IV, perhaps by the Duke and Castlereagh, and I am confident it would have prevented them from pressing the Bill beyond a certain point."

No man or woman is so bad that something good could not honestly be said about him. Even the very bad may not be guilty of the crime of which they are charged. It is the duty of the advocate to say for his client all that could have been honestly spoken by the client himself in his own behalf had he been able. Judge Parry, an English judge, in his *Seven Lamps of Advocacy*, has written that "without a free and honorable race of advocates, there would have been little of the message of justice. Advocacy is the outward and visible appeal for the spiritual gift of justice. The advocate is the priest in the temple of justice trained in the mysteries of the creed, active in its exercises."

Yet reluctance to accept these views has ever been displayed by laymen. The hostility toward an unpopular defendant, more often than not, has been visited upon his counsel. Such was Erskine's fate when he defended Thomas Paine; such was John Adams' portion when he became counsel for the British soldiers charged with the Boston massacre. Such was the reward of

William Seward when, a hundred and eight years ago, in a little
crowded courtroom, he stood up to defend a Negro by the name
of Freeman on a charge of murder. His client was an emanci-
pated slave. The man was deaf and obviously insane, but this,
far from creating sympathy, seemed to accentuate the community's hostility for the poor Negro.

Seward's friends pointed out to him the unpopularity of the
cause and how adverse an effect it might have on his political
career. But Seward swept them all aside and gave the fullest
measure of his strength and his entire devotion to this humble
client. He told the jury that the most degraded human being in
a civilized state is entitled to a hearing.

Finally, he closed, saying: "In due time, gentlemen of the
jury, when I shall have paid the debt of nature, my remains will
rest here in your midst with those of my kindred and neighbors.
It is very possible they may be unhonored, neglected, spurned!
But perhaps years hence, when the passions and excitement
which now agitate this community shall have passed away, some
lone exile, some Indian, some Negro, may erect over them an
humble stone, and thereon this epitaph: 'He was faithful.'"

His prophecy was fulfilled. When he died, these words were
engraved upon the marble over him. What better encomium
could any lawyer have? What higher tribute than these words:
"He was faithful."

Years, however, have not changed the public's willingness to
visit its detestation of a client on the lawyer who defends him.
How persistent is this point of view was recognized by the New
York State Bar Association in July, 1952. Its *Bulletin* declared:
"Public misunderstanding of the lawyer's role in some recent
cases indicates that the Bar should clarify and reaffirm its tra-
ditional obligation to represent and defend the unpopular. It has

always been recognized in the profession that it is the duty of the Bar to see to it that even the most unpopular defendants and those charged with the most repellent of crimes can obtain a lawyer who will do what is possible and proper in their defense. From the earliest Colonial days, this has been a part of the tradition of the American Bar, even as it has in England. Indeed some of the most honored and memorable achievements of the Bar have been in connection with such causes. Adherence to this tradition is peculiarly necessary in times of great public impatience and concern, for in such times the pressure to dispense with ordinary safeguards of individual rights is most intense. . . . No lawyer doubts the duty; the problem is to make sure that it receives more than mere lip service."

And so, at their Saranac meeting, they adopted these resolutions:

Resolved,
1. That the New York State Bar Association recognizes that the right of counsel requires public acceptance of the correlative right of a lawyer to represent and defend, in accordance with the standards of the Bar, any client without having imputed to him his client's reputation, views, or character.
2. That the Association will support any lawyer against criticism or attack in connection with such representation, when, in its judgment, he has acted in accordance with the standards of the Bar.
3. That the Association will strive to educate the profession and the public on the rights and duties of a lawyer in representing any client, regardless of the unpopularity of either the client or his cause.

Echoing the same views, the Association of the Bar of the City of New York in January, 1953, adopted identical resolutions. Throughout the ages, popular distrust of lawyers has been fanned by novelists and dramatists, abetted in these latter days by columnists in many papers. We have learned to bear these strictures with composure, but when one of our own calling chooses to bring obloquy upon us, it is harder to endure. Such were my feelings when I came not long ago upon an article appearing in the December, 1951, issue of the Stanford *Law Review*, written by a Boston lawyer by the name of Charles P. Curtis.

In bald, plain terms he espouses the belief that a lawyer, in acting for others, has the right to lie for his client. "I want," he said in the beginning, "first of all to put Advocacy in its proper setting." If I thought he was right, I would even at this late day take up another calling. Surely all that I have said hitherto must indeed have been ill said if I have not made plain my belief that a good advocate must be an honest man. Ethics to an honorable man come naturally and without conscious effort—like good table manners or ordinarily decent behavior in polite society.

But listen to the views of Mr. Curtis. Having put advocacy in what he calls its "proper setting," he adds two platitudes with which no reasonable person could disagree: "It is a special case of vicarious conduct. A lawyer devotes his life and career acting for other people." True, but how should the lawyer act? Mr. Curtis tells us. "I don't see," he says, "why we should not come out roundly and say that one of the functions of a lawyer is to lie for his client." The occasions when he should do this, he says, are "rare." He should lie, we are told, only when "his duty gets him into a corner or puts him on the spot." A man whose business it is to act for others, the author of this article continues, "finds himself in his dealings on his client's behalf with outsiders, acting on a lower standard than he would if he were acting for himself, and lower, too, than any standard his client himself would be willing to act on, in fact, than any-one on his own." If this is the standard which Mr. Curtis has set for himself, it is one which should be repudiated with scorn and with contempt.

He gives a number of illustrations wherein a lawyer's lying for his client receives his hearty applause. He cites the case of a police inspector questioning a lawyer regarding the where-abouts of his client. "Of course he lies," says Mr. Curtis, add-ing, "and why not?" Still another sample of the ethics Mr. Curtis has espoused is the case of a lawyer who lied to him as a member of a grievance committee. "I remember thinking then," he writes, "that the lawyer was doing just right in lying to me, but I don't know who else agreed with me."

Well, I do not, for one, and there are others. Among these, none has spoken with more sincerity and authority than William Dean Embree, a member of a great New York law firm, a former president of the New York County Lawyers Associ-ation. "I thoroughly and vigorously disagree with Mr. Charles P. Curtis of the Boston Bar," writes Mr. Embree. "The lawyer owes entire devotion to the interest of his client," he continued. "He must use his utmost effort and all his ability for his client. This is the very heart of advocacy; this is the chief glory of the profession. But the lawyer is never required to resort to any step or procedure which impairs his own character or may weaken his standing in the profession or before the courts; no one can ever lie for his client without impairing his character and without weakening his standing in the profession and before the courts."

Mr. Curtis was graduated from Groton, from Harvard Col-lege, and from the Harvard Law School. Where, then, one won-ders, did he acquire his views of legal ethics? Where was he taught that lying is a good thing? Surely not at Groton where Dr. Peabody impressed on every boy that one of the worst things he could become is a liar—not at Groton where not only lying was proscribed, but a peculiar opprobrium was reserved for the sneak who would lie to get out of a tight spot.

Surely Mr. Curtis did not learn at Harvard College that a liar should be countenanced, much less approved. And if, indeed, law was taught at the Harvard Law School in his day in what former Dean Pound has called the "grand manner," it would be a reflection on that much esteemed seat of learning to suggest that lying was applauded there.

I am light-years from suggesting that the writings of Mr. Justice Holmes, who was a kind of household god of the school where he once taught, could possibly be urged as a source to which approval of mendacity could be traced, but I have often wondered whether some of his assertions in the Holmes-Pollock letters might not be just a bit confusing to the youthful mind. "For my own part," wrote Justice Holmes, "I often doubt whether it would not be a gain if every word of moral significance could be banished from the law altogether, and other words adopted which should convey legal ideas uncolored by anything outside the law." As to ethics, he said, "I have called them a body of imperfect generalizations expressed in terms of emotion." Even in the domain of morals, he said that "it would be a gain, at least for the educated, to get rid of the word and notion of sin." He said he was "so skeptical as to our knowledge of goodness or badness of laws that I have no practical criticism except what the crowd wants."

That Holmes' suggested abolition "of every word of moral significance from the law" in any way prompted Mr. Curtis in his advocacy of lying, I do not believe. But, of this I am certain, that far better instruction can be found in the clear and unpretentious lectures of Lord MacMillan. His views of the connection between law and morals are poles apart from the Holmesian philosophy. "I maintain," he said, "that the ultimate justification of the law is to be found in moral considerations." The truth is, he declared, that "in the ultimate analysis the basis of the law is ethical, at first perhaps dimly perceived and concealed under much that is irrelevant, but increasingly realized as civilization advances and becomes self-conscious." Even in rules of law, he said, "which might appear to be morally indifferent . . . there is an ethical element. But when, as often happens from time to time," declared Lord MacMillan, "the law itself presents a choice whether one or the other principle is to be applied, then it seems to me that it is impossible, as it is undesirable, that the decision should not have regard to the ethical motive of promoting justice."

Ethics is the science of moral duty. It deals with the rules of conduct. Noah Webster, as a second definition of the word "ethical," gives this: "conforming to professional standards." The standards of conduct that lawyers must obey are as high, and are as generally followed, as the most exalted rules that govern any men on earth. All advocates are bound by these standards, and they must obey them. They may and should fight hard for their clients, but they must fight fairly. They may and should say all that honestly and honorably can be said for them. They may say it with fervor and all the persuasion in their power; but in saying it they may not deceive, they must not lie.

The advocate must never forget, said Judge Parry, that he is "not only the servant of the client, but the friend of the court, and honesty is as essential to true friendship as it is to sound advocacy." The arms which an advocate wields, said Lord Cochburn, "he ought to use as a warrior and not an assassin. . . . He ought to know how to reconcile them with eternal interests of religion."

Such an advocate was Thomas Erskine. It is just a hundred and sixty-three years ago that in defending Thomas Paine before Lord Kenyon and a jury, he declared: "I will ever and at all hazards assert the dignity, independence, and integrity of the English Bar, without which impartial justice, the most valuable part of the English constitution, can have no existence."

In America, where the stability of all departments of the Government rests upon the approval of the people, it is peculiarly essential that the system for establishing and dispensing justice be developed to a high point of efficiency and so maintained that the public shall have absolute confidence in the integrity and impartiality of its administration. The future of the Republic, to a great extent, depends upon our maintenance of justice pure and unsullied. It cannot be so maintained unless the conduct and motives of the members of our profession are such as to merit the approval of all just men. So runs the preamble of our Canons of Ethics.

I have been observing American lawyers for many years. I know that there is no other group of men in the United States whose record of devotion to their duty and whose obedience to their trusts is worthier of commendation. When one once thought to be an honest man turns out a rascal, he is driven from the Temple of Justice by the lawyers themselves. The conduct of the members of our profession, in general, has been such as to merit the approval of all just men.

And so, in the words of Erskine, I will ever assert the dignity, independence, and integrity of the American Bar.